Empathetic Space on Screen

Amedeo D'Adamo

Empathetic Space on Screen

Constructing Powerful Place and Setting

Amedeo D'Adamo
Università Cattolica
Milan, Italy

ISBN 978-3-319-66771-3   ISBN 978-3-319-66772-0   (eBook)
https://doi.org/10.1007/978-3-319-66772-0

Library of Congress Control Number: 2017950725

Cover design by Jenny Vong

Printed on acid-free paper

This Palgrave Macmillan imprint is published by Springer Nature
The registered company is Springer International Publishing AG
The registered company address is: Gewerbestrasse 11, 6330 Cham, Switzerland

A QUESTION OF DEDICATION

There is a quiet moment in an episode of the sitcom *Gilmore Girls*. A character looks in a mirror and contemplates the 50-ish face looking back at her and says thoughtfully to herself, "This is not what I really look like."

This is true in a specific sense: we see ourselves through a tunnel of memories and moments and not as the simple physical version that someone else might meet for the first time. In fact, we do not just see ourselves this way: we often see those we love and hate through the same kind of tunnel of time, as a kind of alchemical amalgam of past and present. Are we wrong? Deluded? Living in a dream? Is this a flaw or a strength?

Aristotle says that a true friend is a mirror of one's best self, but how is that mirror more true than the one hanging in the bathroom in *Gilmore Girls*? Because the mirror of the self is informed by history, by experiences and their emotional truth.

I experience this true mirror every day in my marriage to my wife. In a real sense I wrote this book through that marriage and its particular intensely shared tunnel of time and memory. After all, she and I have taught together for fifteen years now on three continents, in the beating monsoon rains of Cameroon, on hot sound stages in Hollywood, and in universities and film festivals all over Europe. Threaded through all that is the turns we took producing and directing three tough low-budget films. Meanwhile we've lived through and tried to grasp so many intense social and emotional experiences and crises that it is now frankly impossible for me to say how much of the work on these pages is hers.

But I do know her long experience in drama therapy, with the connection between life and drama, has fixed my attention for so long that this book's fascinations are, like my life, impossible to imagine without her.

And this I think helps explain that moment in *Gilmore Girls*. Our human facility for melding the inner and outer, the past and the present, gives us informed sight, and even a way to see into the future. Though my wife is of course quite beautiful, we've now been married for decades and so I do not see the same person others do. I see what my wife *really* looks like. Every day at a glance I see the woman who was stretching in a particular Thursday dawn along a river two decades ago, the person who once stood up to the Cameroon mafia to save a group of young teens she had been working with, the person who campaigned for Obama, the person who while pregnant with our first child and waiting for dinner in a very slow restaurant after having not eaten all day at a film festival began furtively eating the raw leaves of their decorative herb garden until I caught her. I see the woman who taught me lessons about teaching and psychology and anthropology in so many late night conversations and so many co-taught classes. I remember moments and gestures and acts of generosity that she can't, I can tell you about her help given to strangers and friends and family, memories that I know that if she even does recall she'll dismiss with a wave if I bring them up. I see her empathy, and with that I see how ours are joined. I have witnessed her best and most revealing moments and now I carry them like treasures.

And this is informed sight: this is the true vision of character, the truth of the social bonds underlying an actual person. These bonds create friendships and tie families together. These are the glue of a lived romance, that long braided commitment to a beloved who struggles with you through the valleys and deserts of time. This tunnel of character and memory is what makes up our social and empathetic dedications: like the character in *Gilmore Girls* suddenly realizes, I am a better mirror of my wife than the mirror hanging in our bathroom. I know her tendencies: because I know what she has done, I know what she is likely to do. No mirror has this information, no stranger knows these traits, these triumphs and travails. To see only the present moment shorn of the past is to be blind to the relational truth of people.

So while I can only hope my wife remembers only my all-too-few good moments, I can say this.

I see the truth of you, my love.

ACKNOWLEDGEMENTS

As Manzoni says, "friendship does not pair us off into couples as marriage does; each of us generally has more than one friend, and so a chain is formed of which none can see the end." A long chain of friends have made this book happen. I'm especially thankful to Nevina Satta, Anna Thomas, Andy Bienen, Salvatore Puledda, Gabrielle Kelly, Michael Silver and Jennifer Calder for their years and decades of conversations, encouragement and genuine friendship. Particular thanks to Lisa Perrott for her detailed suggestions and thoughts on this book. A huge molto grazie to Franca Marchi for the talks on Dante and for so much else: without her support this book would not exist. Effusive thanks to Francesco Casetti (for creating the teaching environs in Brescia, Lugano and Locarno where my wife and I have taught so happily for so long), to Max Locatelli, Elena Mosconi, Francesca Piredda, Marco Cucco, Gabriele Balbi, Giuseppe Richeri, and Ruggero Eugeni (for maintaining ideal pockets of teaching) and to Larry Paull, Barbara Boyle, Henry Bumstead, Dick Sylbert, Silvio Maselli, Daniele Basilio, Frank Patterson, Thom Mount, Carolyn Pfeiffer, Pat Olmstead, Mark Debacco and Paul and Diana Kessler for great days working together. To Liz Giuffre, JeanPierre Candelero, Anna Stucchi, Mauro Magatti, Chiara Giaccardi, Anna Caccia and Ian Dixon for their support, to Michael Collier for crafting three wonderful Breadloaf writer conferences, and to my students in Lugano, Locarno, Brescia, Apulia, Royal Holloway, China, Cameroon and Hollywood.

To the teachers I admire who taught with passion and insight: the marvelous Bernard Williams, the generous Joe Volpe, the rigorous

Paul Shrader, and the patient and generous Dan Kleinman, Lewis Cole, John E. Hare and Brendan Ward. A special thanks to James Shamus who took a chance on an immature young student and let me intern and even briefly work for him so long ago at his great company Good Machine. To Lina Aboujieb at Palgrave Pivot, who saw promise in a short Pivot project proposal and for her patience and encouragement, and to Heloise Harding for all her focus and attention. It has been a marvelous experience working this first time with an editor and editorial assistant who really care about helping hapless academics and about producing real work. A grateful thanks also to the hardworking crew at Springer: molto grazie Vanessa Mitchell, Aishwarya Balachandar, Tabea Gueers and Prashanth Ravichandran for the many painstaking corrections. Particular thanks to Chiara Giaccardi for inviting me back in 2011 to speak about my concept of Dantean Space at a 2012 ECREA conference she helped organize at the Università Cattolica.

As an effort to bridge film craft and cultural theory, this book owes much to the many highly-accomplished film craft folks who I've been lucky to work with over the last twenty five years. A more concrete acknowledgement to them makes up this book's Afterwards.

Finally, it seems important to acknowledge some of the great theorists whose life—work inspires us all. I'm thinking here particularly of singular inspirational thinkers such as A.C. Bradley, Gaston Bachelard, Erich Auerbach, E.R. Dodds, and Svetlana Alpers. But most of all to Herbert Marcuse, T.J. Clarke, Carol Gilligan, Martha Nussbaum and those who work on a collective level from the Situationists to the Marxist collective Plan C. These are people who strive to create a knowledge that does not just enrich but that activates, a cultivation of the self where the self extends out beyond today's crippled confines. They embody a long tradition of intellectuals, artists, writers and filmmakers who have chopped vigorously into the alienation, cruelty and false social necessity that crushes down on us all like a great, terrible iceberg, flattening our capabilities and chilling our spirits. They realize with urgency that the task is not to understand our culture but to carve out new spaces of mutual care and richness.

CONTENTS

CHART OF TOPOLOGY

Chart of topology for the myths, plays, novels, films, TV shows and video games we shall be considering in this book.

Chart 1: The Three Forms of Emotional Entanglement in Stories, Films, TV & Videogames

1. DISPASSIONATE space & characters	2. DRAMATIC space & characters	3. DANTEAN space & characters

Story Character's Objectives

External goals	*External & Internal Goals*	*External & Internal Goals*
ie, Kill The Monster,	*ie, Find love, Prove Yourself,*	*(usually dantean goals are*
Rob the Bank,	*Get Rid of Guilt Escape the*	*about facing a traumatic*
Win The Race,	*Past*	*from the character's past.)*
Defuse The Bomb,		
Find The Killer Survive		

Characters

Powerful with little vulnerability	Sympathetic, Vulnerable	Sympathetic, Vulnerable

Emotional Involvement

Low and Adrenalynic	High	Very High

Emotional Entanglement Between Character and Space

Little entanglement (since Character is not deeply drawn)   Deep Entanglement

Use of Spectacle

Strong but Unemotional Spectacle   Low Spectacle   Strong Emotional Spectacle

Exemplary Genres

Action-Adventure, Thriller   Drama, Dramedy   Drama, Horror

Chart 2: Examples of the Three Forms of Space in Stories, Films, TV & Videogames

1. DISPASSIONATE Space   2. DRAMATIC Space   3. DANTEAN Space

Classical Stories

Hercules, Agamemnon   Achilles, Medea   Oedipus, Penthius, Ovid's Narcissus & Echo, Dante's Characters: (i.e. Francesca, Ugolino, Capaneus)

Popular Literature

Sherlock Holmes, James Bond   Most Characters   Miss Havesham in *Great Expectations* Poe's "The Tell-tale Heart" & "The Black Cat", Camus' *The Fall*, Dostoevski's *The Demons*

Narrative Films

Superman, old James Bond Terminator, Speed, Taken   Most dramas and comedies *IE, Casablanca, Gran Torino, etc.*   *Amelie, Aliens, The Dark Knight, Gravity, Psycho, The Third Man, The Official Story*

Documentaries

Manny   *Supersize Me Cutie & The Boxer*   *Tarnation, Elena Waltz With Bashir*

TV

'Thriller' shows like *24*

Most dramas, ie *The Wire*
Friends, Louie, Love

Homeland 1st Season finale

Children's Literature

Stevenson's *Treasure Island*
Journey To The Center Of
The Earth

The Wind In The Willows,
The Hobbit

Francis Burnett's
The Secret Garden

Children's Television

Spiderman, Paw Patrol
Jake and the Pirates
Inspector Gadget

LEGO Friends, BeatBugs
The New Adventures of
Winnie The Pooh
Doc McStuffin

Children's Films

Peter Pan, Mary Poppins
A Series of Unfortunate
Events

Little Nemo, Trilly

Up, Dory

Videogames

Most 1st-person Shooters
Old *Tomb Raider*
Grand Theft Auto

BioShock Infinite
New *Tomb Raider*

Wrath of the White Witch

LIST OF FIGURES

The Building Codes of Narrative Space: The Three Forms of Emotional Entanglements between People and Places in story

Welcome to Dantean Space!: Empathy and Space in *Singin' in the Rain, Legally Blonde, the Pursuit of Happyness* and *Aliens*

In cinema and television empathetic settings stand out above all others.[1] Think of the now iconic gooey dripping tunnels that Ripley stumbles through in *Aliens* (1986; see Fig. 1.2), or the delightful melancholic wonderland of Paris so winningly animated by the winsome protagonist of *Amelie* (2001) (Fig. 1.1). Other examples come to mind—the sewers of *The Third Man* (1949), or Norman's bird-decorated parlor in *Psycho* (1960), or the dark Gotham of certain *Batman* movies, or certain moments in *Homeland* (2011–), *Mad Men* and other television shows. Because we lack a clear account of the power of setting and space we are reduced to describing such narratives as 'atmospheric', 'emotionally moody,' or perhaps somehow illustrating a 'romantic aesthetic', but can we define them more concretely? Why do these settings stand out so memorably in narrative history when so many others, however spectacular and breathtaking and adrenalynic, start to fade from our view as the end-credits roll up? Could we dissect their craft and story techniques, show an underlying unity and even illustrate how and why they differ from other uses of narrative space? In short, what makes these particular spaces so powerful and iconic?

We set out to answer these questions and begin by showing how one unifying aspect of these iconic settings sets them apart from ordinary cinema settings. While the settings of most films pass by as an unintrusive backdrop, or erupt into view as an excuse for adrenalynic escapades or sometimes simply as eye-candy, and therefore have a weak relationship to the film's protagonist, all of the story settings we have mentioned above

© The Author(s) 2018
A. D'Adamo, *Empathetic Space on Screen*,
https://doi.org/10.1007/978-3-319-66772-0_1

Fig. 1.1 Publicity material for the film *Amelie* (2001) showing her ensconced in her bedroom, one of the film's Dantean spaces

are entangled with the emotional struggles of their story's protagonist in a common, specific and identifiable way. We will argue that there is a narrative architectural form, one we will call *Dantean space*, that unifies them all. Understanding this powerfully empathetic resonance of place, protagonist and viewer has many implications, not least of which is that, by focusing on such narratives we begin to also understand the other less powerful forms of space and place in films and television. We learn that there are in fact *three* distinct forms of narrative architecture, three forms that make for viewers a kind of ascending ladder of emotional and empathetic involvement with protagonist and setting. In this book we will describe this topology of forms, showing how it manifests in many different examples, after which we focus on the possibilities of Dantean space.

Any successful account of how empathetic space function in story has to carry implications for all narratives and to offer useful tools for many groups. A useful, robust theory would allow us to excavate the

Fig. 1.2 Ripley, protagonist of the film *Aliens*, enters her Dantean space (*Aliens*, 1986)

machinery of empathy and empathetic space, linking a kind of narrative space that appears across different myths, narrative paintings, novels, films, television shows and commercials. It would allow us to identify variations of empathetic space, drawing out certain underlying narrative structures, revealing the cues, materials and production design techniques commonly used to create these kinds of spaces across media forms. It should also reveal the social implications, if any, of these forms.

That is the goal of this book. This understanding should be useful not only for theoreticians of cinema and television but also provide insights for practitioners in all forms of narrative, including film, literature, plays television and video-games. Tactics found in one form should be replicable in diverse ways across others, and a history of this machinery should begin to be visible. Understanding the empathetic power of a sixteenth-century sculpture or a nineteenth-century painting might reflect and reveal the craft techniques of contemporary empathetic films.

But most of all, any account of empathetic space has to begin with the phenomenon of that rush of feelings we associate with such empathetic moments: it must first set out to identify the phenomenon to be studied. It must offer a phenomenological account that can identify empathetic reactions, group them and give underlying causes.

When the Setting Moves Us: Empathy and Space as Categories

Since we are talking about the specifically *empathetic* use of space we should first distinguish both empathy and space. Films will often use *space* to express something about the story or plot, in some instances without empathetic content. My own favorite example comes in the musical number 'Dream of You' in the musical *Singin' in the Rain* (Fig. 1.3). The scene opens on a room of mostly men, talking relatively quietly to each other, all in black and white tuxedoes. Suddenly our starlet and romantic interest, dressed in a scanty pink outfit, bursts out of a huge pink cake and behind her a gaggle of chorus girls (all wearing pink) invade the room and start throwing pink confetti, then swing round the room dancing in synch and singing loudly as a band strikes up a jazzy medley. Now the characters must shout to be heard over the musical number.

The director, Stanley Donen, and his team have very cleverly dramatized a major plot-point—the film industry's sudden and bewildering

Fig. 1.3 *Singin' in the Rain* (1952): Narrative space without empathy

shift from silent to sound film—by a color change mixed with movement and acoustical change. Thus a technical and social transition which was truly an earthquake for the industry is here represented spatially by a transition from black and white to color in the frame as well as an acoustical shift in volume and atmosphere. However, despite all this machinery of spatial spectacularity there is nothing empathetic in the shift: like most others of its time, this marvelous musical is still a rather dispassionate film, meaning that it does not explore the deep emotional lives of its characters but rather entertains us through spectacular feats, in this case of choreography and music. Our heroine's pink outfit does not make her more empathetic, nor does it signify any deep emotional conflict between her and her love interest.

Compare this scene, though, to a similar invasion of pink into a similarly sombre room. In the film *Legally Blonde* (2002), our ditzy bright main character Elle Woods sits down in her first Harvard Law School classroom and, while everyone else in the room is dressed in sombre colors and opens a laptop, she pulls out a pink heart-shaped notebook and a pink pen with fluffy pink feathers (Fig. 1.4).

Fig. 1.4 Elle's props, spirit and affect empathetically contrast with the cold space of her Law School class in *Legally Blonde*

This contrast introduces a long-running spatial conflict in the film. Because Elle's fun, funny pen and notebook reveal her inner life (her bubbly love of frivolity and her joy in spreading social silliness), they heighten her own antagonisms with the serious space and social group she is entering: immediately we feel this contrast is certain to cause cruel judgements and conflict for her, as in fact it does. These oppositions will run through the realms of Harvard Law School, the film's later law firm spaces and are then fully realized in the sombre space of the court in the film's finale. And so crucial emotional allegiances are being introduced by this fluffy pen and heart-shaped notebook: while we laugh at the surprising and spectacular contrasts, this costume and prop choice makes Elle's character empathetic in four ways. First, it reminds us of how earlier in the film she used her oversized fashion style to help other characters be less serious and thus happier. Second, we see her own faith in herself. Third, we see the coming storm of conflict between her inner and this new outer reality, and fourth, we see her growing underdog/out-group status foreshadowed for the remainder of the film. Unlike the example of *Singin' in the Rain*, here our emotional allegiances are being triggered and shaped by carefully-opposed spatial elements. In both examples *space* is being manipulated, but only *Legally Blonde* uses the spatial change to convey emotion and to evoke our empathy.

Let us now compare two examples where *empathy* is strong but is realized in very different ways. Consider just the trailer for the highly empathetic film *The Blind Side* (2009), a film so full of empathetic moments it is often labelled a 'weeper', but yet where the empathy has no spatial embodiment. There are many empathetic moments in the two-minute trailer—the moment Sandra Bullock's character stops the car to ask the black teenager (who is walking along the road shivering in the winter night) if he has somewhere to go, the moment she puts him up at her house, the moment she learns he has never had a bed, the moment he is ignored at his new school by the little kids, the moment he scores the touchdown and begins to be a hero to the school, and so on. But though this drama is full of strongly empathetic moments, there is nothing especially spatial being done to heighten or embody them.[2] Here empathy is largely expressed through the dramatic interactions and revelations of the actors while the backgrounds serve only as backdrops supporting the plot.

Contrast this with the use of empathetic space in the biopic *The Pursuit of Happyness* (2006). This film centers around Chris, a proud yet poor black man who is determined to create a better life for his 5-year-old son Christopher Jr. and himself by, struggling through an unpaid internship at a stockbrokerage firm while he loses a series of apartments and temporary jobs. Chris and Christopher finally end up being thrown out of their apartment with their belongings locked inside. When little Christopher starts banging on the door trying to get back in, Chris nearly loses it and for the first time in the film physically shakes little Christopher, yelling at him to stop complaining.

In the next scene they end up sitting downcast and depressed on a bench in a subway station. Christopher Jr., usually so upbeat, is now incredibly discouraged, so his father invents a game. Chris pretends they have a time machine and gets his son to imagine they have sent themselves back into the world of the dinosaurs. Now Chris convinces his son that a nearby public restroom (see fig. 1.5) is their cave where they should hide for the night from the dinosaurs. The son falls asleep in his arms as Chris stays on guard, preventing anyone from coming into the restroom. When someone outside bangs on the door, Chris carefully covers his sleeping son's ears with his hands, braces his foot against the door, and silently begins to cry (Fig. 1.6).

Here, unlike in *The Blind Side*, space is being used in clear opposition to other spaces in the film to significantly connect the space to the characters' emotions and problems. The public bathroom space, so cold, hard, rectangular and confining and so flatly lit (Fig. 1.5), is a stark contrast to the way we imagine the boy pictures his caveman cave. That unseen fantasy that took them into this space represents the dad's love and the boy's innocence, but this real room represents not only their loss of any private spaces of their own but also their desperation, the shark that might eat the child's innocence, the hard reality thinly papered over by the dad's quick-thinking ploy and the child's fertile imagination. And then, when an unseen person outside tries to get in, the sound effects of the increasingly insistent banging on the door and the jiggling of the doorknob represent the father's mounting panic, being now both part of the space and also a trigger and a stand-in for the fears he has hidden for so long behind a wall of smiles, stories, fantasies and lies. The fragility of this wall, now about to break, is suggested in the paper towels that he has torn from the dispenser and carefully laid under his son, a

Figs. 1.5 and 1.6 Chris cradling his sleeping son in a public restroom in *The Pursuit of Happyness* (2006)

thin boundary emphasized when Chris, fearful his son will awake, has to cover the boy's ears with his hands to keep him from hearing the rattling of the door and his own sobs. This space, while neorealist, also vibrates with the unseen fantasy-cave that little Christopher has created with his dad's help, making this restroom into a projection of the dad's harsh truth and the boy's innocent fantasy, of their homelessness and mutual care, and of the external and internal conflicts of the dad. By knowing this narrative history we see not just a public bathroom but a space imbued with a father's struggle, love, and fears and a child's innocence as it is threatened by a temporarily staved-off trauma. Here it is the *space* and not simply the dynamic between the characters that provokes our empathy.

EMPATHETIC SPACE DEFINED

At this point we might define the nature of *empathetic space*. An empathetic space exists in a moment of a story that arouses some intense level of empathy in us and where the space is somehow expressing that empathy by embodying the hopes and/or fears of the character. In general, the space becomes more intensely empathetic the more it expresses the emotional conflicts of a character.

One last step is needed before we focus on how empathy can be expressed through space in a narrative: first we must understand how empathy itself functions in narrative.

OUR ENGAGING TENDENCIES: EMPATHY, CHARACTER AND SPACE

What are the underlying story techniques that create empathetic reactions? By beginning with some moments in films like *The Blind Side* or *The Pursuit of Happyness* where we feel a deep and vivid feeling of sympathy, pity, love or yearning for a character or characters, the kind of 'lump-in-the-throat' moment where some of the audience is crying and others are holding back their tears, we can begin to draw out some commonalities, in particular the deployment of a series of dramatic tricks that reappear again and again in scenes that provoke our empathy.

THE MACHINERY OF EMPATHY: TEN STORY TACTICS THAT TRIGGER OUR EMPATHY

We offer the following incomplete list of story tactics, naming some of the stories we look at in depth in the chapters ahead. We tend to feel intense moments of empathy towards characters who exhibit one or more of the following attributes and situations:

1. **They are worth pitying.**
   Legally Blonde, Macbeth, Saving Private Ryan, 50/50, the boy in *The Blind Side,* the child in *The Pursuit of Happyness, Hiroshima*

Mon Amour, Piaf in *La Vie en Rose*, *The Secret Garden*, the child in *The Official Story*, Sy in *One Hour Photo*.

2. **They have done nothing to deserve their emotional pain.**
   50/50, the boy in *The Blind Side*, the child in *The Pursuit of Happyness*, the child in *The Official Story*, *La Vie en Rose*, *One Hour Photo*, *The Secret Garden*.

3. **They are trying to bear up and go on despite their emotional pain.**
   Macbeth, *50/50*, the father in *The Pursuit of Happyness*, *Hiroshima Mon Amour*, the boy in *The Blind Side*, the anti-hero of *Gran Torino*, *La Vie en Rose*, *One Hour Photo*.

4. **They are an underdog in some struggle they are unlikely to win, a competition in which someone else has far better resources and chances to win.**
   Legally Blonde, *The Pursuit of Happyness*, *Little Miss Sunshine*.

5. **They achieve or finally fail to achieve something that they have long struggled for.**
   Legally Blonde, *Amelie*, the father in *The Pursuit of Happyness*, *La Vie en Rose*, *One Hour Photo*, *Little Miss Sunshine*.

6. **They are deeply and increasingly in conflict with very intimate vulnerabilities, struggling hard for the first time in their life to somehow resolve them in order to achieve their objective.**
   Macbeth, *Hiroshima Mon Amour*, *Twilight*, *Amelie*, *The Pursuit of Happyness*.

7. **They have a heart in winter that begins to warm: i.e., they have had no intimacy or social contact for a long time (usually having closed their heart thanks to some big trauma) and now slowly begin to take intimate risks by reaching out to someone or to some community.**
   Amelie, *Hiroshima Mon Amour*, the anti-hero of *Gran Torino*, *La Vie en Rose*, *One Hour Photo*, *Witness*, *The Secret Garden*.

8. **After a long period of hiding their feelings inside, they finally reveal their deep vulnerabilities, fears and intimate secrets to someone.**
   Hiroshima Mon Amour, *50/50*, the father in *The Pursuit of Happyness*, *Amelie*, *La Vie en Rose*, the anti-hero of *Gran Torino*, *The Graduate*, *Pleasantville*, *One Hour Photo*, *Witness*, *The Secret Garden*.

9. **They have been abandoned, which has affected them, and they are reunited with someone who cares about them.**
   50/50, Amelie, the boy in *The Blind Side, La Vie en Rose, Pleasantville, One Hour Photo, The Secret Garden.*
10. **They do something good for someone other than themselves.**
   The friend in *50/50, Amelie, The Blind Side, Gran Torino, The Pursuit of Happyness, Pleasantville, Twilight, The Secret Garden.*

We can make a few distinctions about this list.

First, it is cumulative: as our examples have already shown, often there is more than one empathetic cue working at once in a story.

Second, there is an entire form of story that uses very little of this machinery and does not try to move us to the cathartic emotional experiences of empathy: in Chap. 2 we consider the negative, non-empathetic and invulnerable examples of the classic Superman, Sherlock Holmes and the original James Bond.

Third, there is a clear division in the list between characters who struggle with themselves and characters who struggle with another character or with a community.[3] For example, the first six tactics all make us care for the singular personal struggle and pain of the character: we might call them *tactics of compassionate empathy* since they draw compassion from us for the character herself. But it is important to see that while tactics 1 through 6 can be about a character in emotional conflict with herself, tactics 7, 8, 9 and 10 are different in that they aren't just emotional struggles with oneself but are empathetically *dyadic*: i.e., they involve taking emotional risks and forming a bond with an other. Dramas using these tactics necessarily drag the character into the social realm.

Fourth, we will argue that the tactics are listed roughly in order of increasing emotional intensity; the examples we focus on in this book suggest that the most affecting scenes tend to use the later tactics, with tactic 10 tending to be the greatest trigger of empathy. We come to care deeply for a character who cares for others, particularly if this comes at a personal cost, and this electricity of empathy is quite strong. Even if we never do anything to the benefit of anyone but ourselves in life, it seems that as audience members we love to see others do something good for someone else.

To mark this distinction, we suggest that tactics 7, 8, 9 and 10 be understood as *tactics of communal empathy*, as distinct from the compassionate empathy we feel for a singular character wrestling with her own self and not reaching out to others. This distinction is important for our book because *compassionate* empathy links the examples in Part II while the overtly social form of *communal* empathy is central for the characters of ecstatic space discussed in Part III.

THE COMMERCIAL POWER OF EMPATHY

The Edeka 2015 Christmas commercial[4] illustrates a strong dramatic use of empathy tactics. The story of this short commercial is very tight: an old man gets messages from his family that they are all too busy to come for Christmas, and so he sits alone in grief, triggering our empathy through tactic 1 (Fig. 1.7).

Each of the unavailable family members, scattered across the globe, then receives a message that he has died, and in grief and shock and with some guilt they all arrive for a memorial at his house: we feel their regret and guilt. Now in a dramatic reversal, the living grandfather then steps from around a corner and says gently "How else could I get you to come?" They burst into joy and we leave them sitting around the Christmas table reunited as a family. We see in this minute and a half the adroit use of empathy tactics 1, 2, 3, 5, 6, 7, 8, 9 and we finish our tight empathy arc with a cathartic use of tactic 10.[5]

There is a structural strategy beneath the way this tight story deploys our list of tactics. It begins with compassionate empathy tactics to tie us to the inner problems and pain of an individual character. Then after that empathetic bond is established, the story invokes the communal tactics of showing different characters doing good things for each other and then being brought together. As we shall see, this device of starting with

Fig. 1.7   Edeka 2015 Christmas commercial

compassionate empathy to make us care for individual characters and then building towards communal empathy and a cathartic climax is a very common structure for building empathy in stories.

COMPARING CHRISTIAN IN *FIFTY SHADES OF GREY* WITH EDWARD IN *TWILIGHT*

As we shall see, the machinery of empathy underlies our empathetic bonds to characters, and the relative lack of this machinery in certain kinds of stories and characters helps define a whole category of narrative space. For example, take the difference in our emotional investment in the big confessional scenes of two different protagonists: Christian the billionaire sadist in the film *50 Shades of Grey* (2016) and Edward the vampire in the film *Twilight* (2008).[6]

We begin with a negative example of a film with no commitment to empathetic bonds. The film *50 Shades of Grey* turns on the question of whether the young, vulnerable, virginal, sensitive and middle-class Anastasia should commit to a BDSM (Bondage, Domination, Sadism and Masochism) relationship with the handsome, sexually experienced, BDSM-oriented Christian. Christian's most vulnerable moment*s* comes late in the story when he finally confesses to Anastasia his most intimate secret: he cannot change because he is an orphan whose mother was a prostitute and crack-addict who died when he was just four years old. Clearly, we and Anastasia are supposed to feel pity for him at this confessional moment, but in fact we don't. Why not? It is not that we do not believe him: so far he has been very honest. Instead our indifference results from the fact that this Edgar is a sadist who recognizes this but yet, like some story-book villain, makes no attempt to change, to fight his sadistic impulses and attempt to develop an intimate, romantic, negotiating character (i.e. to have a character arc) that will meet Anastasia somewhere in the middle.

We can note three aspects of Christian's emotional coldness. First, he is unsympathetic in what he wants: that is, to torture and dominate Anastasia. Second, he is an unconflicted character: his conflict is entirely external in that he wants her to observe the strict emotional and power rules of his BDSM contract, and makes this confession essentially to convince her that he is unable to change so she should stop nagging him about it. Third, his backstory feels too generic for us to care: we learn nothing else about his mother or his childhood, making the backstory seem a blatant attempt by the writer to use empathy tactic number 1, perhaps slapping it on late in the writing process to make Christian more sympathetic: it does not seem integral or organic to the drama. We do not simply gather this from some perception of bad writing: we gather it from the invisibility of any real vulnerability in sadist Christian anywhere in the story. For all the allure of his power and handsomeness and promise of experiences, Christian is a dispassionate character, unable and unwilling to form deep social bonds and indifferent to Anastasia's vulnerabilities and emotional needs. As she finally realizes when she walks out of the relationship at the end of the film, there is no way into Christian's inner life, or even any assurance that such a life exists. He can never join her in any inner circle of intimacy.

This sadist differs in some specifically empathetic ways from *Twilight*'s Edward, the handsome and powerful high school vampire who loves the film's protagonist, Bella, but fears that his vampire nature will make him suck all her blood and kill her. In their big tryst scene (i.e., their scene of revealing vulnerabilities and asking for commitments), he warns his beloved to run away, and in fact does his best to show Bella that their love is a terrible idea by revealing his fearsome strength, his predatory power and his addiction to blood. He does this all not to impress but selflessly, out of concern for her and despite his strong desire and love for her. He is also taking a much bigger risk than Christian in making his confession: Edward has spent many lonely lifetimes hiding his identity for fear of being hunted, and so unlike Christian's admissions about his crack-addicted prostitute mother, Edward reveals his vulnerabilities and entrusts his beloved with a dangerous truth that puts him and his vampire friends and family at risk.

Notice how this scene makes Edward empathetic to us in many different ways. First, here we have the use of many compassion empathy tactics—we and Bella feel empathy for him when we learn that this young vampire has been desperately lonely for centuries, waiting for someone like her (tactics 1 and 4). And we also feel compassion when we see that Edward is tormented by a real and painful inner conflict—being in love with Bella but also desperate to kill her and suck her blood (tactic 7).

At the same time, we also feel communal empathy for him: he is opening up to Bella in a way he would never do with anyone else (tactic 8), *and* he is acting for Bella's own good, trying to scare her off even though he wants desperately to be with her (empathy tactic 10: doing something good for someone else at some real cost to himself). By contrast, Christian would never try to frighten Anastasia away in order to save her from his own desires, another sign of the poverty of his character and a reason why his spaces are so emotionally and empathetically empty.

In general, the form of a character defines the form of space in a story. As we will see, the empathetic Edward allows the craft team of that film to create an emotionally rich space in *Twilight*. By contrast, the dispassionate Christian produces the very flat spaces of 50 *Shades*: empathetic spaces cannot be built up around non-empathetic characters.

These examples let us sketch out the spatial topology of narrative that we will develop in the next two chapters.

TOPOLOGY: THREE FORMS OF CHARACTER AND THEIR CORRESPONDING NARRATIVE SPACES

The long array of dispassionate characters stretches back to the beginnings of the Western storytelling tradition. Consider for example the classical example of Hercules and his episodic adventures killing the horrible beasts of his world. More recently there is the classic 1950s Superman, that ever-confident, goodnatured emblem of mental hygiene whose psyche seemed free of all blemish. Think then of James Bond unflappably racing through his adventures in 22 films from the 1960s through the 2000s without a single doubt, guilt or emotional difficulty. Think of other emotionally impervious and invulnerable superheroes like sunny Thor in the film of that name (2011), or the traditional Sherlock Holmes, appraising every detail of a crime scene with Aspergian calm. And of course the FPS (first-person shooter) video-game landscape abounds with such characters. These dispassionate protagonists—usually male heroes—have no emotional vulnerabilities or struggles. There is another commonality: in these narratives the main character is pursuing *external* objectives that have no empathetic relation to these settings, which is why they never move us deeply. As a result the missing pleasures of empathetic bonds are here replaced by the pleasures of thrilling spectacle: Setting and narrative space tend to serve as pure spectacle and protagonists generally move through dispassionate spaces.

By contrast, most film and television narratives are powered by a *dramatic* protagonist, that most common form of protagonist who has both an *external and* an *internal* struggle. As they wrestle with psychological conflicts, identity crises and intimacy issues, these characters are usually found in a *dramatized space*. This is a place that is related to the plot, in

the protagonist's *external* goal, but is *not* deeply expressing her[7] *inner* objectives and struggles: as we can see from our example of *The Blind Side* above and also from the setting in the film *50/50* below, setting here no longer plays the role of empty spectacle, as this can distract from the dramatic struggle playing out in the protagonist's character-based conflicts. Nor is space used to create empathy the way the bathroom did in *The Pursuit of Happyness* (Fig. 1.8).

Many films in the drama and romantic comedy genre fit this model: think of *50/50* (2011), *Spotlight* (2015), *Room* (2015) or *The Intern* (2016). Think here too of the relatively unspectacular sets of most television comedies and dramas, of for example *Transparent* (2014–), *Silicon Valley* (2014–), *Black-ish* (2014–) or *Louie* (2010–). In all of these narratives spectacle may occasionally appear but it is not central to the story-line. This is not simply a question of budget but of foregrounding the emotional conflict playing out between the characters. Experienced filmmakers are aware that a spectacular setting can distract from or overwhelm certain kinds of story-lines and scenes. Here while the *characters* can be highly empathetic, their *spaces* are not.

Fig. 1.8 The film *50/50* (2011) utilizes dramatic space: Ordinary locations with low spectacle. Empathy is instead created first by compassion for the main character, who has to deal with cancer, and then by the efforts of his friend to help

Thirdly, there is the most powerful empathetic form which we see in films like *Amelie*, *Aliens*, and *The Third Man*, forming the narrative space which we call *Dantean space* since, we will argue, it was largely invented by Dante Alighieri in his *Divine Comedy*. In this aesthetic form a character is both *within* a place but is in a dramatic sense also within *herself*. That is to say, the story's setting has become a projection of the character's inner emotional drama, thus allowing us a powerful empathetic access to her inner emotional conflict through sensory, visual and aural means. The image from *Aliens* (Fig. 1.2) illustrates this: as Ripley descends from clean well-lit geometric spaces into the dark, dripping intestinal passages of the *Aliens*, she is also descending into a direct confrontation with her own past, with the death of her daughter, with her own fears of sex and rape and pregnancy and her fears of the organic reality of her own body. The tunnels reflect both her inner and her outer journey and struggle. The same can be said for Amelie, for Norman, for Batman, for the heroine of *Gravity* (2013), and also for so many of the characters we meet in Dante's *Divine Comedy*. They all feature a Dantean space, an aesthetic form where the setting is filtered through and entangled with the emotional aesthetic and point of view of its protagonist. As a result, the setting takes on a dramatic significance that is at the same time emotionally charged, being grounded in the past traumas and joys of the protagonist, and this makes the protagonist a powerful emotional glue between the viewers and the settings of the story.

A film can utilize a location as either a *dispassionate* space, a *dramatized* space, or a *Dantean* space, depending on the nature of its protagonist's dramatic struggles. As we will see in Chaps. 2 and 3, each of these forms is animated by a corresponding form of protagonist. This matters because the first form, dispassionate space, uses no or very weak forms of empathy, while dramatic space uses empathy as a tool of the drama but rarely as a tool for crafting the space: here the machinery of empathy often defines the conflicts between characters but does not find expression in the story space that envelopes them. By contrast, in our third form of space, setting becomes a kind of window into a character, and for that reason Dantean space is itself deeply and powerfully marbled with the tactics of empathy.

This window-like nature also reveals another aspect of Dantean space. While dispassionate and dramatic spaces can both work on different levels of narrative time, revealing the past, playing a role in the present or foreshadowing the future, a Dantean space serves all three roles at once.

It does this specifically because it is a layered character space: it reveals the deep roots of an individual's actions and shows how deeply they are inscribed in character. Take a film like *Amelie*. Essentially every single frame of the film is steeped in Amelie's sensibility, revealing that as an adult our protagonist still lives in the world she saw as an eight-year-old when her mother died violently besides her and her father showed her no physical affection.[8] As we can see from her room in figure 1.1, we feel that part of Amelie is still trapped back in her childhood in the very moment of her mother's death. To see this world of her childhood extending into every moment of her adult life is to see and feel the effects of the earlier time's events on this adult woman: the shade of the past is drawn over the adult Amelie's bedroom just as it characterizes her present-day yet dreamy Paris, telling us that she is still in some sense experiencing the world like a lonely, dreamy child.

Additionally, her charmed bedroom and charming Paris also tells us about what Amelie is likely to do in the future precisely because these spaces are imbued with her own character, with her tendencies and thus her own coming conflicts. These spaces tell us, for example, that she is going to approach every problem she faces with a sense of shy but playful whimsy and a childlike sense of justice and sharing, and that she will identify with anyone she meets who seems withdrawn and vulnerable and childlike. After she has had an episodic series of these adventures, her romantic interest Nino finally shows up: she finds him busy saving the abandoned photo-booth pictures of other Parisians, working as a costume skeleton in a fairground ghost train and showing a puckish joy and interest in the tiny captured moments of ordinary people. Nino is the only other character who shares both Amelie's childlike characteristics and her jouissance; it is important that he also sees Paris as she does, as a playground of flaneur habits, that like her he helps people he doesn't know, that like her he helps people he doesn't know, has a fondness for role-playing, and notices human singularities. Their character parallels and mutual compatibility all foreshadow their final romantic struggle and union: after seeing how their empathetic tendencies all overlap, we feel at the end that we know the future of this relationship, and we empathetically approve. In this sense the film's delightful, childlike, charming, nostalgic Paris is a field of their joint homologies and longings: while grounded in her past it vividly points forwards in the narrative, prophesying their future relationships, conflicts, quirky affinities and romantic choices, to become an empathetic web drawing and keeping them together. And being a space of an empathetic nature, it enlists us in *Amelie*'s struggles and then in her romance.

And so throughout the film we never leave the tunnel of Amelie's character, of her memory, fears, hopes, and innocence. To enter and stay in this narrative space is to stay within Amelie's singular experience and bond to her sensibility in an empathetic way. And because such spaces are so highly singular, they accomplish what Ralph Acampora (2006) posits (in a very different context) as a fundamentally compassionate act: our exposure to such surprising and fascinating interior sensibilities undercuts our ordinary assumptions that there is only one world, that there is only our own sensed world, and this realization of difference necessarily opens up "the possibility of other *Umwelten*–foreign, yet potentially familiar, forms of worldhood."[9] In this way Dantean spaces broaden both our concept of the Other and our ability to project our empathy into others. While Keen (2007) may be right to be suspicious of the claims of various empathy advocates, there is increasing evidence (Burke et al. 2016; Johnson 2012, 2013; Djikic et al. 2013) that exercises in imaginative narrative projection do actually affect and broaden our ability to empathize with others. In other words, while this is a narrative and not a sociological investigation, it necessarily takes us into core questions of the porous borders between readers and viewers, texts and narratives, and places and politics.

BOOK OUTLINE

But before we face those questions we first have to understand empathetic space in some depth. While Part I illustrates our overall approach, Part II pursues the examination of empathetic space across many Dantean examples, genres and forms of narrative. And here we identify a number of variations of *empathetic narrative space*. The first is '*shaded space*' a place where the death of a loved one has come to shade a character's entire world. The second is '*tryst space*', where the emotions of a romantic relationship have become spatialized in a non-generic way that expresses the characters of the couple. A third form, which we find in films ranging from the Death Star of *Star Wars* to the hotel rooms of *Hiroshima Mon Amour*, is '*alienated space*', spaces that show some social or emotional disjunction among characters or within a character. Some alienated spaces are placeless *non-spaces*, in the sense defined by the French sociologist Marc Augé in his analysis of airports and hotel lobbies. Another form of alienated space is '*showcase space*': similar to non-space in projecting a character's alienation, this form is marked by new consumer goods and walls lacking in any human mark, the kind of stage and production design often found for example in the television show *Mad Men* and in films from *Playtime* to *Pleasantville*. A third form of alienated space shows the violation of Oldenberg's Third Space theory, where in shows like *Homeland* or in *Star Trek: Discovery* (CBS, 2017–) we cannot distinguish workspace from homespace or cannot easily find any third-space zones of social life, as we find on the Death Star and in other alienated narrative spaces. We call this form '*work-house space*' to indicate how the pressures of instrumental work have crowded out the needed aspects of home and play from a character's living-space.

This overall analysis reveals some crucial aspects of Dantean space. For example, because Dantean spaces echo with the traumas that originate the story and because they often appear in a story when the character can no longer avoid or control her trauma-caused emotions, they are usually the site of the greatest dramatic tensions in a story. For this reason they are also often the site of the unresolved gender tensions in a protagonist. This is why they make great forensic tools, great red flags, for both writers and theorists. To illustrate this, our last chapters consider the strong social and political implications in this account.

Following on the heels of the analysis of over twenty examples of Dantean space, we begin Part III by asking "Is Dantean space bad for us?" After all, in a majority of the examples we consider in Parts I and II we find characters who are isolated, trapped within themselves by themselves. That marked commonality raises questions like: what are the effects of consuming narratives that deploy Dantean space? Despite its empathetic power, could Dantean space be a peculiarly alienating form of narrative space? Does traditional Dantean space inscribe a specific sense of self and of personal responsibility? Is it a coincidence that Dante's originary landscape is so marked by alienated, atomized and misanthropic characters? Does this form of narration teach us to see ourselves and others in a specific and anti-social way? After all, this aesthetic model of memory was in Dante's poem originally a moral model, one that wed personal history to responsibility and a code of punishment. Could it also have been both central to the development of the western bourgeois subject and also be destructive of social bonds that we value and desperately need today?

In our conclusion we ask if and when empathetic space might actually be good for us. The final chapters use our elaboration of story craft and social theory to highlight a newer variant of Dantean space, a form of storytelling that appears in such striking examples as the novel and films of *The Secret Garden*, the film *Amelie*, and the next-gen video-game *Wrath of The White Witch* (2013–), an innovation that has produced the rather unique emotional response of making its players cry. These narratives exhibit the youngest form of space which we call *ecstatic space*, a socially shared space of enchantment and healing, a form that suggests how story space might generate both socially-shared goals and emotions and a new sense of self. And so we end by seeing how these spaces all illustrate an ethics of care rather than Dante's moral commitments to guilt and bitterness: this leads us to ask whether such examples of ecstatic space might model a new and highly-empathetic public commons. Looking forwards to the future uses and manifestations of empathetic space, we ask if such spaces cannot only mimetically model our inner lives but can also actually extend out into the real world, charming and enchanting it in a way that produces a caring social commons.[10] Certain examples (sculptures by Bernini and examples like *The Third Man* and *Amelie* in cinema tourism) reveal a triangle of emotional entanglement of viewer, protagonist and place. Could such cases link mass-produced emotions to the nature of place? Could we use narrative to entangle people with real places, thus constructing a new shared space and social commons?

And so at the end of our journey, our tale about tale-telling ends by revealing a new path for escaping alienation, escaping our older more gendered forms of both story and political communication, pointing towards a path for escaping Dantean space.[11]

Craft Theory: A Methodological Approach

Before we begin on this journey, it might be worthwhile to describe our methodology. Though the final intent is to treat story and story space as social phenomena and to analyze them within the frame of cultural theory, we have begun by using certain common dramatic screenwriting terms, such as character and objective, to define a topology of forms of narrative space, avoiding at the outset even the simplest sociological concepts such as identity and subjectivity. The intention is to ground our analysis within the very Aristotelian methodology used by those who devise our novels, plays, TV series and films. Our justification for it is simple: when you set out to theorize about any field or activity, it is best as a rule to stay initially as much as possible within the working vocabulary of that field instead of immediately importing concepts from another body of work. In this way you are more confident of capturing the essence of that field's activities. And so in Part I we first focus on the Aristotelian and craft methodology that underlies the story phenomena we are trying to explain.

We then use that methodology—which we call Craft Theory—to reveal the logic, practice and impact of story space. In Part II we use this approach in a close reading of many examples of story space across many media. Here too we assume that Aristotle's story theory is central to the narrative design of the majority of today's narrative filmmakers and television creators, and so we seek to ground our theoretical tools in that body and history of theory. However, this book certainly does not assume that Aristotle's theories comprehend all useful thinking on aesthetics and culture: once we have deconstructed the phenomenon through its own terms and aesthetic history, we relate these craft techniques to the work of theorists of social space such as Augé and Oldenberg and to other social theories, such as recent work on hauntology by Fisher and others.

Finally in Part III we synthesize this craft-based approach with other historical and theoretical investigations in order to reveal the larger critical implications of these forms of space. In fact we argue that the insights extend not only across all forms of narrative, encompassing theater, literature, web series and video-games, but also have implications for how the self and the social are themselves constructed.[12 – 16]

THE HEART'S CAVE

Finally, this journey into empathetic space is a journey away from realism into guilt, into bitterness, and sometimes into the sight of the innocent. And hopefully this journey will help reveal not only our empathetic vision but how empathy is central to our lived lives and social structures.

As I hoped to hint in the book's dedication, empathetic space is a space informed by character, meaning it is a present informed by our experience, using the past to ground and deploy our present fears, hopes and dreams. Usually empathetic space in its most common, Dantean form helps us see the risks and rewards of people and situations. But sometimes the present becomes so steeped in and clouded by the past that it occludes aspects of the present, and so this capacity of ours can often lead to delusion and breakdown, becoming a journey into dream and nightmare, into illusion and delusion, into a subjective vision clouded by a trauma.

And yet, though empathy carries many risks, and though some of us avoid empathy like the plague and try to cut it out of ourselves because it makes us vulnerable and commits us to others, the capacity to experience it is actually crucial for our singular and collective survival. Empathy is more than a bridge between drama and life, more than a morality and a technique for creating social bonding, more than just the radar and record of intimacy and vulnerability, and far more than a collection of aesthetic tricks or storytelling tropes. Although, as storytellers have shown, it is also a mental tool that can break under stress, leading to all kinds of interesting aesthetic results, and the pain of empathy can lead us to hide in a cave of the heart for all our lives, that risk does not define this risky access to the world. In ordinary life empathy is a powerful and predictive tool for us. It is the best way we have to shine a light into the other, and then shine it back into ourselves. Empathetic space is not just the cave of the heart; we possess this tricky, slippery and frankly, dangerous aesthetic form because it is an essential form of knowledge.[17]

NOTES

1. This book builds on work I've presented and published in the past. The first is "Dantean Space and the Cities of Cinema", which is reprinted in the book *Media and the City* published in 2013 by Cambridge Scholars Press. I first presented that essay at the Ecrea "Media And The City" Sociology Conference in Milan in February 2012 and, in refined form, at the European Conference on Aesthetics in Prague in 2013. The second essay, "Narrative Space in Films and Videogames", was presented at the international Media and Sociology conference "Spectacular/ Ordinary/Contested Media City" at the University of Helsinki on May 15–17 2013. The third essay, "Dantean Space in The Gendered Homes of the Television show *Homeland*", was presented at the Feminist Media conference "Console-ing Passions 2013" at De Montfort University in Leicester, England. The core argument in this essay was also presented at the 2013 MLeague International Symposium "Media and the City" held at Ryerson University in Toronto, Canada and a Dantean Space analysis

of Batman and superheroes was accepted for presentation at the 2016 Superhero Identities Symposium at the ACMI in Melbourne Australia organised by Angela Ndalianis and others.

2. Even in the moment where the boy walks through the cold, the cold is not dramatically visible but is present only through his shivering performance.

3. We might also note that the first three tactics mark relatively passive characters while the rest of the list mark active characters.

4. https://www.youtube.com/watch?v=4_B6wQMd2eI, accessed May 1, 2017. Consider also the Wells Fargo Commercial "Learning Sign Language" (https://www.youtube.com/watch?v=DxDsx8HfXEk: accessed May 1, 2017). It too uses dramatic space, and also rises towards a catharsis of empathy tactic # 10 while first using tactics 1, 3, 4, 6 and 7 to make us care about the characters.

5. For another empathetic commercial see Apple Computer's "Frankie's Holiday" (https://www.youtube.com/watch?v=DxDsx8HfXEk: accessed May 1, 2017).

6. (We find it useful to compare these two films because compare them because *50 Shades* began as a piece of fan fiction on the *Twilight* website and resembles that film's structure in many ways.)

7. Note on general pronouns: since there is still no commonly accepted solution to the question of the right pronoun to use to cover general cases, throughout this book I have chosen to use both male and female pronouns to describe general cases.

8. Many moments of post-traumatic stress disorder are doubtlessly Dantean moments. But the broader definition of Dantean moment should include, first, the sense of being not only psychologically damaged by that earlier moment but even sensuously stuck in that earlier surrounding. An experience of betrayal can be so severe that a person is forever phobic about commitment, but this phobia isn't the same as the sensuous memory of the warm white sands under your feet as you rose over the rise on the beach and discovered your lover in the arms of the lifeguard. Second, it admits the possibility that one's whole personae is in a real sense unable to go beyond that stage of life, but an individual can remain childlike in his needs and cares and outlook, like Amelie, even though this is not necessarily bad or something to be cured. These two aspects distinguish Dantean moments from the psychological experiences of PTSD, though certainly the phenomena often overlap in drama and life.

9. Acampora (2006): p. 12.

10. The commons is a long-standing concept in economics and sociology and refers to spaces, whether actual or virtual, that are held in common usage by a community and that are subject to social conflicts requiring some

regulation or standards of use. Under some definitions, both the internet and the earth's sky are examples of zones that are social public commons. Among the many theorists in this area is the economist Elinor Ostrum, who won the Nobel prize in 2009 for her work on the commons.

11. There are other approaches as well that this study owes a debt to but which its approach differs from. Many efforts to analyse narrative space have deployed either the approach of Bakhtin (which puts time and the plot at the centre of analysis) or of Lefebvre (which posits sociological use as the determiner of meaning). Both of these approaches stress the social uses and categories that a space connotes. Another approach, especially common to film and television studies, has been to focus on the geographic mis-en-scène and framing of a space. Clearly in this study we are beginning at a different point: we propose that *character* be considered as a central if not primary indicator and determinator of a story's space's meaning. While of course acknowledging the crucial importance of other approaches, we propose ours has a number of useful dimensions. We continually try in these pages to relate theory to practice: we try to follow— and to reinforce and clarify—the methodology of the subject matter under examination, which is a fairly important justification for any methodology.

12. For example, on the construction of race, place and narrative space on sitcoms, see D'Adamo (2017).

13. By focusing only on empathetic space, we try to work phenomenologically up from character and focus on a certain emotionally powerful phenomenon in the viewer. Moreover, we do not argue that all narrative space is empathetic: we do not claim that narrative space always functions to express character, or that it always expresses the story's core conflict. Instead we try to identify stories that provoke no or very little empathy and to explain why and how they work so differently and why they attract such a different viewership. For this reason we place narrative space within a threefold topology that reveals a gamut of empathetic machinery at work in our stories. We feel this helps explain the roles and links between character, plot, emotion and place in specific examples. Initially we leave other forms and categories out of our analysis except where they enable powerful insights on specific noticeable tropes of empathetic space across many different examples. Here we deploy the spatial insights of Augé, Oldenberg and others.

14. Our hope is to be part of the project that Keen speaks of, to help fill in the current "gaps in our knowledge of potentially empathetic narrative techniques" (Keen 2007: p. x), even if we generally do not follow her excellent direction into analyzing how in-and out-group status can affect a particular aesthetic effort at creating bonds of empathy. Aside from some beginning work in our final chapters, we in general do not explore the role of these empathetic tactics across the boundaries of gender, race,

nationalism, age and so forth (the focus of, for example, Hollan and Throop 2011). This book is only a step in that direction, proposing an initial methodology and a focus on the specific narrative phenomenon of empathetic space.

15. Although we argue that Dante's work is an excellent way into empathetic space, and at times we make the historical claim that he was pivotal in the spread of empathetic space, this book is in no way intended as a work of Dante scholarship: there are far more scholarly road-maps available for that journey (see, for example, Durling and Martinez 1997; Kameen 2009–2010; Pearl 2009; Pertile 2007). Our main goal is pragmatic in nature and not entirely unlike those often made for the chronotope. That concept is considered useful to the extent it is productive for sociologists and semioticians. Perhaps, we propose, if a study is *also* pragmatically useful and insightful to the *makers* of narrative, that is in and of itself a kind of additional evidence for claiming to reveal some deep structure of narrative. Perhaps we need a new standard of truth and communication in a specific kind of narratological studies, one we call Craft Theory Studies, which overtly links the methodologies of the makers and the explicators of narrative. That is at least the additional standard we strive for ourselves in this study.

16. This work also builds on concepts I have suggested in earlier work. In one (D'Adamo 2015b) I proposed the existence of an "intimacy corridor" that was produced when a character in a set script (whether a singer, a newscaster or a subject of a documentary) broke down and left the script. In another essay (D'Adamo 2015a) I suggested we need various concepts, such as that of "inter-emotions", to describe the phenomenon of emotions and emotional memories that can break away from our Cartesian tradition and reveal how these phenomena exist not so securely in a subject's or a singular character's experience but rather across subjects and in the social realm. Expanding on Aristotle's brief intriguing comment that a true friend is a mirror of your best self, I proposed we recast the emotional language of aesthetic constructions in a more Heideggerian fashion. While avoiding that claim directly (I develop it in forthcoming work), this book is an initial attempt to establish a foundation for those investigations and has implications for the study of social bonds.

17. Dedicated to Joe Volpe for being such a generous teacher.

BIBLIOGRAPHY

Acampora, Ralph. 2006. *Corporal Compassion: Animal Ethics and Philosophy of Body*. Pittsburg: University of Pittsburgh Press.

Alighieri, Dante. 2006. *The Divine Comedy*, trans. and ed. Robin Kirkpatrick. London: Penguin.

Aristotle. 1986. *Poetics*, trans. S. Halliwell. Chapel Hill, NC: University of North Carolina Press.

Augé, Marc. 2002. *In the Metro*. Minneapolis: University of Minnesota Press.

———. 2004. *Oblivion*. Minneapolis: University of Minnesota Press.

———. 2016. *Everyone Dies Young: Time Without Age*. New York: Columbia University Press.

Bakhtin, Mikhail. 1981. *The Dialogic Imagination*, ed. Michael Holquist. Austin, TX: University of Texas Press.

Baxter, Charles. 2012. Undoings: An Essay in Three Parts. *Colorado Review* 39 (1): 96–110.

Burke, Michael, Anezka Kuzmicova, Anne Mangen, and Theresa Schilhab. 2016. Empathy at the Confluence of Neuroscience and Empirical Literary Studies. *Scientific Study of Literature* 6 (1): 6ff.

Burnett, Francis Hodgson. 1961. *The Secret Garden*. William Heinemann.

Creed, Barbara. 1990. Alien and the Monstrous-Feminine. In *Alien Zone: Cultural Theory and Contemporary Science Fiction Cinema*, ed. Annette Kuhn. London: Verso.

D'Adamo, Amedeo. 2013. Dantean Space in the Cities of Cinema. In *Media and the City: Urbanism, Technology and Communication*, ed. Simone Tosoni, Matteo Tarantino, and Chiara Giaccardi. Newcastle upon Tyne, UK: Cambridge Scholars Press.

D'Adamo, Amedeo. 2015. The People Beyond Mars: Using Robinson's Mars Trilogy to Understand Post-scarcity. *Thesis Eleven* 131 (1): 81–98.

D'Adamo, Amedeo. 2017. That Junky Funky Vibe: Quincy Jones' title theme for the sitcom *Sanford and Son*. In *Music in Comedy Television*, ed. Liz Giuffre, and Philip Hayword. New York and London: Routledge.

Dickens, Charles. 2002. *Great Expectations*. London: Penguin.

Djikic, Maja, Keith Oatley, and Mihnea C. Moldoveanu. 2013. Reading Other Minds: Effectsof Literature on Empathy. *Scientific Study of Literature* 3 (1): 28–47.

Durling, Robert, and Ronald Martinez. 1997. Notes. *The Divine Comedy of Dante Alighieri: Volume 1: Inferno*. New York: Oxford University Press.

Egri, Lajos. 2005. *The Art of Dramatic Writing*. New York: Bantam-Dell.

Field, Syd. 2005. *Screenplay: The Foundations of Screenwriting*, rev. ed. Delta Press, New York: Bantam Dell.

Hauge, Michael. 1991. *Writing Screenplays that Sell*, reprint. New York: Collins Reference.

Hollan, D.W., and C.J. Throop. 2011. *The Anthropology of Empathy: Experiencing the Lives of Others in Pacific Societies*. New York: Berghahn Books.

Johnson, Dan R. 2012. Transportation into a Story Increases Empathy, Prosocial Behavior, and Perceptual Bias Toward Fearful Expressions. *Personality and Individual Differences* 52 (2): 150–155.

————. 2013. Transportation into Literary Fiction Reduces Prejudice Against and Increases Empathy for Arab-Muslims. *Scientific Study of Literature* 3 (1): 77–92.

Kameen, Joseph. 2009–2010. Darkness Visible: Dante's Clarification of Hell. *WR: Journal of the Arts & Sciences Writing Program* (Issue 2).

Keen, Suzanne. 2007. *Empathy and the Novel*. Oxford: Oxford University Press.

Kim, Sue. 2013. *On Anger*. Austin: University of Texas Press.

Lefebvre, Henry. 1992. *The Production of Space*. Oxford: Wiley-Blackwell.

Miller, Frank. 2016. *The Dark Knight Returns*: 30th Anniversary Edition. DC Comics.

Ostrom, Elinor. 1990. *Governing the Commons: The Evolution of Institutions for Collective Action*. Cambridge, UK: Cambridge University Press.

Pearl, Matthew. 2009. Dante and the Death Penalty. *Legal Affairs*, Jan.–Feb.

Pertile, Lino. 2007. Introduction. *Inferno, The Cambridge Companion to Dante*, ed. Rachel Jacoff, 2nd ed., 70–73. New York: Cambridge University Press.

Shonfield, Katherine. 2000a. The Use of Fiction to Interpret Architecture and Urban Space. *Journal of Architecture* 5 (4): 369–389.

Shonfield, Katherine. 2000b. *Walls Have Feeling: Architecture, Film, and the City*. London and New York: Routledge.

Steinby, Liisa. 2013. Bakhtin's Concept of the Chronotope. In *Bakhtin and his Others: (Inter) subjectivity, Chronotope, Dialogism*, ed. Liisa Steinby, and Tintti Klapuri. New York: Anthem Press.

Tolkien, J.R.R. 2011. *The Hobbit*. New York: HarperCollins.

Wallace, Lee. 2011. *Lesbianism, Cinema, Space: The Sexual Life of Apartments*. London and New York: Routledge.

CHAPTER 2

The Empty Man of Action vs. The Active Heart: Dispassionate and Dramatic Characters from *James Bond* and *Sherlock Holmes* to *Little Miss Sunshine, Hamlet* and *The Hobbit*

DEFINING CHARACTER

Since we are describing empathetic space as an expression of character, we now tackle the fundamental question of drama:

What is character?

The term has been defined in many conflicting ways. The confusion over defining this core term of drama is found across the literature: consider Hawthorn (2017). The conflict, though not the resolution, is nicely spelled out in Moller (2017, p. 56), where she points out that for decades many have rejected the idea that the concept of character can even be a useful critical category. "Like the idea of unitary selfhood, "character" was dismissed as an anachronism and "as much an ideological construct as other basic concepts of western "logocentrism" (Hillis Miller 1992, 31). Generations of students have been taught that character analysis—in particular the sort of character analysis that deals with fictional characters as if they were real people—is, at best, a naively mimetic undertaking." This insight about a central ideological divide over such a core term helps reveal the division that now exists in universities between the schools of narrative craft and those of narrative theory. Despite this excellent critique, however, even Moller has some trouble giving a clear and simple definition of the term character, instead summarizing Forster.

© The Author(s) 2018
A. D'Adamo, *Empathetic Space on Screen*,
https://doi.org/10.1007/978-3-319-66772-0_2

We suggest that character, in both life and literature, is composed of the tendencies in the actions of a person. What do we mean by "tendencies"? Those patterns in the desires, hopes, dreams, approaches, impulses, tactics and techniques of a person. Why is character so important to us as humans? Simply because the past tendencies in the actions of a character also tends to predict how a person will act in future situations, and this is often the most important information we need to know in the most important situations we face in life.

Imagine you meet Jim, a very interesting fun guy, in a local bar one night. Your conversation goes on for hours: you find you've so much in common and Jim is smart, fun, interesting, insightful and clearly loves talking with you and you feel you're yourself funny and smart with him. And so a friendship starts: you meet at the bar every two or three days for a few weeks.

Then one night when it's raining your car breaks down just twenty minutes outside of town so you call Jim at the bar and explain the problem and ask him to come pick you up. And he gives excuses. You press him and he says "Look, the bar's really hopping tonight: can you call someone else? I'd love to do it but ... anyway, let's meet up tomorrow night, how's that sound?"

In this moment, you realize the difference between Jim's great personality and his character. It turn out that Jim is what's known as a fair-weather friend, someone who loves to be around you when all is good but who won't be there if you ever need him. Now you have learned about Jim's tendencies, and you learned about them by putting him into a situation where he had to choose and this revealed something hidden about who he really is. It revealed his character—Jim is very self-centered and selfish, and thanks to this insight into him now you're careful not to take this new friendship too far. Suddenly gleaning the difference in a friend between a projected scintillating, fun personality and an underlying selfish, egocentric character is a lesson at the heart of many dramas in life and literature: this insight is for example there at the core of Holly's relationship with Harry in *The Third Man*, lies at the core of the protagonist's first girlfriend in *50/50*, and also in Paul Reisman's character in *Aliens*, and is the revelation at the center of many romantic stories. And the reverse is also often true: think of how many forbidding, unfriendly personalities then reveal a strong and helpful character hidden underneath?

The example of Jim shows how crucial character is for our social bonds: think of the pressing practical importance of such questions as, will this friend be generous and giving? Will this leader be trusted to be brave and loyal to the group? When I leave town on a short trip, can this lover be trusted not to sleep with my friend and can this friend be trusted not to make a move on my lover? These are questions about what this person is likely to do, an extrapolation I make based on what I know they've done. It is a question of the predictability and the trajectory of a person's tendencies. It is a question of character.

The biopic *Raging Bull* (1980) illustrates this in a painful and comic moment. Down on his luck and all alone, the retired boxer Jake La Motta needs to raise some money. So Jake gets an idea: he has a very valuable trophy, his old jewel-encrusted Boxing World Championship belt. Jake takes a hammer to his esteemed trophy belt and smashes the jewels off and then takes them to the pawnshop. The owner patiently explains that the jewels are not worth much but that the belt would be worth a lot. But of course, as even Jake now realizes, he has destroyed the belt and so has destroyed his own chances once again. His forlorn slouch in the scene as he realizes this seems like a revelation of character: he seems to realize that this action of his, destroying the belt, manages to sum up his whole overall character and story.

From the start of our tale Jake has been a boxer to his core: he tends to solve every problem by hitting it with all the force he can. This marked tendency which has come to define his life certainly worked great in the ring—it won him the bejeweled world championship belt, for example, but the same tendency didn't work so well in his two important relationships, the bond with his brother/manager and with his wife. When he had a conflict with them he struck out physically and as a result is now permanently estranged from them. At this point in Jake's life he has begun to realize and take responsibility for his guilt, and so the destruction of the belt, done in a growing fury, also feels like Jake is punishing himself for his own choices. A kind of brilliant mis-en-abîme of Jake's entire story, this broken heraldic trophy becomes a perfect expression of all his tendencies and choices and of their good and bad results.

THE CENTRALITY OF DETECTING CHARACTER FOR SURVIVAL

Character is at the very center of our dramas for one excellent reason: evolution. All of us, from the moment we are born, have a driving need to perceive and understand and predict the tendencies of the people all around us. We need to know who to trust, who to fear, who will feed us, who to depend on, who to love and befriend and shun and hate. We need to learn to read and predict and diplomatically interact with characters in nearly all situations in life; we need to know and predict their goals, tactics and methods. It is a major challenge to be born into a human community without being able to understand the communication system or detect character. Detecting character is not so easy thanks to the many-faced evolution of personality (a social mask that purports to reveal character but is really a dissimulation). It seems even the most perceptive of us can be fooled by someone, to expect tendencies that are not actually there, and the results of this mistake range from disappointment to divorce to death. At the same time we know it is dangerous for us to reveal our own tendencies: this can allow others to predict and manipulate us, and so it becomes important for us to recognize, exert, regulate and hide parts of our own character. And of course, as Jake LaMotta comes to realize, it is also hard to see inside ourselves, to see our own character: to even begin to see the most obvious and awful patterns in our own tendencies we often need the stress of a drama. Often we can only see our own actions when they are reflected in the cold faces of our disappointed friends, of our estranged families, in our own smashed trophies lying broken in our hands.

The Social Circles of Intimacy

And so in life we are careful about revealing our character. I do not reveal my mistakes, my secret fears or hopes or secrets, just to anyone I meet: some tendencies I can reveal to a distant friend, others to a close friend, others only to a trusted brother or parent or lover, someone who has been there for me in the past, who has a proven tendency to keep secrets. There are in fact a series of concentric rings of trust, rings of revealing character tendencies which we might call the rings of intimacy. Someone slowly becomes a good friend by building and observing the circle over years through many rainy nights and stormy days. Only after the test of time will I trust her with my character flaws, my mistakes, my vulnerabilities and insecurities.

Character Arc Defined

Recognizing flaws can lead to a struggle to change, which is also not easy: in fact to inculcate new habits and new tendencies is extremely hard. In the children's novel *The Hobbit*, when Bilbo Baggins leaves his comforting hobbit hole he is a coward who faints when he hears a scary story. But then through some rough, painful, frightening experiences, he gradually changes: after being caught by trolls, chased by goblins, fleeing Wargs and cowering in Bearn's house from a giant bear, Bilbo can finally face the spiders and then a dragon and then a war. And so as characters from Bilbo to Jane Austin's heroines show us, we can learn step by step to be courageous. In both life and drama character is deep and strong but like a hard metal it can be slowly worked into new shapes. This process of a major change in one's tendencies is called a *character arc*.

Inner and Outer Goals, Objectives and Conflicts Defined

So far in our definitions we have avoided invoking any historically laden term like "the self". But we now suggest that the human trick of personality, the false mask of projecting character, and also the concept of the rings of intimacy, both open up a distinction between external and internal desires, goals and struggles. A struggle to change one's intimate secret tendencies is often labeled an "inner conflict" or an attempt to achieve an "inner objective" to distinguish this from struggling to achieve an objective in the world, which is often called an "external objective" (Hauge 1991). One person might become a Doctor to gain respect, another to gain community, another to feel worthwhile, another to gain money and security, another to gain power. External objectives are powered by internal objectives but do not mirror them: as we see in the film *Legally Blonde*, the protagonist Elle struggles to get into to Harvard Law School (an external objective) not to get a law degree but to prove to her ex-boyfriend that she's worth loving and marrying (an internal objective).

Intimacy is a key term here in distinguishing these two types of motives. A relationship with intimacy requires trust, a sense of safety in revealing vulnerabilities, hopes, fears and dreams. Internal objectives play such a central role in drama because it is risky to reveal these intimate tendencies to someone: we keep our intimacies hidden from larger social circles because we fear how they might be used against us. Think of being in high school and being afraid to tell someone about a crush you have on a certain person.

The risk that circles our intimate hopes and fears, the concern that they might become public in a bad way that hurts us, means that intimacy and vulnerability usually increase as a relationship grows stronger: they are a kind of glue that can strengthen a bond between two people. As we noted earlier, the bond, the level of intimacy in a relationship, is usually calibrated as appropriate to the other's place in our concentric social circles of trust—the roughly concentric shrinking rings of neighbors, co-workers, friends, close friends, family, lovers and spouses. And over time a relationship can travel in either direction through these circles (which are not always fixed or in exactly this order). The more intimate a revelation is, the smaller the circle, the greater the level of risk being taken and so the greater the trust being placed on the person receiving it. And betrayals of an intimate trust and of intimate secrets sever the bonds, leaving painfully-torn hearts.

Also, sudden violations or disruptions of these circles of intimacy also cause drama. A wedding can bring someone entirely new into a somewhat stabilized group of family and friends, and the effect is rather like a new giant planet entering a solar system that then disturbs all the old orbits. Marriages always cause problems and changes and collisions in existing relationships, which is one reason why weddings are so often at the center of dramas. But other large events can disturb these circles as well, bringing new tests and allegiances. For example, the threatened failure of a business will often challenge the hierarchies and circles of trust in a group (*The Big Night, The Godfather*). So will the revelation of any complex betrayal. Imagine you heard that a young man in your neighborhood had an affair with his father's business partner's wife, and then had one with her daughter. Anyone who heard only these facts would know that this betrayal is guaranteed to cause uproar across the circles: that there will be drama, that suddenly all the old bonds of trust are threatened in some way, and so all the circles in these two families will need to be redrawn. Knowing nothing else about these people, we understand this is a dramatic situation, that vulnerabilities, insecurities and intimacies will be shaken loose, that characters will be challenged and relationships changed. We also know that these families will probably want to hush up this situation as it reveals too much intimate character information.

Moreover, to meet someone who wants to ignore the socially accepted gradations of intimacy and barge prematurely into an intimate circle is usually alarming, and hints at some inner imbalance of emotions and a promise of hidden future dramas. If you are on a blind date with someone and he offers you the key to his apartment or shows you that he has already tattooed your name on his arm, you know that a lot of drama, in his past and potentially in your future, lies just below his strained smile. Usually the circles of intimacy must be carefully negotiated and if someone can't do this properly, he is probably wrestling with internal conflicts that tend to push him into messy choices and dramas.

After providing this rather simple account of character, intimacy and vulnerability, let's see how these concepts map onto the Western dramatic tradition, which purports to be a great instruction manual for understanding character in ourselves and in others.

Dispassionate Characters and Dispassionate Space

Intimacy and internal objectives are missing in a whole class of stories. Consider now the shared singular characteristic of protagonists such as Hercules and the classic versions of Sherlock Holmes, James Bond and Superman, or think of the lead character of many children's shows from the classic Spiderman (ABC 1967–1970) to today's *Paw Patrol* (*Spinmaster* 2013–). These characters all possess only clear external objectives—monsters to kill, mysteries to solve, bombs to defuse, enemies to destroy—and have carefully been shorn of most signs of an inner emotional life. Reflecting this simple clarity of purpose, such characters possess remarkable powers to change their world and have no internal emotional goals to struggle with or achieve, no intimacies to cover over, no vulnerabilities to protect, no emotional conflicts to slow them down as they charge forwards through their highly elaborated and exotic worlds. They are in a sense emotionally invulnerable, possessing an inner strength that mirrors their external imperturbable strengths. We will call this form of character a *dispassionate* character.

These characters also have something else in common. They tend to solve problems with 'high stakes', an inexpert term of story craft which means that their goals are very pressing matters of life and death. The 'high stakes' often involve numerous members of the public, usually with no cohesive intimate bond: our hero must save the 747 plane before it crashes, then he must go on to save the country or the planet or the universe. In other words, often the people who need to be saved have no personal intimate conflicts or connection to the hero.

Not surprisingly, these heroes tend not to focus on problems or conflicts inside the smaller, more intimate circles: we are fascinated by them not because their struggles are so like our own but rather because the lives of so many hang on their success. Their journey needn't be about working on inner problems because the outer ones are so pressing. These characters also tend to lack a clear character arc. Hercules and Sherlock Holmes are essentially invulnerable with no inner conflicts and so have both no particular tendencies that must be changed and no impetus to change. The classic Superman is the exemplary case. As shown here in Fig. 2.1, the strong stance of Superman shows he is never in doubt, never ashamed, never guilty, never afraid of intimacy, never in a personal crisis of any kind. His problems revolve around the proper techniques for stopping this week's super-villain. His only vulnerability, a weakness in the presence of Kryptonite, is itself a physical external problem. Try to imagine Superman crying, or cringing over a memory from middle school, or dealing with a wife who has breast cancer. He does not have the inner emotional machinery to engage in such dramas. Thankfully for him, he also doesn't have the time: he has to rush off to defuse a bomb or thwart another super-villain.

Fig. 2.1 Superman, who lacks vulnerabilities and intimacies and internal objectives but is never lacking in external objectives like Save the Planet, Stop the Villain, etc.

Though their roots extend far into classical storytelling these dispassionate characters continue to save our worlds in cinema and television today: consider for example the first film of the successful Marvel franchise *Thor* (2011). Like Superman, Thor has no emotional problems to grapple with, no fears or guilt, no intimacies to confess to a lover in bed. His big turning-point is the moment he decides to sacrifice himself for his friends, but this is not a dramatic change demanding some new hidden strength he never knew he had: nothing before this moment has led us to think of him as weak or insecure or even selfish. From start to finish of the plot, Thor is simply a god with the sunny smile and look of a buffed surfer dude who once again saves our universe from some very one-dimensional enemies.

The same can be said about most versions of both Sherlock Holmes and James Bond prior to the 2000s: before the social trauma of 9/11 such characters appeared in film after film solving murders and saving the world without ever being noticeably marked in any psychological way by their tireless efforts. Such characters tend not to have character arcs, since there is no inner emotional struggle to overcome, no problematic tendencies of action that require changing. They therefore make great central characters for film franchises because they are known, fixed characters, always ready to be wheeled out for the next mystery or battle, the next foe and the next show of fireworks.

There are also dispassionate heroes who lack any of the extraordinary powers and methods of these characters but who are just a plucky brave version of an everyman. Consider Jack, the hero of the 1994 hit *Speed*. Jack thinks fast and solves problems and jumps into save others, but he has no special abilities. He also has only the slightest of discernible emotional arcs: perhaps he is learning through his adventures with Annie (his romantic interest) to trust a partner and no longer go it alone. We might read this change into his story, but aside from a few thrown-away lines Jack's commitment issue is a very slim emotional problem with no scenes of dramatic conflict dedicated to it. Our examples also reveal something else: by traditionally skewing male, such dispassionate characters have also helped define masculinity itself as invulnerability.

It should not surprise us that dispassionate characters and stories appeal largely to audiences who have no interest in the puzzles of emotional intelligence: instead the appeal of these characters is that they allow us uninterrupted fantasies of power and social importance that play out in spectacular manipulations triggered by their conflict with their antagonist. We wish we could fly, or fling a mountain at a bad guy, or be valued and cheered and feted by a relieved galaxy. As a result such characters elicit no deep sympathy or empathy. However adrenalynic they make us feel, we never cry over the travails of Superman.

Mirroring their emotionally denatured form of character, and heightening the fantasy of power that carries the viewer past the emptiness of their emotional life, these tales are full of dispassionate spaces: spectacular barriers and opponents for these characters to battle against. The emotional fireworks are produced from this impact, and so we can say that the external goal of the character shapes the space of the story into emotionally empty external spectacle. Here spectacle is usually deployed to dazzle and create an adrenalynic reaction: Superman lifts buildings, Thor blows up the Bifrost Bridge, and Jack skids and slams his way through *Speed*'s spectacular explosions. But of course while buildings explode, no heart is ever harmed or warmed: we do not see any wrenching emotional scenes and never find ourselves crying over tragic events. When death takes place it is almost always only to propel the next adventure with vengeance. And so we feel only adrenalynic jolts and, at best, we marvel. Dispassionate and Dantean space each have a corresponding form of Spectacle: Because empathy is largely missing, dispassionate spectacle is thus deeply different from Dantean spectacle, which is an individualized expression of a character's past joys or traumas and thus is imbued with an emotional dimension and with a far more elaborate construction and conception of the self. But first we must look at dramatic characters, the most common form of character in today's plays, novels, films and televison shows.

DRAMATIC CHARACTERS AND DRAMATIC SPACE

By contrast to their dispassionate brethren, *dramatic* characters do depend on the machinery of empathy, and are characterized by three differences from dispassionate characters.

1. They tend to pursue much more prosaic external goals like "Get the Job!" or "Win the Dance Contest!".
2. They do so with an active, conflicted heart; for example, they wrestle with confidence or guilt or loneliness or a need for love or to prove themselves.

3. They usually have character arcs: they usually either undergo a change in their tendencies or resolutely refuse to change, and an answer to this question of whether they will change marks the end of the story.

Let's examine the first difference, which is simply the very size of the external objective being pursued. Like dispassionate characters, dramatic characters are also actively trying to achieve some external goal, and often with the same urgency but, unlike the save-the-world high-stakes goals of dispassionate characters, the goals of most dramatic characters are the kinds we ourselves are likely to experience. Examples of common external dramatic goals include "get the guy/girl!" (*Hiroshima Mon Amour, Once, Notting Hill, Knocked Up*), "fix the broken relationship!" (*Casablanca, La Notte*), get into college (*Say Anything*), plan a friend's wedding (*Bridesmaids*), win a contest (*The Full Monty, Little Miss Sunshine, Pitch Perfect*), or save the family farm or restaurant or bank or protection racket (*The Big Night, The Godfather*).

Generally speaking, we have far more to learn from watching someone solve a dramatic conflict than a dispassionate conflict: we are unlikely to ever need to save the entire from world or stop a mad bomber or a war with the frost giants, but we often need to fix a friendship or save a business or plan a wedding. Such goals and problems engage our emotional intelligence while dispassionate goals and problems engage our adrenalynic reactions and our fantasies of power. In other words, dramatic characters generally try to face problems similar to ours armed only with abilities somewhat like ours while dispassionate characters use powers and abilities we know we will never have to solve problems we know we will never face.

Second, dramatic characters differ from their dispassionate brethren because they grapple not only with an external problem but also with an internal objective, such as to overcome a particular guilt or fear, or to realize some underlying desire. And now just as we noted that the domestic, familiar, prosaic nature of dramatic external goals engage us in ways that dispassionate goals cannot, we also see a parallel form of inner engagement and recognition. The *self*-reflective struggles and conflicts of dramatic characters are familiar enough to engage our emotional intelligence in a way dispassionate characters (who lack such vulnerabilities and concerns) cannot.

There is a third distinction that often holds as well: the worlds of the two kinds of characters are usually rather different. The dispassionate character's world can be a result of special skills: Sherlock Holmes lives in a world of clever and dangerous murderers, of microscopic observations and unique, surprising forms of knowledge about the ordinary; Thor lives in a mythological homeland. And this is the fantasy aspect of many dispassionate worlds: they function by such different rules from our own that they can be enjoyed without fear that our viewing pleasure will be interrupted by anything reminding us of troubling emotional or practical problems.

The rise of the Novel and the modern theater have somewhat sharpened the distinction between the thrilling fantasy stories of kings and heroes and the stories of ordinary life. Though novels and modern theatre helped make dramatic characters into the most common form of protagonist in our stories, they did this largely by their emphasis on the specifically *domestic* dramas of their new middle-class and working-class audiences. These dramas are generally not about the struggles of a Hercules or the downfall of a king but focus rather on the conflicts in, say, a middle-class or working-class family. Slowly the older tropes of dispassionate stories were shunted into the tropes of adventure stories and thrillers, genres that have become the province of children and teenagers.[1]

This too has helped mark the general distinction of spaces we associate with the two forms of character: as the scope of story conflicts changed so did the role of spectacle. Compare an audience watching Hercules wrestle with dragons to an audience watching a husband and wife wrestle with their disappointments and thwarted longings as they argue about the cost of her new dress and his flirting with her friend at the bar. Ibsen's play *A Doll's House* (1879) would not work well if just behind the couple we saw through a window a raging battle between armies playing out in the hills behind the house. With this placement of dramatic characters in domestic settings, story space must lose some of its spectacularity and serve the drama in new ways. When the external problem—be it dragon or armies—turns into a stack of overdue bills and a tendency to drink too much, dramatic space *must* recede to a supporting position and not distract us from the emotionally complex drama playing out in the foreground.

THE DRAMATIC CHARACTERS AND SPACES
OF *LITTLE MISS SUNSHINE*

Let's look at some examples of dramatic characters in some depth. The film *Little Miss Sunshine* (2006) is a dramedy (a drama with some comic elements) featuring dramatic characters existing in non-spectacular dramatic spaces.

As we can see from Fig. 2.2, the little girl who opens the movie stands alone before a television in a small cheaply panelled, sparsely decorated living-room. She is rehearsing the hollow sentiments of some beauty pageant winner, carefully practicing the woman's false, inauthentic performance. Right away we learn that the little girl is an innocent, that she is not being supervised and that she is not a typical beauty, and we grow afraid that her goal to be like a beauty pageant winner will damage her permanently.

Next we meet her father, far away at some community college, giving a motivational lecture on how to be a winner and not a loser. The audience is small and uninspired by his talk but he struggles to smile and soldier on, trying to sell his book and his 'Be a Winner in Life!' philosophy as the bored room empties out.

Now we cut to his son, a teenager doing workouts alone in his room under the baleful glare of Friedrich Nietzsche, who has been painstakingly drawn with a sharpie on a bed sheet. We soon learn the son wants to be a fighter pilot and this is part of his training.

Fig. 2.2 A typical location from the film *Little Miss Sunshine*, a dramatic space using low spectacle

Now we meet the family's grandfather who locks himself alone in the toilet to do drugs.

Next we meet the mother, alone in her car, driving fast while nervous and agitated: she lies with irritation to her husband as she speeds to the hospital.

At the hospital her brother, who has tried to cut his wrists, sits alone in utter depression. The hospital wants to keep him but he has no insurance and no money so she will have to take him in. Soon we will learn that he has lost both his college teaching job and his lover and wants both back.

All of these six figures have individual struggles and goals but only the little girl's and the suicidal brother's are overtly empathetic at the start. Slowly, though, we realize that they also share some common antagonisms. Each is found separate and alone in a location, and slowly we begin to see how this isolation expresses a common antagonist: they are each alienated, all lack love and care, and all are threatened by poverty and loss. Though each has their own separate *external* antagonist—the beauty competition, the book publisher, the military pilot program, etc.— all have a unified *internal* antagonist, which is expressed in many places but also in the dramatic spaces of the film. As we come to realize their common danger we feel a compassionate empathy for them all. Moreover, although each has his or her own separate external objective and singular inner objective, by the end of the film's set-up all six characters commit to a unified external objective, rallying around the compassionate goal of getting the little girl to the beauty contest and helping her to win.

In a film that opens with an announcement that everyone must fight to be a winner and each has a specific individual goal, we are surprised when it turns out that every single one of these six very sympathetic characters clearly fails in a very real sense to achieve what they want. The son permanently loses his chance to be a fighter pilot. The father loses his book contract in no uncertain terms and, after giving up all hopes of publishing has no idea what career he ought to pursue. The wife, who wanted a divorce, changes her mind and loses her chance to start a new life free from her shallow husband. The wife's brother learns he has no chance to gain his old job or his old lover back and faces professional ruin. The grandfather dies and is stuffed unceremoniously into the minibus trunk. And the little girl rather spectacularly loses the contest, marking the resounding failure of this family's joint goal which underlay the entire road-trip.

But despite this range of failures, something remarkable happens in this film. In most stories when six main characters each and all lose in both their separate and their joint struggles to achieve external objectives, we are in a tragedy. Yet the ending of *Little Miss Sunshine* is very uplifting and positive. Why? Because while the six characters each and all fail to achieve their *external* goals, they each and all resolve their *internal* conflicts: they overcome their alienation and loneliness and unify as a family and help and find love in each other. Thanks to a confining, narrow unified and unifying space as imperfect as this family, the ancient cheerful VW van with its stuttering engine and its broken sliding door becomes the emblem of their growing and very empathetic communion: our compassionate empathy for each which has been growing in the first two acts now changes into communal empathy for all in the third act. And this is what matters to us: since these are fully-realized, vulnerable dramatic characters and not dispassionate characters, we care far more about their *internal* objectives and struggles than we do about their external objectives.[2]

GENDER BIAS IN DISPASSIONATE AND DRAMATIC STORIES IN BOOKS FOR CHILDREN

As we noted above, dispassionate characters tend to be male while dramatic characters have a far less noticeable gender bias and, to judge from a quick glimpse of a few examples, this bias seems true even of children's media. *Jake and the Pirates* (Disney Junior 2011–) and *Inspector Gadget* (DIC 1989) both feature confident dispassionate male protagonists and are full of spectacular adventures. By contrast, a dramatic show like *Doc McStuffins* (Brown Bag 2012–) features a girl protagonist who is committed to an ethic of care and solves problems among her toy friends in her backyard. Similarly, the dramatic show *LEGO Friends* (LEGO 2012–), set in the ordinary life of a small town, features five main female characters who are drawn with enough depth and difference for the show's plots to be about learning to be honest with yourself and others, solving emotional problems among members of a group, and various other inner conflicts and issues of intimacy and trust.

Empathy Invades the Dispassionate Story: Recent Cross-Over Pressures

Before we move on to Dantean characters and their forms of empathetic space, it is worth taking a moment to consider a large cultural shift in Western films: in the last two decades many of our traditionally dispassionate stories have become inflected by dramatic characters and character arcs. For example, although superheroes have traditionally been dispassionate characters, they have increasingly become dramatic characters, ever since the cross-demographic financial success of Sam Raimi's *Spider Man* (2002). *Spider Man* accomplished this feat (and the resulting box-office success) by bringing a new level of emotional realism to the character's relationships to his parents and to his romantic lead.[3] In fact, Peter Parker's superhero persona and spectacular adventures aren't introduced until over an hour into Peter's story: in that first hour we learn that Peter is vulnerable, under-confident and always emotionally reaching out to his romantic hope, and then when he tries to do the right thing we see him inadvertently becoming responsible for his uncle's death, acquiring a crushing guilt that makes his later superhero struggles both empathetic and purgatorial. This newer narrative architecture has greatly changed the demographic appeal of certain superhero franchises, bringing in women and other groups that had tended to be largely uninterested in genres dominated by dispassionate characters.[4]

Spiderman's success was followed by the successful reinvention in 2004 of a dispassionate science fiction adventure show as a dramatic series. While staying within the mythological outlines of the old *Battlestar Galactica* (ABC 1978), the re-imagined 2004 series took place in a far more dramatic universe with many well-drawn relationships and emotional conflicts, becoming a six-year critical and commercial hit for the Sci-Fi channel.

In 2005, this change was further marked by the remarkable success of director Christopher Nolan's film *Batman Begins*, which put emotional vulnerability and a dramatic therapy arc at the very center of the superhero franchise. We discuss Nolan's film in depth in the next chapter.[5]

Perhaps the most striking moment in this shift came in the shocking opening sequence of *SkyFall* (2012), the twenty-third film in the James Bond franchise, when Bond was accidentally shot by his partner, a woman agent. Shaky, unable to shoot straight, shorn of his usual swagger and confidence, a newly vulnerable Bond was created, a dramatic character now gifted with inner conflicts, and for the first time in the franchise a Bond film became peppered with affecting dramatic scenes and even occasional flashes of Dantean space. Like Abrams' *Star Trek* reboot (see note 5), *Skyfall*'s director Sam Mendes bluntly stated that this film too was inspired by Nolan's reworking of Batman into a dramatic character.

We also see this sea-change on television in the Marvel superhero universe. *Jessica Jones* (2015–) is a superhero who is nonetheless a dramatic character, a lonely, bitter alcoholic wrestling with issues of intimacy and trust. Despite her physical invulnerability and her continual need to save others from the bad guys, every episode is also a drama unfolding around relationship problems. Similarly, the show's noir atmosphere is not only serving as a series of codified visual cues intended to trigger genre expectations: the dark city Jones inhabits is also a reflection of her own dramatically-grounded state of misery and depression.[6]

Two explanations seem plausible for this recent melding of aesthetic forms. One is the resulting expanded demographic: combining dispassionate franchises with dramatic protagonists can terrifically expand a film's audiences. But there are plausible social explanations for why dispassionate franchises have become increasingly dramatic in their form and execution. One is the historical trauma of 9/11, which by undercutting the myth of US invulnerability introduced new uncertainties into our collective imagination. Another turning-point was the economic crisis that began in 2008, which brought so much precarity to the everyday lives of ordinary people. It is perhaps no surprise that since the crisis started so many previously invulnerable heroes have become vulnerable and self-reflective: perhaps audiences living with a new and constant sense of precariousness may find such vulnerable dramatic superheroes easier to identify with than their older dispassionate counterparts.

Another effect of this recent change in form that many have observed is that high-quality, non-spectacular drama has been pushed off the big screen in the last two decades and has taken over cable television.[7] For all the accolades and critical successes of a *Spotlight*, it is today very hard in Hollywood to make a mid-range budget drama that doesn't contain many spectacular elements. Arguably partly this is because the dispassionate form has been corrupted so that spectacle can now express inner struggles.

A last wrinkle worth mentioning here is the success of the dispassionate and yet highly empathetic film *Wonder Woman* (2017), the most recent product of the growing realization in the Hollywood studio culture that women now make up a much larger proportion of the ticket-paying audience in genre-demographics that had been conventionally understood as young and male. On one level *Wonder Woman* (2017) is a typical dispassionate film, but our enjoyment of it is also highly empathetic for two specific reasons that stand outside the film's dispassionate story-structure. First, many of us are thrilled to see a woman finally taking on the superhero struggles that are nearly always given to men in our story culture, and this feeling grows stronger if we watch little girls in the audience cheering. This makes us feel empathy on three levels: first, we see an underdog community being recognized and growing out of its oppressive, restricted circle. Second, we see innocent children in the audience being given positive role-models and a vision of a world where they too have a greater sense of self and equality. And third, in our adrenalynic enjoyment we also feel a deep approval of the ethical and pedagogical work of the filmmakers.

While taking place in a sense outside of the film's story frame, this rush of both compassionate and communal empathy is a central part of the design of *Wonder Woman*'s marketing campaign and of the film's planned and realized critical and audience reception: it is a mutual moral assent between filmmakers and audience, a clearly signaled promise of empathetic pleasure, announced and agreed upon largely in advance through the film's trailers, posters and reviews. These hooks are of course socially selective, pulling in people of certain social and political persuasion even as they fail to appeal to others. In other words, people of different political and social commitments are drawn to certain kinds of story participations that promise certain kinds of empathetic experiences.

This distinction between dispassionate and dramatic modes extends from story out into the culture at large. As both producers and audiences understand, a film's director often strongly signals what form of narrative space a film will have, and this signaling can reflect a gendered demographic following.[8] Though we deal only passingly with video games in this book, a similar distinction runs through that realm as well: though this is perhaps a gross oversimplification, FPS games often have a dispassionate story while many RPG games attempt to create a dramatic character with increased emotional investment from the player.

And so we make another assertion: this book argues that on some level these forms of dispassionate, dramatic and Dantean stories are not only story forms but also frames of reception: that is, anthropological circles of empathetic reception within our fractured culture. These frames, with their power to direct empathy, gender and allegiances, are laced through our media and military economies. In media, empathy both is a tool of market share and a web for creating imagined communities (Anderson 1983, 2016) and so unpacking its machinery helps us deconstruct its increasingly prevalent commercial and political uses.

In that spirit we now move on to see how empathy functions in our *third* aesthetic form: the *Dantean* character who moves through the emotional miasma of *Dantean* space.[9]

NOTES

1. In passing, we point out that our definition of dispassionate stories is different from the concept of escapist stories. To take children's literature for example, a dispassionate tale such as Stevenson's *Treasure Island* is largely based in reality, while a dramatic tale like *The Wind in the Willows* is in a magical land of animals who, however, are continually wrestling with their loneliness, their friendships, their pride and jealousies and self-doubts. Dispassionate characters can be involved in realistic stories and dramatic characters can power escapist fantasies: the different distinction we make here is about the presence of inner objectives. The boy hero of *Treasure Island* is dispassionate: resolutely shrugging off even the death of his own father, he has no discernible inner conflicts and simply must be resolute, brave and smart enough to defeat the pirates and get the treasure. By contrast, the adventures of Mole and Rat and Toad in *The Wind in the Willows* are dramatic: always emotionally conflicted and drawn with a level of emotional realism that belie the tale's fantastical elements. Moreover, these adventures are punctuated by dialogic character insights: the animals evince a remarkable empathetic astuteness about their own and each other's characters and limitations even as they show great concern for the roles of strong friendships and good neighbors. In other words, the distinctions we wish to draw are between external and internal conflicts and not between escapist and realistic stories.

2. Consider another example: the bare bones of the plot of Shakespeare's play *Macbeth* can be described in a shallow but accurate way as a kind of dispassionate tale. In this version, three clever evil witches meet a moderately successful and contented man who has just won the great favor of his king. They then fool him into both committing evil and engineering his own destruction: they make prophecies that seem to predict his grand success as

king but which, just as he acts on them, each in turn then twists like an eel to correctly predict his, his wife's and his kingship's downfall.

If this was the core of the tale, if Macbeth's story was simply about how an unlucky king duels with clever witches, the play would be simply a dispassionate tale with fantasy elements. However, Shakespeare's tragedy is so unsettling and so memorable because, though it features some spectacular elements such as the witches, the ghosts and the battles, and some logical puzzles like the prophecies, it is largely dramatic in the sense we are arguing for. Macbeth himself is a dramatic character with fierce inner struggles: he first struggles to be a good vassal while trying to keep his ambitious wife's respect, then he wrestles with the conflict between loyalty and personal ambition, then he must watch helplessly as his clever wife and co-conspirator drifts off into madness just when he truly needs her most, and finally when she commits suicide he must deal with his resulting grief and guilt and finally find his own inner strength and resolve.

These personal struggles transform Macbeth's external problems, which by themselves might otherwise be just as otherworldly to us as those of Thor's mythologic kingdom, into dramatic situations. It is exactly Macbeth's particular relationship issues with Lady Macbeth and his inner struggles over gaining and holding power (struggles one might find in the corporate world, in a military career, a boy scout troop or even an academic senate) that makes his settings feel vivid and alive. These inner struggles make us pay attention to every nuance of every moment of the characters' lives.

In other words, the two forms do mix: dramas can use the elements of dispassionate stories, but the core distinction is over the nature of the character at the heart of the story because that nature determines the uses of spectacle. Moreover, because we are given access to Macbeth's intimate fears, his indecisions and his ghosts (all dangerous for a king to reveal), and then witness his loss of his wife, we feel compassionate empathy for him. Without this window on his intimate conflicts we would find it hard and unpleasant to watch a monster engaged in murder and then plunging a kingdom into blood and war. Thanks to vulnerable moments like his marvelous speech about indecision (in Act 1, scene 7, where he stands "upon this bank and shoal of time" trying to decide whether or not to kill the king), his battles become *dramatic* ones, struggles with problems we can all recognize and that are in no way the sole province of steadfast superheroes and fearless kings.

Note now that nearly everything we have said about Macbeth can also be applied to the protagonist of the TV show *House of Cards*.

3. The famous upside-down kiss in the film became iconic because it unfolds within a clear romantic drama and because Peter is a sympathetic character

with real vulnerabilities and losses; he is an under-confident outsider who has been bullied, who then loses his father through an accident he caused (see empathy tactic 1 in our list of empathy tactics in Chap. 1). He also completes his character arc not simply by saving the world but also by sacrificing his love for Mary Jane, his romantic interest, out of care for her (empathy tactic 10).

4. To see this demographic shift, see for example http://time.com/49440/box-office-reports/ also http://www.hollywoodreporter.com/news/box-office-woes-age-gender-718812.

5. Another landmark in this shift was the 2009 'reboot' of the *Star Trek* franchise by J.J. Abrams, itself powered by Paramount executives who were impressed at Nolan's efforts and wanted a similar treatment of another classic and typically male-oriented franchise (https://www.pressreader.com/usa/los-angeles-times/20090504/281990373470874, accessed May 1, 2017). Though the original TV series anchored by Captain Kirk and the subsequent film franchise was clearly dispassionate in nature and audience, Abrams' blockbuster film challenged all this from its starting moments. Opening with a giant space opera set-piece, its fierce, spectacular space battle soon twists surprisingly into a tearjerker, which ends when Kirk's father sacrifices himself and his starship to save Kirk's mother just as she gives birth to baby Kirk. For traditional *Star Trek* fans this empathetic melodrama between Kirk's father and mother—a new origin story which managed to be operatically emotional, serious, exhilarating and ridiculous all at once—announced that the franchise will now feature a much more dramatic Kirk. This protagonist, having grown up fatherless and out of control, is both more spontaneous, more antisocial and more damaged than the original Kirk and so must spend more time navigating social relationships. Spock too is far more dramatic: burdened with a heavy grief missing from the original series, fiercely bullied as a child for being half-human, he self-exiles himself from Vulcan society, and then is unable to save his own mother who dies in front of him as his entire planet is murdered. As a result he has a moving emotional breakdown and must relinquish command of the Enterprise to Kirk. This new franchise also often features issues of emotional turmoil and self-examination among the crew, playing dramatic chords never seen before in the earlier Kirk-based series or films.

A similar dramatic fate has befallen Sherlock Holmes. Unlike most of the 200+ films made in the traditional dispassionate vein of Conan Doyle's original stories, the BBC series *Sherlock* (2010–2017) has repeatedly put the bonds between Holmes and Watson and of Holmes and his brother Mycroft into emotional crisis. The intent of this humanisation of Holmes, who originally never strayed from the emotions of a sociopath (and the many empathetic scenes this choice then made possible) has expanded the audience considerably beyond that of children's literature and mystery buffs.

Even US military recruitment advertisements have recently shifted to some degree from the dispassionate mode to incorporate dramatic story lines. Take a traditional type of recruitment video like the 2014 video to "Apotheoisis" (https://www.youtube.com/watch?v=MFOilBZvfeA, accessed May 1, 2017) or the 2017 commercial "241 Years of Battles Won" (https://www.youtube.com/watch?v=fiDvqdY7Edg, accessed May 1, 2017). In their mix of impervious, invulnerable men saving the country, placeless emotional music and adrenalynic spectacle and editing both are in many ways indistinguishable from a dispassionate summer blockbuster. Now compare that to the character arc from fear to fearlessness of "Leap," the 2008 Marines video (https://www.youtube.com/watch?v=uwaskivJrZE, accessed May 1, 2017).

6. See for example producer Richard Gladstein interviewed by Collider: http://collider.com/producer-richard-n-gladstein-the-hateful-eight-pulp-fiction-interview/, accessed May 1, 2017.

7. This is not a work of Dante scholarship but rather sees his work throughthe lens of later narrative craft. While some Dante texts are mentionedin the bibliography, my own favourite is a website edited by and with anextensive and thoughtful commentary by the scholar Teodolinda Barolini.https://digitaldante.columbia.edu/, accessed May 1, 2017.

8. For example, Michael Bay is a consummate dispassionatedirector while Lisa Cholodenko is among Hollywood's finestdramatic directors. It is unlikely that they would be in competition forthe same project simply because each works for a very different audience,with different forms of story and with very different gender conceptions.One expression of this is that Bay simply does not craft inner dramasand specializes in creating a certain Manichean moral universe ruled byspectacular battles of force. By contrast, Cholodenko does not portray characters driven purely by external objectives, nor does she make simplemoral distinctions, nor does she depend on music to inform us ofemotions, nor does she execute large spectacular displays with complexsoundscapes that mix hundreds of tracks. If Cholodenko were to tacklethese technical aspects of big-budget spectacle, the resulting spectaclewould almost certainly be an expression of the inner emotional conflictsof her well-drawn characters as they wrestle with questions of how tobetter care for, communicate with and relate to each other. As a result,each director's following shares a kind of reception that distinguishes itas a culture of sorts: Bay's is a dispassionate culture and Cholodenko's isa dramatic one, which is to say that each following has a different relationshipto empathy, cinema pleasure, morality and to

community ingeneral. We will speak more about dispassionate, dramatic and Danteancommunities in Part III.

9. Dedicated to Thom Mount for all the adventure.

Bibliography

Alighieri, Dante. 2006. *The Divine Comedy*, trans. and ed. Robin Kirkpatrick. London: Penguin.

Anderson, Benedict. 2016. *Imagined Communities: Reflections on the Origin and Spread of Nationalism*. London: Verso.

Aristotle. 1986. *Poetics*, trans. S. Halliwell. Chapel Hill, NC: University of North Carolina Press.

Baxter, Charles. 2012. Undoings: An Essay in Three Parts. *Colorado Review* 39 (1): 96–110.

Blacker, Irwin R. 1996. *The Elements of Screenwriting*. London: Pearson.

D'Adamo, Amedeo. 2013. Dantean Space in the Cities of Cinema. In *Media and the City: Urbanism, Technology and Communication*, ed. Simone Tosoni, Matteo Tarantino, and Chiara Giaccardi. Newcastle upon Tyne: Cambridge Scholars Press.

Doyle, A.C. 1998. *The Adventures of Sherlock Holmes*. Project Gutenberg ebook #1661.

Earnshaw, Steven. 2007. *Handbook of Creative Writing*. Edinburgh: Edinbugh Univesity Press.

Egri, Lajos. 2005. *The Art of Dramatic Writing*. New York: Bantam–Dell.

Field, Syd. 2003. *The Definitive Guide to Screenwriting*. London: Ebury Press.

Grahame, Kenneth. 1998. *The Wind in the Willows*. Ware, UK: Wordsworth Classics.

Hauge, Michael. 1991. *Writing Screenplays that Sell*, reprint. New York: Collins Reference.

Hawthorn, Jeremy. 2017. *Studying The Novel*. London: Bloomsbury.

Hillis Miller, J. 1992. *Illustration*. London: Reaktion Books.

Miller, Frank. 2016. *The Dark Knight Returns: 30th Anniversary Edition*. DC Comics.

Moller, Liz. 2017. Character. In *Literature: an Introduction to Theory and Analysis*, ed. Mads Rosendahl Thomsen, Lasse Horne Kjaeldgaard, Liz Mllen, Dan Ringgard, Lillian Munk Rosing, and Peter Simonsen. London: Bloomsbury.

Shakespeare, William. 2003. *Macbeth*. Washington: Folger Shakespeare Library.

Stevenson, Richard Lewis. 2000. *Treasure Island*. London: Penguin Classics.

CHAPTER 3

The Frozen Ones: Dantean Moments, Characters and Space in the films *Aliens, Amelie, Sunset Blvd, Batman* and others

As we pass through our lives we sometimes meet people who strike us as frozen in a specific moment in theirs. It might be a 40-something woman who reveals a certain childlike innocence or a 60-year-old school teacher who exhibits the mercurial mischievousness of an adolescent. It might be a frowning waiter who seems caught in teen anger, or perhaps a gentle friend whose defining moment came in college when he crashed his car and others were killed, or the aging revolutionary, our favorite college professor who even in her seventies still yearns to recapture that joyful moment and spirit of the spring of Paris in 1968, a passionate moment that in some ways she cannot (and never wants to) get beyond.

Sometimes their actual bodies seem frozen. My friend knew a man who, ten years before she'd met him, had been on a hiking trip with his father on a mountain. He had talked his father into taking the hiking trip for health reasons: his father was both an alcoholic and obese. Unfortunately, half-way up the trail the father had a heart attack and, though the son carried him down the mountainside, this took hours and his father died during the descent. When my friend met him years later, this man had a slouch in his body, an atlas-like tragic air that was there in his very posture and movements, as if still carrying his father's heavy weight. As this bowed man told his story, slouching at a bus-stop outside a bar, he was clearly also still struggling down that hot mountain trail.

There are certain intense experiences, actions and desires that have the power to freeze us, or anyway part of us, in that intense moment of time. It is as if the brain has such a flush of emotions—of fear or hope, hunger or

© The Author(s) 2018
A. D'Adamo, *Empathetic Space on Screen,*
https://doi.org/10.1007/978-3-319-66772-0_3

yearning—that then whip into a storm in the brain, causing deep and permanent connections to form. A special romantic summer, that particularly-horrible Christmas, those weeks of blood on that tour in Iraq: these are storms of joy or pain that can then become our sensibility, our pivotal moment, and even the foundations of our ethics, our politics, our personality and bedrock character. By shaping the way we see all experiences, places and situations, it becomes our permanent subjectivity, a sensibility, a way of understanding and filtering everyone we meet and every place we ever inhabit from that moment forwards. That moment can make us into someone who maintains the hope and innocence of a child or alternatively it might craft the heart of a pathological child-molester. When such shades of death, love and hate settle in our bodies and our minds, they can be gifts or curses, causes or cages: they can define or destroy our lives. And we have little recourse: often only years of love, adversity or therapy can loosen their hold.

Thankfully life is not exactly full of such experiences: Dantean moments are a remarkable and very specific subset of our life's many emotional and passionate moments. Our emotional moments unfold continually and can range from a passing anger at a driver who cuts you off on the highway to the rich experience of falling in love. A couple has a romantic evening on a beach at sunset, a boy has his first sexual experience, or a woman has a short, intense but forgettable fight with a co-worker at work. These can be lived, intense, real emotional, even passionate experiences. They can and are often there even at the center of major dramatic turning-points in one's life, and we see this often in stories and films. But the subjective stamp of such emotional moments is momentary. They may endure in memory and in their effects on our choices and commitments, but they are not Dantean moments.

DEFINING DANTEAN MOMENTS

Dantean moments are more than momentary because they are branded into the person, creating an afterimage, a history, enduring and echoing and shaping later experiences. Thus they are more defining and complete aesthetic experiences because they can inform so much of one's later life. Dantean moments are thus not simply an experience or a moment or a chapter of a life: rather, they include the afterglow of that very unusual emotional experience.

In short, no matter how dramatically important or fiercely intense a moment might be, this alone does not make it a Dantean moment: their distinguishing characteristic is that they actually shape later moments, they can live on in memory (though they needn't) but more importantly they live beyond memory since they become a frame of experience itself. In fact, as all of our dramatic examples in this book will show, this is how they become so determinative of one's most dramatic struggles in life, and this is why they are so dangerous and also why they are so prevalent in drama. In essence, Dantean moments create a sensibility and thus shape a history in a character.

Let's move from Dantean moments, which are real, to the invention of Dantean characters and Dantean space, two forms of aesthetic representation that were largely invented by Dante. Consider for example the bloody-faced Ugolino, one of the more famous of Dante's characters, a clear victim of a dark Dantean moment which he recounts in sparse but harrowing detail.

DANTEAN CHARACTERS

We meet Ugolino deep in Dante's Hell, where he is trapped up to his neck in a twilit frozen lake, gripping his victim Archbishop Ruggieri and enthusiastically gnawing through his skull (Fig. 3.1). Ugolino sees Dante stops chewing and wipes his gore-covered mouth on Ruggieri's hair. He then tells in crisp vivid detail the trauma that binds him permanently to his victim here in the ice.

Back in life in the city of Pisa, Ruggieri the archbishop was once Ugolino's ally in political struggles. But then he betrayed Ugolino and boarded him up in an abandoned tower with two sons and two grandsons (Fig. 3.2). Soon the children died of starvation, but not before begging him to eat their bodies. Hunger was stronger than grief, and he ate their flesh before dying himself.[1]

Once he has told his brief story, Ugolino enacts its dramatic ending: he returns to obsessively dining on the archbishop's brains. Virgil and Dante walk on, leaving the pair frozen together like this for all eternity.

After hearing Ugolino's story, we grasp an entirely new dimension of how and why he and Ruggieri are here in the ice like this. They are both trapped by and in their past actions, by and in their old lived selves, by and in the chilling horror of the events that took place in that tower's sealed room. But these two characters are not only trapped in that past Dantean moment of the cannibalism. It is crucial to notice that they are also both now trapped in a Dantean space, a dimly-lit

Fig. 3.1 Dante and Virgil on the frozen lake in the Ninth Circle of Hell where they meet Ugolino trapped in the ice (illustration by Gustave Doré)

space of nearly complete immobility, frozen together in ice up to their necks, bound in the endless tableau of this cannibalistic embrace. This ice-bound space is seen and felt by us through Ugolino's emotional perspective: it shows up through eyes shaped by those spirit-freezing moments alone with his children's bodies in that silent, dim-lit prison-room in that forgotten Pisan tower. The two imprisonments are joined: the icy lake is informed by, imbued with, and in a sense created by that Pisan cell and its terrible events. In a psychologically real sense, Ugolino can never escape that cannibalistic moment in his shuttered tower: that torturing tower sped him directly into this specific personal space in Hell, a space he will never leave because it is burned too deeply into him. And so this is a space of double vision, one linking Ugolino's constant present to the arresting actions within that past Dantean moment.

Fig. 3.2 Ugolino in the tower as his children die of starvation (illustration by Gustave Doré)

Ugolino's double-visioned space is not unique. Many of the characters in *The Divine Comedy* tell vivid tales of a specific past trauma, revealing themselves as still stuck like a fly in amber in that past Dantean moment while bound now in a specific and corresponding Dantean space. For example, in Canto 14 Dante meets Capaneus, a famously angry warrior from myth who was so overcome with fury in one battle that he directly attacked a god. Capaneus, still proud and unchanging, says "What I was in Life, I am now in Death", while sitting inert inside a cage of flaming bolts. He means that the raging anger that defined his character in life— a fury powering his fighting prowess and rebellious nature and finally directing his famous death—has now become the cage that surrounds him.

A similar extrusion of an inner emotional struggle comes in Canto 7, line 123, where a great swamp of the resentful lie trapped in muck. One of the imprisoned explains that "[In life] we ... nursed in ourselves sullen fumes, and (thus) come to misery in this black ooze." Again, an inner emotional pattern has become physicalized into a prison.

Many of Dante's prisoners exhibit such a sublime, special architectural beauty of setting that they have become fixtures of the Western imagination. Consider the embodied stories of figures such as Francesca. We meet her as she is buffeted about on winds with Paolo, her brother-in-law and lover in life. She tells us of how one day when she was alive she was reading a romance with Paolo: swept up by the romantic story, they kissed. When their affair was discovered by her famously cruel husband he murdered them both with a sword. Now she and Paolo are forever unable to forget or to consummate their adulterous love: unable to recover from her husband's severing sword that divided her from her lover and both of them from life, she drifts here forever with Paolo, unable to touch or to leave her lover.

Elsewhere in Hell Dante meets other suffering figures, such as Farinata, a heretic now ensconced in a fiery tomb, or Pier della Vigna, a suicide transformed into a bleeding tree. This remarkable parade of iconic sufferers provokes us to ask: what do the memorable Ugolino, Capaneus, Francesca, Farinata, and Pier della Vigna all have in common? In fact, like so many others in the *The Divine Comedy*, they all share one characteristic: whether trapped in burning crypts or suicide trees or in a cage of their own anger, their inner lives and past actions are reflected architecturally and physically in this new dramatic space that now encases them. And so as a group they come to define a new dramatic form: such characters, each entangled within a *Dantean space* of her own, tell their tales from within themselves (Figs. 3.3 and 3.4).

As a result, Dante's Hell is not just a bad place to be: unlike the generic burning pits of Old Testament Hell, the Inferno is a place where the traumatic memories of its inhabitants actually generate its architecture. This makes it a highly individualistic place, a zone peppered with memory-cages where sufferers exist in a singular space that is distinctly theirs, one that is architected and made manifest by their specific values, fears, traumas and actions back in life.

This is also why such characters stay with us so long after we forget the rest of the poem's complicated fourteenth-century agenda. We remember such characters so vividly because their space in Hell is a powerful evocation of their story in life. Their tales are psychologically realistic and their past trauma is alive and breathing all around them.

Figs. 3.3 and 3.4 Farinata the Heretic Pier della Vigna the suicide tree (illustration by Gustave Doré)

DANTEAN SPACE AND EMPATHY

To appreciate Dante's brilliant narrative trick, consider how it perfectly meshes with our earlier list of empathetic machinery and our discussion of intimacy. When Dante invites us to consider the spectacular physical situations of Francesca and Ugolino, he is simultaneously drawing us directly and intimately into their inner emotional circumstances of deep regret or guilt or sacrifice, and into the intimate historical moments that they would normally never tell anyone about but which sped them here into their personalized Hell. We experience the Dantean moment they tell us about because that moment, that antagonist, that very *struggle* is right there before us: it is imprinted all around them and they are still wrestling with it. His aesthetic invention is a powerful technique for emotionally suturing us to these characters because their vulnerabilities and passions and hopes and fears are splayed all about them. Their inner selves are extruded like an exploded diagram of their emotional lives, their intimacies revealed to us as if we were their confessor. As a result these characters in their cages made of vulnerability, guilt and regret are each a kind of Venus fly-trap of compassionate empathy.

Dante's trick also opened a new box for storytellers and artists: now they could express how an environment can be both memorable and empathetic because it is a deep communicating medium of character. Soon Bernini, Poe, Dickens and others would take advantage of it, and today Dantean characters and their weird corresponding spaces represent a new, third form of emotional mimesis in the Western canon: in Dantean space the character has both an inner and an outer conflict, but—and this is Dante's new invention—the character is now found in a peculiar projective space in which *inner* struggle has become *outer* struggle. With Dante's help we make a great point-of-view jump, seeing through a character's pained eyes to find an architecture, a production design, a sensual sonorous space shaped and constituted by—even breathing with—her past actions, traumas, guilt, desires and memories.

THE DEAD HEART BEATS ON: DANTEAN SPACE IN POE, DICKENS AND HITCHCOCK

Arguably Dante was the first dramatist to truly understand the role of psychological trauma in freezing a person's life in a specific vivid moment of pain and anxiety, the first to notice how some people have certain kinds of experiences that then travel along with them, coloring and shaping every perception, every moment, every drama of their lives. Today the deep psychological uses of Dantean space are seen across a wide spectrum of stories but the most powerful use is in dramatizing the backstory of a character, and usually one whose development has been frozen in a specific traumatic moment in the past.

How else can we understand Miss Havisham, that hostile, tragic, gothic figure in Charles Dickens' *Great Expectations*? When we meet Miss Havisham we learn she has suffered a terrible event. As a young wealthy woman she met a handsome man who wooed her and promised to marry her. Then at twenty minutes to nine on her wedding day, in the midst of her excitement and euphoria, a letter arrives from her fiancé. It tells her that he has left and defrauded her.

This betrayal became her heart's fatal Dantean moment. We meet her as an old woman, (Fig. 3.5) still dressed in her wedding dress, trapped for decades now among the rotting remains of her wedding banquet with all the clocks stopped at twenty minutes to nine. Her Dantean

Fig. 3.5 Miss Havisham trapped in her own hellish Dantean space in Charles Dickens' *Great Expectations* (*Great Expectations*, 2012: Dir. Mike Newell)

moment, the emotionally violent abandonment, architects her Dantean space, this gloomy room with its wasting cake and tarnishing silverware which becomes her cage of memory. For decades afterwards she does not leave her house, never gets out of her wedding dress, never clears the table laid for the wedding feast, and never lets go of her plan to take her revenge against all men.

There are many other such examples in our story canon. How else can we describe Poe's narrators in two of his most famous short stories *The Tell-Tale Heart* and *The Black Cat*? Or Norman Bates of Hitchcock's *Psycho* in the moment shown below (Fig. 3.6), sweetly talking with Marion in his parlor as his stuffed birds loom above him, manifestations of the stuffed dead mother who sits in that basement room in the house above them on the hill, a stuffed murdered mother who also lives on in his head controlling his homicidal thoughts and deeds?

Aliens

And consider Ripley of the *Aliens* franchise. Ripley's Alien spaces are complex Dantean spaces that she actively fights her way through. At the start of *Aliens* (1986) she wakes from a decades-long sleep in cryogenic

Fig. 3.6 Norman's parlor, a hellish Dantean space, in Alfred Hitchcock's *Psycho* (*Psycho*, 1960: Dir. Alfred Hitchcock)

suspension in a drifting spaceship to discover that her daughter has grown old and died. While coping with this grief, Ripley increasingly struggles to master her own horrible memories of the deaths of her fellow crew and her flashback-like nightmares of being impregnated and having an alien burst out of her (a terrifying birth she witnessed in *Alien* (1979), the first film of the franchise). We see through her recurring nightmare, shown below in Fig. 3.7, that that memory now serves as a Dantean moment for her. This nightmare also reminds us that Ripley has just learned of the death of her daughter, whom we never see.

As Ripley grows stronger as a character on this journey, she also moves from the safer, sterile spaces to spaces that are darker, more organic, and more dangerous. Then finally she battles through her own fears of giving birth as she descends into the dripping, organic mother Alien's nest to kill this evil mother. An active protagonist who takes on the external goal of saving a child, Ripley also wrestles with internal conflicts that become clear as she finally faces her own Dantean space.

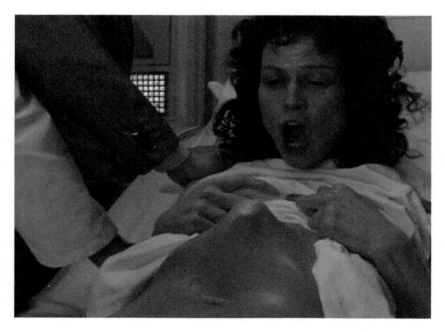

Fig. 3.7   Ripley's nightmare of giving birth to an Alien (*Aliens*, 1986)

As has been pointed out many times in film criticism, her journey in *Aliens* is from one distinct kind of architectural space into another. In the earlier parts of the film she is in rectangular, mechanical, well-lit, sterile white spaces that are safe (Fig. 3.8).

Increasingly, though, tension rises as Ripley must enter dark, rounded, organic, dripping, blackened intestine-like spaces that are controlled, occupied and ecologically transformed by the Aliens.

Finally, in the penultimate scene when she must descend into the heart of the black, dripping, living nest of the Alien mother to retrieve her own daughter-figure, she at last faces her own fears of birth, death and bodily violation.

Consider the space where Ripley fights the mother of the Alien as she also wrestles with her own fear and desire to be a mother. Here the Alien creatures and their lairs are vicious living emblems of Ripley's deepest fears about sex, motherhood and human bonds, and so here she finds the innocent little girl surrounded by intestines, gestating baby Aliens and even a birth canal. By the time she has entered the tunnels of the Aliens (Fig. 3.9) it is as if she has descended into her own body cavity.[2]

And why does Ripley go on this journey to face her deepest fear? She does it to rescue the knowing innocent girl, Newt: Ripley and her journey into her own fears is highly empathetic because she is doing

Fig. 3.8 *Aliens* (1986)

something good for someone else at very high cost to herself. Ripley's action and journey is communally empathetic.

Both *Amelie* and *Aliens* use Dantean space extensively. *Amelie* uses it from beginning to end, while *Aliens* highlights the power of its use in the second half of the film by starting with spaces that are realistic and all the exact opposite of the Aliens' lair and then descending into their nightmarish Dantean zone.

While these films use Dantean space for very extended sequences (in fact Amelie never leaves her sensibility), other films use Dantean space only in singular scenes. Consider for example *The Official Story* (1985). This powerful Oscar-winning drama revolves around a middle-class Argentinian couple raising a little girl they adopted some years before in

Fig. 3.9 *Aliens* (1986)

the middle of the worst years of the country's military dictatorship. At first all seems fine but then slowly the wife, Alicia, begins to ask herself if her adopted daughter Gaby might be a child of one of the murdered *desaparecidos*. This is a difficult suspicion for her since, if true, it means her husband may have been far more deeply involved in the crimes of those years than she thought. She, like most of the country's middle-class, is unsure just how brutal those years were.

And then the film's turning-point comes. The five-year-old Gaby is playing in a large walk-in playhouse in a bedroom while a party is going on downstairs in their house. Some young boys with plastic guns are playing on the stairs outside and the boys spontaneously charge into Gaby's playhouse while yelling and pretending to shoot. Gaby reacts in a completely surprising way by going into a screaming and sobbing fugue. Sucking her thumb, she has to be rocked to sleep by Alicia.

This incident is a scene of revelation for Alicia: in this moment we witness like her that a fundamental traumatic moment of Gaby's has accidentally been re-enacted and as a result a door has been thrown open onto the situation of one of the many Argentinian families that were tortured and killed. Gaby's own horrifying personal history, the junta's past history of crimes, and Alicia's own deepest fears of losing Gaby and facing her husband's fascist past are all triggered by the children's play.

Note, though, how our cinematic access remains limited to Alicia's point of view and to realism. Here we do not get any flashbacks or special sound effects to convey Gaby's experience: rather we stay entirely in the world of an incident observed by a concerned mother at a party. But note that though the boundaries of neorealist drama are observed, giving this moment its ordinariness and its force, at the same time the playhouse serves as a Dantean space on two levels. It is obviously vibrating with the imprinted, never-seen memory of a night years ago when Gaby's parents were arrested. But it also now emotionally and historically colors the actual house of Alicia, our film's protagonist. This house, which was until now just a dramatic backdrop is now imbued with the destroyed home of Gaby; its shade now falls on this actual house, haunting it and revealing the past violence and violations of her husband's friends and of the Junta. After this moment Alicia begins to question the official story and stumbles towards the truth, and simultaneously stumbles away from her house and her marriage. Her husband, trying to keep her from leaving, tries to turn their house into an actual prison, smashing her hand in a door and breaking it. But she escapes nonetheless and in the end is free, marching unbowed in the public square with the mothers of the *desaparecidos*, mothers who have lost their own children, all stand-ins for their own disappeared as Alicia now chooses to be for Gaby's murdered parents.

This is a film where empathetic machinery is used to characterize the hidden history of a place. Gaby's playhouse is not just a vivid transference-object for her own traumatic memory, and is not just a metaphor foreshadowing Alicia's own household's future. This space also becomes a vivid emotionalized stand-in for the historical record: here the story's spaces vibrate not only with the shades of the story's dead characters but with the actual *desaparecidos*, the historical dead now thrust into the country's dark political unconscious. We will see this same use of empathetic Dantean spaces to rewrite and re-enliven actual history again in Chap. 6 when we examine the film *Hiroshima Mon Amour*.

The Hidden Cauldron: Dangerous Dantean Characters

As we see in the case of little innocent Gaby, a Dantean character can be a hidden danger to those around her. She is a secret emissary from another time and place and drama, concealing a bubbling emotional cauldron of the past that other characters do not suspect because they lack any cognitive, sensual or emotive access to the truth inside her. We viewers may be given none or some or all of this access ourselves, and the examples we explore in this book reflect many variations, different kind of glimpses of a Dantean character and his or her hidden cache of Dantean moments.

For example, let's compare two films of strikingly different tone and genre but that offer two quite similar Dantean characters. In both films a Dantean character tries her best to pull others into her cauldron.

The first example is the comedy *Young Adult* (2011) a drama with a Dantean character that nevertheless remains always in dramatic space (we do not go inside her subjectivity), while the second example is *Sunset Boulevard* (1950), where a similar Dantean character brings us and the protagonist remorselessly into her Dantean space, with fatal results.

Young Adult

Young Adult is a sharp-eyed character study of Mavis Gary, someone who was unable to mature and is stuck in her own adolescence, a fact announced in the poster's tagline "Everybody gets old. Not everybody grows up." Mavis, the 36-year-old protagonist of this dramedy is a divorced, alcoholic, and deeply bitter writer of a failing series of Young Adult novels. She returns to her hometown when she gets an invite to the baby shower of Buddy, her old flame from high school, who is about to become a father. We soon see that while all of Mavis's old classmates have matured and changed since high school, she has not; the fiercely jealous and spiteful Mavis is stuck in the emotional zone of high school and tries to break up Buddy's marriage and get him back. In the end she fails and is humiliated in the process, which finally forces her to face her own spiteful ugliness, loneliness and alcoholism. Only a last-minute, deeply misguided pep-talk from Sandra, a fan of her fiction who is also hopelessly trapped in her own mid-teen emotions, gives Mavis the false strength to cling to her old bitter dysfunctional self and return to her delusion.

At first the reason for Mavis's overall conflict with her mature and compassionate peers seems clear in the film. Initially it seems that, unlike everyone else in the film, high school was a wonderful period for Mavis, a time of glory days when she was beautiful and popular and socially powerful and felt loved by Buddy, and that she has kept this world alive for herself by continually re-envisioning it in her failing Young Adult series. A distinction in styles of dialogue also backdates her sensibility: the screenwriter Cody reserves a clever cutting sharpness of tone for Mavis's dialogue, and this fixation with a bitter, teen-like sarcasm helps place her character back in high school where the art of wounding words had such a large role. By contrast, the film grants the other characters a grounded sensibility, a patient niceness and a lack of sarcasm in their dialogue, and this gap further isolates the protagonist, throwing her into emotional relief and staring alone across a bitter gulf at the world of the present.[3]

For all these reasons we know that Mavis badly misses high school and is in real ways still anchored there. But late in the story we learn something else: at the baby shower for Buddy's new child, Mavis reveals that in high school she too was pregnant from Buddy but then lost the baby in a miscarriage. Now it becomes clear to Buddy and his compassionate wife that Mavis has never recovered from this: she is stuck in 19-year-old events, social relations, joys and loss, and now the news about him having a baby, the news that drew her here to begin this extended comic psychodrama, takes on an entirely new and far more empathetic tone.

They are filled with a compassionate and communal empathy for her, an emotional offer which she quickly rejects.

Young Adult makes clear how dangerous a Dantean character can be. Though it stays within the confines of a drama and never enters Mavis's own perceptions directly—it never gives us a sense of Dantean space and stays largely within dramatic space—it does show how Mavis is a vortex into the past. Led by her own immaturity, she threatens to drag Buddy and others out of their own happy lives and back into the sick, socially-infectious emotions and relations of high school, trying to get everyone to dance to her own tune, to act in her own outdated social scripts. She is a modern-day Miss Havisham, only Mavis's frozen decaying room of mental furniture lies not in an aging mansion that the other characters can enter but remains hidden from their view in the scenes of a series of Young Adult novels mouldering off-screen in a bookstore's remainder bin. The film shows a Dantean character but stays largely outside of her inner life to remain in Dramatic space.

In this way Mavis's story differs from that of Norma Desmond in *Sunset Boulevard*, who in so many other ways she resembles.

Sunset Boulevard

When we meet Norma Desmond, the protagonist of the film *Sunset Boulevard*, she is an aging former film star hiding in her aging mansion. Like Mavis only "real big", Norma was once very popular, once at the top of a social hierarchy, once the most beautiful and famous woman in her world. A former silent-film star, she, like Mavis, still lives in a glowing construction of her own past: hers is not a series of novels but the old silent films she continually projects in which she is the star (Fig. 3.10). And she too threatens to suck everyone else, and particularly the man she loves, out of a happy healthier life and into her withering fantasy, into a past that is long gone.

Sunset Boulevard is an interesting Dantean space film. Its protagonist is an out-of-work screenwriter named Gillis. He is down on his luck and needs a bed to sleep in. The film is structured in five sequences and each sequence opens with a different bed, with each bed a stepping-stone leading closer to the Dantean heart of Norma Desmond. After a final desperate bid to escape, he finds himself floating face-down in her pool, his final resting-place.

Fig. 3.10   Norma in her private cinema showing Gillis her life as a silent cinema star

When we first see Norma's house with him we are already meeting her: Gillis actually describes it as feeling just like Miss Havisham's room, as if a person was frozen in the past, only here the past is the fabulously wealthy Hollywood of the 1920s. And then he enters the house itself: like Miss Havisham's wedding banquet room, this mansion is both frozen in time and falling apart. Its gothic airs—the organ wheezing in the corner in the wind, the dead monkey in the coffin (a foreshadowing of Gillis's gothic future), the silent butler—all refer back to the expressionistic silent-film era where Norma is frozen. An air of unreality is created by the grotesqueness but also by a technique that is a common hallmark of Dantean space: in a small moody metalyptic break of realism, we hear a wavering bed of notes as score for twelve full seconds before it is revealed by Norma as coming from an old organ. Apparently the wind is continually blowing backwards through it.

Gradually we learn with Gillis that Norma's Dantean moment is not a trauma exactly, but it is also not exactly a moment of joy. Norma's crucible was her silent-film stardom, a cage made of klieg lights, billboards and fan letters, a sickness of the overfed ego and of a kind of false, isolating and ephemeral love. As a now-forgotten former cinema star, she is a pronounced morbid example of the actors' desire for applause and attention. We meet Norma twenty years after the end of silent films still watching her own old silent films, still seeking out that lost joy, still racing after that lost adulatory crowd, and maintained in her Dantean space by fan mail and by the ministrations and support of her butler. In what may be the finest slow emotional revelation in cinema history, we then learn with Gillis that the butler was actually her director and then, most startling of all, that he has been writing all her fan letters, thus feeding her sense of fame and her delusion that she can make a comeback.

This revelation makes everyone more tragically empathetic. While the butler maintains the atmosphere, keeping Norma safe in her delusion out of love and concern for her, Gillis slowly joins this duet, stepping one-by-one through the circles of intimacy, from stranger to manipulative, deceitful screenwriter-for-hire, to friend, to confidant and member of her social circle, someone worthy of sharing a deep secret in order to be a confederate, to becoming a lover and a kind of co-conspirator in maintaining her delusion. She changes too; at first ordering him around and dressing him like a minion in her own play, she then shows her vulnerability to Gillis, finally opening to him sexually in a way that he cannot in good conscience extract himself from. The glue of intimacy grows stronger and stronger, giving a sense of a closing web, until when he tries to wake her from her delusion, to yank her out from her Dantean space into reality, Norma has to shoot him to prevent him from leaving her intimate circle, to prevent this supporting player from walking out of her play, escaping her desires and tearing the sfumato penumbra of her fame. In the film's last shot and surrounded by cops and reporters, Norma descends into madness: echoing Narcissus she walks into her final close-up, walking into fame, into her past, and into a complete psychic break with reality (Fig. 3.11).

And now we can see more parallels and difference between *Young Adult* and *Sunset Boulevard*. Both Mavis and Norma attempt to impose their own two-decades-old personal reality onto the world. While Mavis has her own novels to imagine and browse through, Norma has her own old films, finally disappearing into them in her last gauzy moment.

Fig. 3.11   Norma descends into madness as she walks into her final close-up

And while Mavis has her Buddy to pull into her world and shore it up, Norma has her Gillis. But while Mavis is poor, Norma is rich: Norma can build her own mansion and fill it with a silent-cinema aesthetic which she maintains by shutting out anyone who might not agree with her frozen world. She can pull Gillis into her world and hold financial power over him, while Mavis has no such power over her Buddy. Norma is a modern version of the rich and powerful Miss Havisham, the would-be failed puppeteer of Pip and Estella.

ROLES OF NARRATIVE SPACE

It may be useful now to recap by listing some of the roles space plays in a narrative:

Existing in one or more of the following dimensions, a space can:

1. Serve as simply a non-obtrusive backdrop imbued with a sense of place.

2. Reveal a character's or an antagonist's past.
3. Reveal a character's or an antagonist's inner hopes, desires, guilt, or fear.
4. Reveal a character's or an antagonist's external objective in the present.
5. Foreshadow the future.
6. Entertain or engage, usually by being beautiful or sublimely spectacular.
7. Reflect clear genre tropes and cues.

We will return to this list of roles in our later chapters, but for now we can apply it to spaces in our examples. We suggest that *dispassionate* spaces (i.e., those spaces created to surround and support the roles of dispassionate protagonists) tend to play mainly roles 6 and 7. Such spaces accompany shallowly-drawn characters and generic locations, as in films featuring Thor, most early Bond films and many Marvel Universe films.

By contrast, *dramatic* spaces are not spectacular and can often be a backdropped place that does not markedly intrude on, comment on or inform the foregrounded drama, as we can see from the settings in *50/50* and *Young Adult*. *Little Miss Sunshine* also generally confines its spaces to backdrops, though as we pointed out in our description of the opening sequence, they often carry markers of the poverty, alienation and personal failure that are the film's antagonists. Dramatic spaces can play a number of the listed roles at once but tend to remain unintrusive while most dimensions of meaning play out in emotional beats in the dialogue and action between the characters.

In contrast to both, *Dantean* spaces tend to overtly play the listed roles 2 through 7 at once, which is part of the secret of their cinematic and emotional power. We discussed the examples of Amelie's Paris, Miss Havisham's rotting banquet in *Great Expectations*, Poe's rooms of horror, and Norman's parlour with its looming stuffed birds in *Psycho*. These spaces are vivid and memorable because they provide such a rich empathetic layering of dramatic meanings. *The Official Story*'s playhouse starts as a background space but then bursts into a kind of bright emotional fire as it suddenly stands in for both Gaby's past violated home and Alicia's future violated home. Here the playhouse simultaneously works on the first six levels, creating an intensely empathetic scene of revelation and care between Gaby and Alicia that will then become a central turning-point in both of their lives. As emblems of

Figs. 3.12 and 3.13 The Batman Franchise, anchored in the Purgatorial Dantean space of Bruce's parents' death (*Top*—The Dark Knight Returns, graphic novel by Frank Miller. *Bottom*—Batman: The Dark Knight, 2008: Dir. Christopher Nolan)

character-forming memories, Dantean spaces vividly link past, present and future time. We will explore this phenomenon, which we call the *Characterological Manifold*, in Chap. 4.

Batman

We see this layered effect of Dantean space in many genres. For example, consider the Dantean characters and Dantean moments of *Batman*.

Remember that unlike most superheroes, Batman's origin story is a clear Dantean moment. When the protagonist Bruce Wayne is eight and is walking home in the city at night with his parents they are confronted by a mugger. As we see in the illustration from Miller's graphic novel (Fig. 3.12), the child is a helpless witness to his parents' murder.

Brooding along in his room that night, Bruce swears to a life fighting crime and meditates: "Criminals are a superstitious, cowardly lot, so my disguise must be able to strike terror into their hearts. I must be a creature of the night, black, terrible ..."[4] By coincidence a bat suddenly flies through the window, and the young traumatized Bruce is inspired to develop the persona of Batman, a persona that shows he is trapped forever in the traumatic night when his parents were killed. For the rest of his life he will fight crime, endlessly trying to unwork his dreadful origin story; as the poster for one of Nolan's films shows (Fig. 3.13), every action Batman takes and every subway overpass and skyscraper of Gotham will relate back to the violence of that alleyway where he lost his parents. In this world Batman never really does face his demons; his Gotham is an overtly hellish place where the character is forced to forever fight against his past, striking out against many aspects of their original trauma but with no appreciable progress or chance of escape. Like the hero of *Aliens* and the secret antagonist of *Psycho*, like Ugolino endlessly and obsessively gnawing on the archbishop's skull, Miller's Batman will skulk these streets forever.[5]

THE TRIPLED LENS OF CHARACTER: THE THREE LAYERS OF TIME IN DANTEAN SPACE

Note the layers to such empathetic spaces. Such spaces are not just double-lensed, i.e., they don't simply reveal the past and play a role in the narrative present. These spaces *also* reveal and are constituted by fundamental events in the life of the sufferer that reveal and reflect the sufferer's character itself. And, following Aristotle, we understand that character is constituted by the tendencies of behavior of a person, by the ways she tends to act or refuse to act in life's important situations.[6]

There is a real difference in a Dantean space, as we see when we consider either Amelie (with her animating, contact-improvisational dance through her adult enchanted Paris) or Ripley (with her determined penetration of the Aliens' dripping, nightmarish lair) what is being revealed in the character's past is also being experienced by the viewer as the narrative proceeds in the present, while simultaneously being entangled with the future of the protagonist. By virtue of wordlessly, sensually communicating the past, present and future goals yet staying within the character's sensual point of view, a Dantean space brings us into a unique, close and highly empathetic identification with the character's intimate guilts, fears or desires. This phenomenon (often felt as in these examples via an atmosphere of quiet enchantment or living nightmare) distinguishes them from both disPassionate and dramatic characters and spaces.

DANTEAN SPACE, RATED G

We often have children as the *subjects* of Dantean space in stories made for adults (think of *Batman*'s 8-year-old Bruce, Gaby in *The Official Story*, Mary the heroine of *The Secret Garden* or Amelie). It is harder, though, to find Dantean space in films or TV shows that are made *for* children. Of course, the vivid power of Dantean space can be dangerous for children: it would be traumatic to show this audience a vivid story about a trauma. Anyone who has tried to read the novel *The Secret Garden* to their children immediately realizes that it is written in another century. Opening on the crippling Dantean moments of its eight-year-old protagonist, the story begins with a realistic scene in which the main character's parents die of disease and all other caregivers run away and abandon the little girl Mary to die of hunger and neglect: she is threatened by poisonous snakes while starving alone in an abandoned house of the dead. Today's children's stories simply do not have this level of harrowing realism.

But even in children's films there are exceptions. For example, the film *Up* (2009) uses compassionate empathetic space by beginning with a highly empathetic opening sequence that shows a couple's romance, marriage and struggles and then ends with the death of the wife. The

Fig. 3.14 The moment of release and ascension, of past and present, in *Up* (2009)

surviving husband, the film's main character, comes into the main story with his heart plunged into winter, a grumpy social isolate feeling terribly guilty that he was never able to take his wife on the exotic trips of exploration that she dreamt of. What's worse, he is soon falsely accused of a crime and is about to be forced from his home by a large corporation. Thanks to the machinery of empathy working in all of these story elements, our allegiances are now empathetically aligned with this mean old man. The film then launches into its main action when he unfurls his secret scheme: he floats the house from its moorings with thousands of tethered party balloons (Fig. 3.14).

This emotionally spectacular moment is highly empathetic because of the history of balloons in the relationship (the husband and wife first met thanks to a balloon) and because his action so strongly evokes and embodies the dreams of his dead wife. In this explosion of color and flight in the frame, we are plunged into an empathetic experience of her joy and his release from guilt as his old memories come alive with a new ending.

Toy Story

Another use of Dantean space comes as the third act starts in the film *Toy Story* (1995). Buzz Lightyear, the co-protagonist in the film, has been for the last two acts in conflict with the main protagonist Woody over many things, but a central comic tension has been that Buzz is convinced he is not a toy like Woody but rather a real astronaut, a hero who can fly. Now as the third act begins Buzz happens to see a TV commercial for Buzz Lightyear toys. He is shocked. To refute the evidence of this commercial, Buzz then jumps from a railing trying to fly up to an open window high above the house's stairwell. When he falls hard, detaching his plastic arm, the revelation of being a toy that cannot actually fly hits him with the force of the hard tile floor.

Woody later finds a shattered Buzz raving deliriously while drunk on imaginary Darjeeling tea at a dolls' tea-party (Fig. 3.15): Woody pulls him away and then for the next ten minutes of the film has to take care of this mentally injured, utterly demoralized Buzz. But Woody never gives up on Buzz, and by the film's end with Woody's help Buzz has integrated this shock into his old character, his bravery and sunny outlook now married to a more mature self-understanding and a new bond of deep friendship with and appreciation for Woody. From this moment forwards Buzz stops being a dispassionate action hero and becomes a dramatic character with an inner life.

Fig. 3.15 Woody rescuing Buzz from the revelation of his vulnerability in *Toy Story* (1995)

Dantean space is present here only as a threat in this film, but its crippling nature is clear. If Woody had not intervened, had not ministered to Buzz's psychic shock, the astronaut would still be trapped in that moment, like Ugolino or Miss Havisham, drinking Darjeeling tea and raving about the Star Academy for the rest of his toy days.[7]

Notes

1. Ugolino's story, including the death with his children and grandchildren, is based on real events.

2. Creed, 1990.

3. Note that *Juno* (2007), Cody's earlier elaboration with Director Jason Reitman, is marked by a blanket use of this form of dialogue: all the characters speak with the same cleaver archness, granting the entire film a kind of overall sensibility that seems to originate in the young protagonist. This relentless wall-to-wall cleverness of dialogic tone does suggest convincingly that you are in Juno's world, as if every relationship was filtered through her fun sly sensibility.

4. Bill Finger (w), Bob Kane (p). "The Batman Wars against the Dirigible of Doom", *Detective Comics*, 33 (November 1939), DC Comics.

5. This origin is stressed in different ways in different versions of the Batman story, creating quite different versions of empathetic space. Consider the versions of the Batman myth in, for example, Tim Burton's breakout superhero film, in Frank Miller's version in the Dark Knight graphic novels, in Nolan's film trilogy, and finally in the TV show *Gotham*. Neither the campy original television show nor the franchise-birthing 1989 version directed by Tim Burton dwell on Batman's powerful origin: not surprisingly, those Gothams are characterized by dispassionate space, display of quaint and campy gothic production design, with Burton's city made up of gothic and noir tropes deployed in his signature caricaturish style. By contrast, Miller's version is a rich and powerful Dantean space. Miller's convincing neoFascist Batman is prone to grief and guilt over the death of Robin and then experiences a transforming flashback to his parents' death that is presented as a Dantean moment in harrowing detail (Miller 1986, pp. 21–26). This Batman is a frightening and psychologically grounded character. Deeply bitter, cynically sure of his rightness and of the world's blackness, hating the liberals who have destroyed his city, Miller's Bruce Wayne is brother to Mickey Spillane's Mike Hammer: both authors create an anger-torn, death-dealing hero whose mental pathology finds its mirror in his world's social pathology and both heroes are right-wing authoritarians ready to cleanse this fallen world in blood to set it right.

By contrast, Nolan's *Batman Begins* opens the trilogy by deepening the emotional realism and the trauma of young Bruce's origin story while also granting it an operatic dimension. Young Bruce falls down a well and is attacked by bats, and his father, silhouetted against the sky must drop down to him to rescue him. This kindly father than takes him to the opera with his mother, but the Wagnerian figures on stage, who wear batlike costumes and flit about on ropes, trigger Bruce's anxiety and so he asks to leave. The parents then exit the opera house by an alleyside door and the murderous confrontation with the mugger unfurls as dictated by the Batman canon, only in this version little Bruce actually does bear some responsibility for the death of his parents. Black bats now subtly present everywhere in little Bruce's world, but never as caricatures or as theatrical devices as they do in Tim Burton's world: drooping wet black umbrellas at the funeral, the broken shadow of a jutting faucet on a wall, the distant cracking of a glacier's ice are all realistic graphic and acoustic elements that are never heightened enough to interrupt the emotional realism of the story. (These cracking sounds will remind a cineaste of the thunderclaps that accompany the shattering of the walls behind Catherine Deneuve in Roman Polanski's *Repulsion* (1965).

In the rest of the film Bruce must go through all sorts of tests and training in order to overcome and properly integrate his ghosts and fears and memories. It is an overt therapy arc which is then married to the time-tested plot of a kung-fu acolyte in training, but it never quite eliminates Bruce's need to both fight and to be the darkness: it never eliminates his lust for revenge, for violence, which return in shaded suppressed form to power the later two films of Nolan's trilogy.

The success of Nolan's Batman films not only imitated the dramatic innovation of *Spider Man*, bringing a dramatic arc and an inner emotional struggle to a character who had been dispassionate in earlier cinematic versions. Nolan's Batman went further, following Miller's graphic novel in anchoring his persona in the Dantean moment of his parents' death, and then characterizing the space of Bruce Wayne's Gotham as a Dantean space. Nolan's *Batman* trilogy is also a Dantean world, but here the past is present in more subtle and sublime form because Bruce is embarked here on his own therapy arc: Bruce Wayne must first struggle to master his fears and his emotions before becoming *Batman*.

In contrast to these examples of a dispassionate and a Dantean Gotham, the pilot of the television series *Gotham* (Fox 2014–) opens with a dramatic killing of Bruce's parents. The effects of this on the boy is largely to make him serious and stern, but oddly enough the series does not show young Bruce melding this trauma with the bat-in-the-room episode the same night, as in the original origin story. Pushing off young Bruce's fetish with bats and darkness to later seasons of the show, the series remains a dramatic show that instead focuses on police detective Jim Gordon; and its dank 1970s version of Gotham (oddly supplemented by cell phones) is a noir city, a largely dramatic backdrop for Gordon's own moral struggles. (Though the show sees the city dramatically, like a moody cop-show, it too tends towards grotesque casting of secondary characters ala *Barfly* and *Dick Tracy*.)

6. At this point one can argue that a dispassionate or a dramatic space can also reveal the past. Think of how Thor has flashbacks to his relationship with his brother Loki, or how Bilbo thinks in certain moments about his comfy Hobbit hole while dueling with Gollum or fighting Spiders in Mirkwood: obviously these moments can show contrasts and the progress of the story

7. Dedicated to Anna Thomas, with Resolution.

BIBLIOGRAPHY

Alighieri, Dante. 2006. *The Divine Comedy*, trans. and ed. Robin Kirkpatrick. London: Penguin.

Aristotle. 1986. *Poetics*, trans. S. Halliwell. Chapel Hill, NC: University of North Carolina Press.

Burnett, Francis Hodgson. 1961. *The Secret Garden*. London: William Heinemann.

Camus, Albert. 1991. *The Fall*. Vintage Books.

Creed, Barbara. 1990. Alien and the Monstrous-Feminine. In *Alien Zone: Cultural Theory and Contemporary Science Fiction Cinema*, ed. Annette Kuhn. London: Verso.

D'Adamo, Amedeo. 2013. Dantean Space in the Cities of Cinema. In *Media and the City: Urbanism, Technology and Communication*, ed. Simone Tosoni, Matteo Tarantino, and Chiara Giaccardi. Newcastle upon Tyne: Cambridge Scholars Press.

Dickens, Charles. 2002. *Great Expectations*. London: Penguin Classics.

Dostoevski, Fyodor. 2003. *The Brothers Karamazov*. London: Penguin Classics.

Dostoevski, Fyodor. 2004. *The Idiot*. London: Penguin Classics.

Finger, Bill et al. 1939. "The Batman Wars against the Dirigible of Doom", Detective Comics, 33 (November 1939), DC Comics.

Gardiner, Eileen (ed.). 1989. *Visions of Heaven and Hell before Dante*. New York: Italica Press.

Hauge, Michael. 1991. *Writing Screenplays that Sell* (reprint). New York: Collins Reference.

Lansing, R. (ed.). 2000. *The Dante Encyclopedia*. New York and London: Garland Publishing.

Miller, Frank. 2016. *The Dark Knight Returns: 30th Anniversary Edition*. DC Comics.

Tolkein, J.R.R. 2011. *The Hobbit*. New York: HarperCollins.

CHAPTER 4

Character Vs. Emotion: How Music and Sound define Space in the films *Little Miss Sunshine*, *50 Shades of Grey*, *Twilight* and *Secretary*

ON DISTINGUISHING CHARACTER REPRESENTATION FROM EMOTIONAL REPRESENTATION

One of the most powerful story moments in the Western classical tradition comes at the start of the tale of Aeneas, the Trojan hero of the *Aeneid*, who will lead his people from the ruins of Troy to search for a new homeland.

His story begins in the fiery night of Troy's destruction when the Greeks have jumped out of the Trojan horse and are fanning out to destroy the sleeping city. The young Trojan warrior Aeneas wakes and runs out from his house to find the city burning and the marauding Greeks killing the sleeping men, women and children all around him. At a certain moment in the battle Aeneas, realizing there is no hope for the Trojans, makes a fateful decision: rather than stay and fight this lost battle, he will instead take his father Anchises onto his shoulders and carry him through the burning streets out of the city to safety.[1] There Aeneas gathers the Trojan survivors and leads them away from the last flickering flames of burning Troy, starting on a long Mediterranean sojourn full of challenges and dangers that ends only when he settles them all on the banks of the Tiber river in Italy and founds the city of Rome.

The tableau of Aeneas's first fateful step—the moment when the son bends, lifts his father onto his shoulders and sets out into the roaring flames of Troy—is often represented in classical iconography: it has repeatedly been painted and sculpted and is invoked by Shakespeare in

© The Author(s) 2018
A. D'Adamo, *Empathetic Space on Screen*,
https://doi.org/10.1007/978-3-319-66772-0_4

Julius Caesar.[2] This fascination with Aeneas' action springs from its revelation of his strong, virtue-driven character: foreshadowing his role of gathering, defending and sheltering people, his shouldering of his father reveals how he will then shoulder the fates of the Trojan refugees. As the refugees themselves sense, this first step among the roaring flames will eventually lead Aeneas to found Rome, revealing his wise judgement and devotion to others—character traits that any desperate group will need in a leader as they set out on a dangerous journey into the unknown. Thus the dramatic tableau of Aeneas carrying his father is a moment of revealed character, showing the actions he tends to take even under extreme pressure. It reveals his tendencies and not just his emotions.

Now contrast that image with other iconic images from Western art, such as Munch's *The Scream*, that expressionist image of a figure whose hands clutch cheeks and whose mouth opens in a scream of anguish. Or compare Aeneas's bent form to Rodin's many character-less sculptures such as *The Kiss*. Rodin's sculptures do not show a dramatic moment in a specific character's life: instead they strive to represent a universality of momentary emotional expression. In Munch's scream and Rodin's kiss we know nothing of the story of the figures, nothing of who they are, of what led to this kiss, of what will result from that scream: here figuration is freeing itself from the narrative logic of character expression. These expressionistic figures, purposefully shorn of the conditions of a specific life, embody only the intense emotions of a vivid moment. In short, Aeneas's arched back reveals his character while the arched back of Munch's screamer or Rodin's kissers instead reveal only emotion.

The Emotional Music of *Lego Friends* and the Character Music of *Little Miss Sunshine*

Now we can extend this distinction between representations of character and of emotions to the elements of cinema. Though it may seem far removed from story space, a brief look at film and television music can help us distinguish the character function from the emotional function in the construction of empathy. After this brief foray we can more clearly see how the same tactics are used to construct character space (and its refined use in Dantean space) as opposed to emotional or psychological space in cinema and television.

We begin by looking at the musical scores of two six-character ensemble stories, starting with the children's television drama *Lego Friends* (Duckling A/S, 2014 -). This show has six main characters and many secondary characters and different episodes will feature different pairs of friends as they have moments of halting confession or painful self-realization or apology. But under disparate scenes in different episodes we hear the same musical sting, the same short refrain. In other words no matter what specific character is experiencing that emotion, the same delicate music cue will play under these scenes to indicate intimacy or sadness or resolution: the music cue indicates a commonly-experienced emotion rather than a specific protagonist's singular character.

Now contrast this *emotional* scoring with the elegant *character* scoring of the opening of *Little Miss Sunshine*, the scene we examined closely in our second chapter. The film's opening theme 'The Winner Is...', playing uninterrupted, introduces each of the film's six characters in turn and gives each a specific leitmotif that informs us about her or his character. Through choice of instrument, quality of attack, nature of melody, style and speed of playing, and number of instruments performing at once, these six variations in characterization inform us of what each character wants, how he or she faces their struggles, and where they sit on the protagonist/antagonist divide in the story that is about to unfold. A short analysis of how this works will help us contrast this kind of character-based scoring with the generic emotional scoring for an ensemble show like *Lego Friends*.

'The Winner Is ...' theme is composed of a repeating synth-based two-tone pulse refrain of 16 beats that each last a bit under 30s before repeating. Over this and falling on the repeats, a new lead instrument comes in exactly as each new character is introduced to grant each character his or her singular leitmotif. For example, as we first meet Olive, the little girl, a piano begins a delicate yet hopeful refrain: we learn from this motif that Olive is innocent, that some sadness will feature in her story but that she has a good chance of triumphing in her struggles.

As the music completes her short scene and begins the next refrain we meet her father Richard, who is musically characterized by a series of plucked strings playing a step-rising melody that mimics his chart (projected just behind him) of how to win in life. His own aspirationalism (a unifying antagonist in the tale) is here characterized by the rising Rossini-like plucked strings: we know this style, inherited in film comedy from opera buffa, means that this character and what he believes in and embodies is both comic and suspect.

With the next refrain we meet Dwayne the son, doing push-ups. He is characterized by the sharp attack and militant march of a drum-riff which informs us of his character's objective: we will soon learn that Dwayne has a strong drive to become an air force fighter pilot. The drum-riff has a visual analogue: as he adds a last crosshatched mark to a very long record of uniform, crosshatched marks, we see he has been marching steadfastly day-by-day towards that goal.

With the next refrain Edwin the grandfather is introduced. He is characterized by a slow dragging sythesised cello as he does cocaine. Edwin's inner struggle to carry on against age—a conflict that will soon kill him—is heard quite clearly in the sardonic, tired cello, which also seems to express a somber warning.

Next we meet Sheryl, the Mom, as she drives, jittery and frenetic, puffing desperately on a cigarette as she argues hurriedly with husband Richard on the phone. All the musical refrains we have heard now come in together, giving the musical impression that Sheryl, while nervously juggling her driving, smoking and talking on the phone, is also struggling to juggle everyone else's problems and isn't sure she can keep this up.

Completing the film's elegant character overture and rounding out the title sequence, we now meet Cheryl's desolate brother Frank, who sits on the suicide ward with his wrists bandaged: Frank's leitmotif is a sad set of strings, marking both his loss of love and life and his Euro-sophistication as a Proust scholar. As the strings complete their melody the film's title comes up in three ironic punctuated musical beats over Frank's shockingly distraught face.

Now we can see the difference between the music in *Lego Friends* and *Little Miss Sunshine*. *Lego Friends'* gives us glimpses of an emotional *experience* that, while subjective, *is not specific to a particular character*, while by contrast the leitmotif approach of *Little Miss Sunshine* reveals not so much the *emotional* experiences of the characters (though it does of course do this to some extent) so much as a predictive, foreshadowing and long-term *set of tendencies* being revealed or formed in *each particular character*. While doubtlessly the two approaches often overlap, still we can see the difference: emotions pass but ingrained character tendencies remain.[3]

UNDERSTANDING THE DIFFERENCE BETWEEN EMOTIONAL
REPRESENTATIONS AND CHARACTER REPRESENTATIONS
BY APPLYING THE CHARACTEROLOGICAL MANIFOLD

Any element in a story—be it a fluffy pen or a pink outfit, an action like that of Aeneas to hoist his dad on his shoulders, a sting of music or a painted wall or a line of dialogue—can play at any number of levels of meaning. We now introduce the concept of the *Characterological Manifold*, a diagnostic tool for identifying layers of meaning in a dramatic element, be that an action, a line of dialogue, a prop, a location and so forth. In the characterological manifold an element of narrative is meaningful if it[4]:

1. Reveals the past
2. Advancess the story in the present, usually by revealing either the objectives of the protagonist(s) or by revealing the obstacle or threat to the protagonist(s)
3. Foreshadows the future of the story
4. Reveals character
5. Reveals relationships
6. Entertains or engages, usually through spectacle or comedy.

The more of these layers present in a dramatic element, the greater the sense of meaning, and generally speaking, the more meaningful elements we grasp, the more our understanding of the characters increases. Analogously, the more complete this manifold, the more our sense of empathy for the character increases. To apply this to some of our examples so far, we can see that the painting *The Scream* by Munch demonstrates categories 2 and 6. Unlike the images of Aeneas, we know nothing of the past, of the future, of the character or of the relationships of this screaming person: its very vagueness lends it openness of interpretation. By contrast, the painting of Aeneas gives us 2–5. If we compare our previous examples of costume elements from *Singin' in the Rain* and *Legally Blonde* (see Introduction) we notice that the pink costumes of *Singin' in the Rain* give us only 2 and 6, while the fluffy pink pen in *Legally Blonde* gives us 2 *thru* 6.

Similarly, the sad emotional music-cue of *Lego Friends* gives us 2 and 5, while the leitmotif cues of *Little Miss Sunshine* give us 1 *thru* 6.

The point is simply that a story is a tunnel of signifiers connecting to each other, a web where even time and space are themselves expressing various levels of these six elements. Like emotional detectives we are trained to look for clues, finding them planted in production design, in lighting, in music, in dialogue, and then we use that information to understand the space's narrative nature and role and depth and what might happen next. Character can but does not always play a big role in this.[5]

In this account, a narrative is a kind of tunnel where sometimes time and space themselves are processed through character. As examples like *Secretary* and *Apocalypse Now* will reveal, even space and time shrink or expand to express a character's memory, fears, hopes, desires and emotions: they can stretch or collapse or migrate towards order or chaos because the character's past or present is bending them. Like the tunnel that Ripley runs into in *Aliens* or the beach Miller storms in *Saving Private Ryan* or the streets Amelie dashes through on her missions of mercy and romance, this tunnel of narrative is laced with and structured by emotions and memories and goals and desires and fears, and this is why we can speak of empathetic space, why these spaces make us cry and then swell with a mirroring empathetic pride or joy. We mirror not just the character's emotions but the characterological aspects of the spaces we have been brought into. Almost always in the process of developing a project, a novel or script or teleplay evolves towards a richer expression of this manifold: the process of rewriting and revision is largely about how these six levels of meaning can be more densely and richly expressed from scene to scene, and scenes that cannot express more than one element are usually cut.[6]

SPACES OF ROMANTIC TRYST

Let us look at the space of the tryst in romantic films. A tryst space is any space that a couple chooses for their most intimate emotional and vulnerable revelations. This space usually reflects something central about their mutual attraction because it allows them to feel comfortable and intimate, but tryst spaces can also be chosen for other emotional or character reasons and can be a dispassionate, a dramatic or a Dantean space. They are also often specially treated spaces in a film, spaces of heightened cinema power where sound design, music and the shape, materiality and volumes of a space all interpenetrate to create just the kinds of enveloping narrative space we are most interested in examining.

Eroticizing the space of a couple's tryst has its own long history. Think of the lovely purple bruise lining the wall of the apartment in *Last Tango in Paris* (1972), a single erotic sign of an otherwise rather

ordinary backdrop: arguably this very ordinariness and the bare quality of this uninhabited, unoccupied place heightens the intensity of the
sex, of the need by the two characters for their act to express transgression. Sex, this location seems to say, can happen at any time, between
anyone, and to two complete strangers. This aspect of the location quietly expresses 3 and 6, simultaneously foreshadowing the purpose of the
space and being mildly spectacular. Not surprisingly, since it expresses
nothing about their characters and their relationship, this watermark is
memorable but holds no empathetic power.

By contrast, think of the tryst space in Luhrman's *The Great Gatsby*,
where Gatsby's baroque display of flowers plays as a very in-character
offering to his beloved Daisy, softening the place as if it were his own
heart he is asking her to enter. Being an intimate gesture that carries
some risk of rejection, Gatsby's flowery space expresses 2–6 and very
much supports the empathetic machinery of the scene. Gatsby's creation
of space here is simultaneously authentic and sincere, yet also a generic
and over-the-top use of a cliché, a mis-en-abîme action that defines
Gatsby's own prismatic character.

THE CHARACTEROLOGICAL MANIFOLD IN LOCATIONS AND MUSIC

Let's compare three different spaces of romantic interplay in three quite
different films, *50 Shades of Grey, Twilight* and *Secretary*. We use these
three films because they have often been connected through their many
parallels: in fact *50 Shades* is often thought to be a remake of *Secretary*
and, as we've noted, actually began as a piece of fan fiction for *Twilight*.

50 Shades of Grey

We began to study this film in Chap. 1 where we pointed out the lack
of any machinery of empathy in this film. But the film's use of space and
character also helps us begin to give a technical definition to the idea of a
shallow story, a term often thrown around and sometimes applied to *50
Shades*, itself a clear example of dispassionate space.

Note how in this film the locations are simply either emblems of
Anastasia's ordinary middle-class life or of Christian's high level of
wealth, but carry no clear personal history: they do not inform us about

either's character (Fig. 4.1). As we can see, Christian's lavish apartment is indistinguishable from the suites of some recently built upscale hotel. There are no signs of personal history, singular tastes or even of habitation: like photos in an architectural magazine, there are also no marks or smudges or scratches anywhere. Even Christian's sex room itself is just a characterless place full of off-the-rack sex toys that all look fresh from the sex shop and right out of the box. The idea seems simply to show that Christian's world is an envelope of his wealth. Taking any element of these spaces, we find nothing with a rich characterological manifold. His bedroom, dull to look at, tells us nothing of his past, nothing new about his present, foreshadows nothing about their future aside from the expected, gives us no character or relationship clues. Even the sex-toy rack in his hidden room, the film's only actual spectacular element, carries little emotional information. Some elements are somewhat spectacular and its presence is a promise that we will see Anastasia laid bare and bound, and its presence shows her growing interest and acceptance of what he wants, but beyond this no real emotional attachment is being created.

One of the problems with these locations is that they do not seem even lived-in. In Chap. 9 we will see this kind of alienating production design, this plethora of unconsumed consumer goods, in other films and TV shows such as *Mad Men*, where this design strategy serves a different

Fig. 4.1   A typical space of Christian's house in *50 Shades of Grey* (2015)

very specific purpose: to throw the characters into relief and reveal their inner conflicts.

But here this is not happening for one reason: the characters in the foreground have no inner depth and no internal conflicts, and so we cannot perceive alienation by contrasting them with the background. Nor were these locations chosen to astonish the audience by their wealth and sweep; even this spectacular impulse was muted. Why might this be? Since the story cannot express any plausible empathetic reason why Anastasia wants to be with Mr. Grey, if the spaces were truly impressive and astonishing expressions of his wealth and lifestyle, *they* would become the reason Anastasia wants to stay with him—a hunger after wealth then that would have made her very unsympathetic. Because the filmmakers have not given her any real reason to love him, his wealth now becomes a quandary: somehow she has to love him despite his billions and despite their obvious inequalities in the master–slave relationship he wants and which the money reinforces, while at all times Anastasia has to somehow be seeing beyond all his emblems of power and see some other more equitable bond, one that he simply does not want.

The strange shallowness of character in *50 Shades* is not produced by the actors nor really by the director. As a glance at the novel shows, there is no backstory to play here (giving some weight to the criticism that this story might be a rewrite of other films). Certainly the novel's rather famous lack of characterization has carried over into the film, crippling the work of the production design team as well as stymying the genius of the film's composer Danny Elfman.[7] Elfman's soundtrack functions only to express emotional beats and genre tropes, becoming perhaps the most generic and least specific work he has produced to date.

However dull, the film is a very useful object of study because it helps us understand what character and the characterological manifold is by showing us a well-crafted film with a clear plot that is yet bleached of nearly all character and thus has nothing to express in its locations or its music. As a result of the emptiness of this characterological manifold, this is a dispassionate use of space engendered by dispassionate characters, and dispassionate characters sit uncomfortably with romance, which tends to be about emotional intelligence and issues of trust, power-balance and solving problems of intimacy, which are all missing here. There is one odd result of bringing such a high level of talent to realize such a low level of story: in the end

Fig. 4.2   The tryst space in *Twilight* (2008)

it is unclear if this undramatic drama is a film with two very under-characterized characters, or if this is a decently-drawn but undramatic portrait of two incomplete people.

Now we can move from a dispassionate to a dramatic tryst space (Fig. 4.2).

Twilight

Midway through the teen romance *Twilight* (2008) the vampire Edward takes Bella to the woods to convince her he is too dangerous for her to love. The scene is shrouded in mountain mist and set among redwoods and great moss-covered stones. The lovely and rather unique location, with its eerie light and its wild mix of living and dead elements, serves the story on many dramatic levels. The different elevations and branching tree-limbs allow Edward to spring from tree to tree while the great big tree-roots which he yanks out with his bare hands showcase his strength. The mist manages to give them the privacy they need, isolating their small grove while softening both light and sound, granting another excuse to maintain the film's commitment to a preponderance of reflected and diffused light that makes their faces moon-like and softened. Meanwhile the grey granite rocks are largely covered by great patches of green moss that soften their hard texture and outlines, hinting at the suppressed erotic impulses of our couple.

And so this location is not just a pretty backdrop: it serves clear dramatic purposes. Though it undoubtedly has some understated elements of spectacle, the grove is also a practical use for blocking, an excuse for shows of strength and agility (revealing Edward's beast-like killer's side, the antagonist to their love) while also granting a physical explanation for a romantic lighting scheme. This tryst space expresses categories 2, 4, 5 and 6, offering a far richer space than those of our last example. However, though the soft moss covering of the rocks grants a faint and almost erotic romanticism, by and large this scene does not express character: this location, perhaps the most entangling of any in the film, cannot echo with the deep character needs or struggles of these two characters in the resonant and Dantean way our next example does.

Secretary

We can contrast *Twilight*'s mountain grove with a different location where yet another troubled romantic pair struggles to work out issues of power and love: the office in the BDSM romance *Secretary* (2002). The director Steven Shainberg and the film's production designer, Amy Danger, faced a problem: they knew their budget would be minuscule ($4 million, with a star like James Spader attached). Realizing something like the sentiment of famed producer and theorist James Schamus (the former head of Focus Features) that in low-budget productions "the budget is the aesthetic", the two planned a low-budget solution to crafting the office itself, starting their planning two years before production began.[8] Knowing they would need to shoot largely in one space, the film makers opted to construct an unrealistic, heightened character space which, by holding different but complementary character longings for each of the two romantic characters, further draws them together while separating them from the film's other characters. The opposing characters, who all share a conventional antagonism to BDSM relationships, are also linked by being associated with dull, conventional spaces, heightening their antagonism to our struggling couple.

The result is a dual character space, a tryst space that expresses the wants and needs of both characters in the romance. *This* Edward's office is full of plants to emphasize his love of watering plants (an attribute of gardening which helps humanize his otherwise highly unsympathetic need to dominate). More interestingly, this office also resembles the home that Lee aspires to live in with her boss. Thirdly, through its earth tones, friendly volumes and softened surfaces it contrasts sharply with the harshness and artificiality of the world beyond the office, a contrast designed to make clear that Lee would rather be here than anywhere else in her life. Through all of these and other craft-choices, the character needs and objectives of our pair have become clearly elaborated in the space and the sound design of the film: in fact this space is deeply shaped by both sound design and music. This overall design helps convey the sense that these two characters belong nowhere else but here, together.

For example, the physically nest-like, private nature of this office-space is also heightened by the acoustic design, carefully justified by the lush yet homey production design. Consider the dramatic effects of the remarkable deadness of sound in the office, a deadening effect lacking all echoes that is explained visually by a lush carpet, thick velvet curtains and cotton drapes over the windows, and the large plush furniture. This allows for an odd and intimate sound mixing that lacks any added room tone (i.e., a quiet background hum or buzz). Not only does this create the heightened sense of every brush of clothing: it also eliminates any background tone that might mask the small excited quavers of the aroused protagonists' voices (Fig. 4.3).

The acoustic intimacy this allows permits a very specific kind of performance by our couple, a style that lets them reveal their longings for erotic power-relations. Thanks to this dead hush Edward can utter commands to Lee in an intimate near-whisper even from across a long room.

Fig. 4.3 The office, the tryst space in *Secretary* (2002)

Moreover, soon their conversations take on the low quiet of bedroom talk, spoken quietly in fear. This fear is of their desires and each other, and not simply of being overheard by other employees beyond the long hallway. In later scenes they often speak at very low volume, implying that they are standing much closer to each other than in fact they often are, again giving us the sense that they are psychologically linked.

This space's oddness is also not just a reflection of Edward (though since we never see him in any other space we do wonder if he can survive in a space that he doesn't rigorously control). It also becomes a space that Lee loves, an emblem of homeyness that she cannot find anywhere else in her life. And so here the ordinary gendered spatial definitions in which the exterior is a male domain and the interior a female one[9] (Shonfield 2000a, b; Wallace 2011) has been somewhat short-circuited by a careful overlay of the spatial distinction between work spaces and home spaces. The breaking of that boundary allows the space to leave realism and cease to be a dramatic backdrop and becomes a Dantean space of joint trust and daring, a space of relationship growing increasingly pregnant with the shared, divulged, intimate disjunctions of our two main characters.

THE CHARACTER MUSIC OF *SECRETARY*

Moreover, the way we are to understand this peculiar space is given to us by another element: the opening theme and much of the later music are also crucial for bridging character and space in this film. The music informs us of the couple's sense of this office, becoming a roadmap of the couple's dance, taking us into the game they are playing and their own sense of its lushness and forbidden qualities.

We hear this character information from the first furtive beats of the opening theme, in its teasing tense percussion, which is soon joined by a quickly-plucked violin that reminds us of a tango. The song then turns comic when a repeating pock-pock, with a faint hint of rubber suction as in opening the stopper of a bottle, both remind us of Edward's repeated butt-slapping of Lee while also dramatizing that something has been stoppered up and is being released. Now a sardonic rubber-banding bass begins to plod its way through the growing chorus of percussive stings, followed by a rattle-snaking maraca that takes us on a kind of careful step of a jungle hunt. This cartoony, comic sound effect then happily introduces some musical tropes of maze-running (the exoticized balalaika-like strings and the Ventures-like guitar clashes that remind us of the themes of 1960s spy-films). Meanwhile the hissing echoes of the tics set against the softened attack of the synthesizer keyboards and other returning instruments all build to a more urgent chorus. And now all of the fade-ins and fade-outs of passing exotic percussive instruments reminds us of walking slowly and carefully, and then[10] with increasing urgency, as if on a journey through some dark funhouse.

This long suspenseful rising run finally[11] relaxes into a tender, languid stretch released from musical time. Now a new element is introduced as some synth ghost-voices join in, connoting something tender and perhaps sexual taking place. These breathy beds of synth never grow strong enough to imply actual orgasm (note that Lee and Edward never fully complete their dance by consummating their desires), a musical trope which has many cinema-music references. And with the rising synth ghost-voices the theme changes completely. Just as sexual overtures in a relationship tend to eventually lead to emotional terrain, the song completes its tense build-up and releases us into the sad tender musical tropes associated with intimate scenes of longing and memory: now airy notes hang in the style of delicate new age soundscapes where each element is granted a different layer of echo, giving us a sense of an opening-out, layered space of relaxation and release reminiscent of sad, tender, poignant moments.

This theme is a window on the emotional lives of our main characters: when in each other's company in this office they feel they are in an exciting game together, a game of flirtation and sexual hints, a dance. It also informs us that neither is dangerous or intends harm to the other and that the entire thing should be regarded with comedy and indulgent irony, an adult game that just might lead to tender emotional connection as well as to sexual release. This character music transforms the office, showing that when character is revealed through score this information can fundamentally change our grasp of the space the character is in. Character music and empathetic space, we argue, are often inextricably combined.

THE CHARACTEROLOGICAL MANIFOLD AND DISPASSIONATE MUSIC SCORES

This difference in narrative music amplifies the difference in space that exists across genres. A dispassionate, spectacle-driven film like *An Unfortunate Series of Events* (2004) depends so deeply on *emotional* scoring for one specific reason: its characters are not deeply drawn but are instead rather generic, and so character scoring is impossible here. In general, generic characters are lacking in grounded backstories that grant them a sense of uniqueness of place and a complexity of inner conflict. And for now we can state a general heuristic rule: the more deeply-drawn the characters (such as the well-drawn characters of *Little Miss Sunshine*), the more the music can emphasize and comment on character, while the more generic the characters, the more the situations tend to decide the moment-by-moment scoring of the music: if the characters are generic the music tends towards emotional scoring.[12]

Emotional Space and Character Space

Now we can describe how this division between emotional expression and character expression is also a spatial division in narratives. We will also suggest that films that use emotional music also tend to use spectacular dispassionate spaces, and for the very same reason: there is little character to express, and so both the space and the music tend to stress only the emotional beats of story.

There are many textbooks and examples on how to create the moment-by-moment experience of emotional space. As we have noted, there are spotting sessions during which through rescoring or editing a music score is used to emphasize certain emotional moments, heightening kisses, or cuts or twists of the head, or shots of the approaching out-of-control explosives-laden truck, or of the monster emerging unscathed from the firebomb. Similar work is done with color-correction and with digital manipulations of backgrounds, focus and even atmosphere. We often find that an author or director or game-designer tries to heighten a character's moment of sadness by setting it in the rain, or by creating certain soft lighting, or by framing the character as all alone, or by doing all of these to emphasize loneliness. These devices are a staple of today's media narratives, and the intent is of course to communicate the character's emotional experience to us on a sensory, spatial level. Such examples run the gamut from emphasizing adrenalin to expressing emotions.

Since these devices are of course the very same ones that are used to create Dantean space, the two aesthetic techniques are easily confused. After all, both emotional space and Dantean space involve manipulation of space, color, sounds and musical energies to draw us into the

character's emotional point of view (POV). But there are radical differences between the intent and effects of the two approaches. They differ
on a deep structural level in the nature of the screenplay and the funda-
mentals of the story. *Emotional space* is often a situational and reactive use
of space, while the Dantean use of space is a projection of tendencies and
engraved aspects of character, and as we have pointed out in the case of
Aeneas and of film music, the *moment-by-moment emotional experiences*
of a protagonist differs from the *character* of that protagonist. Clearly on
some deep level and in many cases, moment-by-moment uses of psychological space are connected to character—they are the push-and-pull that
can (but needn't) deepen or change a character's tendencies. But while
there is this possible link between the two forms, it's important to tease
out the longer-term and character-based nature of Dantean space.

In most contemporary narratives emotional space, like emotional
beats of music, takes us temporarily from narration into an emotional
moment and then back out again. This jump can often interrupt our
enjoyment, when it is used by an inelegant storyteller, desperate editor
or sound designer whenever it is convenient or necessary to heighten and
signal the emotional beats of a character's arc.[13]

Using Dantean space to inform us of the lifelong effects of a Dantean
moment is a distinctly different enterprise on three levels. First, Dantean
space permeates a tale and is thus a more rigorous use of POV simply
because a Dantean moment is both an experience itself *and* the frame for
later experiences. The filmmaker can then decide when to stand outside
of the character's Dantean POV and when to enter into it, when to bring
the singular aesthetic of a character in to dominate the overall shape and
aesthetic of a story. In our examples in the following chapters, *The Third
Man* overtly enters space imbued with character in its sewer sequence
and its extraordinarily-long final shot, *Aliens* does this intermittently in
the first two acts and for a long continuous stretch in the third when
Ripley fights her way through the lair of the aliens, and *Amelie* never
leaves the main character's own childhood Dantean moment. A quick
glimpse of the stills from *Amelie* shows this (see Figs. 1.1 & 10.10):
her childhood, her adult apartment, her workplace, and all of Paris are
aesthetically united. When the continuities within a person's POV are
dramatized over different stages of a story, a certain specific and unifying
aesthetic effect is achieved: now POV begins to become a film's artistic
form. Thus Dantean space can often bring an overall visual and sensory
unity to a story.

Secondly, this continuous form is not adopted to create a unified *visual* aesthetic—the way for example noir tropes unify the dispassionate *Sin City*, or grotesques, drought and bricolaged costumes and cars unify the spaces of *Mad Max* by expressing the external, commonly-shared antagonistic precarity of that world. Because a tale with Dantean space is grounded inside the protagonist's point of view and relates to her core conflict, the visual and sensory envelope links the core inner *dramatic* contrasts, obstacles and antagonisms of the story to the protagonist, bringing a further level of *dramatic* unity to the narrative. The stills from *Aliens* shows this dramatic aspect of the visual and sensory. *Amelie* also expresses this clearly: the continuous enveloping spectacle of innocence, child-toy colors, and delicate nostalgia has a deep and unifying emotional dimension, a strong role in the storytelling, because it is grounded in the opening montage of Amelie's childhood. The fact of her mother's death and her father's emotional abandonment shows us that the adult Amelie's sensibility is stuck in her childhood because that is also where her heart and hopes are stuck. Amelie's sensibility is thus a direct expression of the film's core antagonist conflict, expressing in fact the very spine of the tale, and this makes these uses of cinematography and production design and music all work more significantly than if they were simply creating eye-candy; i.e., creating isolated moments of emotional space. The marriage in Dantean space of these two aspects—the visual/sensory and the dramatic—is a marriage of the objectives of the character and the memories and sensibility that shapes a character's point of view. Thus it is a bridge between the visual, spatial and sound elements of a story and the core drama of the characters. This synthesis is another aspect of this marriage of content and form in Dantean space.

Thirdly, there is simply the multiplying nature of our emotional identification with a character that can come from our *continual* re-occupation of his point of view. Moving from a traditionally realist narrative to step momentarily into the experience of the world through a character's eyes is a fascinating and sometimes shocking experience: most filmmakers and storytellers heighten emotional beats to create just this effect. But note that *Amelie* presents a very different experience. Once we recognize that the overall tone of the film is continually informing us of how Amelie experiences life, we realize the film never leaves her *Dantean* point of view even for a moment. In a sense we feel we become Amelie, an intense form of empathy. The importance of this will be explored in later chapters.

So far we have argued that space in cinema is inflected by character and emotions, and so whenever the musical score expresses these, it is also inflecting the space of the film. In fact, we will argue soundtrack music not only functions differently when it is harnessed to dispassionate, dramatic or Dantean space but that there are certain codified forms of music that tend to be found in dispassionate space that do not really support Dantean space.

As we move from dispassionate, dramatic and Dantean narratives across the gamut of empathy, we generally find an increasing level of personal characterization in the music. In dispassionate films—take for example the standard Marvel superhero film—the music tends towards a more generic, codified quality, while dramatic and Dantean films tend to a much more heterogeneous and multi-layered, and often a quite singular use of music, as the examples of *Little Miss Sunshine* and *Secretary* reveal.[14]

We might assume that because music in dispassionate films often exhibits a placeless, nonspecific and generic quality, this simply results from using lower-paid uninspired composers (who perhaps have learned their craft in TV). But in fact this dispassionate musical form is necessarily imposed onto such narratives for two reasons. First, the audiences tend to be younger and so their acoustic vocabulary is simpler, often coming from television shows and thus based on the codified musical cues of clear emotional expression prevalent in children's and teen narratives, which are themselves often dispassionate and plot-based and lacking deeply-drawn characters.

The second, more complex reason for this form of generic music in dispassionate narrative is simply that the dispassionate characters of these films tend to lack inner struggle and vulnerabilities and complex personal histories. Any music that expresses the world of a dispassionate character cannot express inner objectives and struggles, simply because there are none to express. This means that these characters also lack the developed backstories that would grant them not only personal histories but also the distinct musical tastes, references and codes that can only grow out of a complex, rooted identity.

We sketch this out at such length to once again use dispassionate form as a negative example that helps us understand dramatic and Dantean forms. By contrast to, for example, the dispassionate, shallowly-emotional music of *Thor*, in dramatic and Dantean films we tend to hear music that takes us into the hidden character tendencies, goals and struggles of the characters. It also can express and take us emotionally into the layered history, experiences and social and economic identity of the characters. It can inform us of their backstory and of their own sense of values, place, allegiances and acoustic heritage. We have seen this in both *Little Miss Sunshine* and *Secretary* and will find further examples, particularly in our later look at the film *Apocalypse Now* in Chap. 7. And by expressing character, music choices can also characterize the space, often giving it another dimension of meaning. Arguably this kind of music, which tends to be rich in the characterological manifold, is for that reason also more empathetic.[15]

Notes

1. The Aeneid, Bk 2, lines 710–725.
2. Act 1, Scene 2, lines 114–116.
3. We cannot ignore the fact that as a film *Little Miss Sunshine* has had months if not years of work in the scoring, while an episode of a TV show like *Lego Friends* is typically made in a matter of weeks. Unlike composers who work for television, a film's composer usually has far more time to focus on characters as opposed to only on emotions. In fact, on many TV shows there is no final pass by a composer: instead the editor or sound designer simply grabs a cue from a list of pre-made musical cues and then fits and shapes it into the emotional moments in the edit.

    It is also worth mentioning that music has long been at the center of the work of Jonathan Dayton and Valerie Faris, the husband-and-wife team that made this film.

    Another aspect of production intrudes here to emphasize which form can be deployed: while *character* scoring in the form of leitmotif can often take place before the film is shot, most *emotional* musical spotting is done in post-production. Though composers have usually seen the script well before shooting began and have usually already scored key scenes, the emotional spotting of the film is a process that usually comes late in the edit when the picture is largely locked. Now the director, producer and composer will sit down as the cut unfolds and try to mark emotional moments where score music can be slid in to heighten the emotional experiences of the scenes. Still, while there are a number of reasons for these different uses of music, neither the length of the production nor the moment of the music's creation can by themselves explain the overall tendencies we find in musical scoring between these two roles. Genre, demographics, film tone, and the level of development of the characters themselves are also all factors that help determine whether a score will depict character or not.

4. Thought he roots of the concept go back to Stanislavski, some of this list can be found in Cohen & Sherman, 2016.

5. We can compare this manifold with the concept of the Kantian space–time manifold that underlies the concept of the chronotope. In Bakhtin's day this concept was perhaps the best available to understand the nature of the human processing of time, and a narrative seemed also a kind of tunnel of processed time, and so the two were equated, or at least the Kantian manifold was taken to be something between a foundation and a metaphor. We don't suggest this research is foundationally flawed: instead we stay out of these fierce debates (which lie at the heart of phenomenology) and simply start from a very different practice-based foundation. Instead of the categories associated with the concept of manifold, we start with those we use in revision workshops for analysing scenes. Drawn largely from Stanislavski's advice for actors who are trying to grasp their character's relation to a scene, this characterological manifold can be applied with clarity to any element of drama to reveal characterological lines of causality and emotion, of motivation and memories.

6. And yet, as we will see in our chapter on alienation, an element or series of elements can also be purposefully denuded of these layers of meaning to convey a sense of alienation around the character.

7. His title for "A Spanking", for example, has no particular acoustic reference to anything about either of the characters, and arguably this generic result is not his fault: with no character to work with, no sense of place and no emotional specificity, or backstory to work with the music, like the location, has very little to express or expand upon and so it is rather clearly limited to genre expression and to marking emotional beats.

8. John Calhoun (2002, October). "Spank You Very Much", *Entertainment Design*, 36:10, pp. 8–10. Retrieved April 1, 2011, from Research Library Core. (Document ID: 204894041)

9. A division elaborated by Katherine Shonfield (2000b)

10. At minute 1:40.

11. At 2:30.

12. At the same time, sometimes emotional scoring seems to be determined by the age, relative sophistication, and emotional demands of a film's demographic. For example, we might consider the scoring for a film with a similar demographic to *A Series of Unfortunate Events*, such as *Fantastic Beasts and Where To Find Them* (2016). Like *A Series ...*, the score of *Fantastic Beasts ...* is similarly emotional, constantly underlining beats, antagonists and situations without very clear character-work. Arguably, this is done not because the characters are shallowly drawn (they are more deeply-drawn than Rowling's *Potter* series, for example). Instead the score is emotional for both genre reasons and because of the relative

musical sophistication of its young audience. Its intended demographic of children and young adults, which is not very attuned to the tropes of the musical canon and thus not very capable of hearing subtle comments of character, also depends on the score to always reassure the viewer by constantly placing her in a clear emotional position regarding the plot.

13. When clumsily done, these shifts in forms of representation only signal the emotions of the scene without moving us: in such cases we often feel manipulated by the author, filmmakers or game designers.

14. When we speak of a generic quality of dispassionate film music, we mean a number of related characteristics. First, there is that quality of clear underlining of oppositions: the music first divides the world into the good and the bad. Second, it tends to underline the emotional moment-by-moment beats of the story: it informs the viewer that the character-feels scared right now, and feels sad now, and feel reassured now, and so the viewer should too. This role has come to define the music of classical Hollywood films: think of E.W. Korngold or Max Steiner, two exemplary Hollywood composers from the 1930s and '40s who both helped formalized and codified classical strains into a kind of dictionary of emotional messages. Today John Williams is perhaps the most famous practitioner of this form of narrative music, but Howard Shore and others also work in this vein.

Finally, such music often uses a large orchestra of studio musicians to create an enveloping "epic sweep" that we have come to associate with certain big-budget Hollywood films filled with spectacular locations and set-pieces.

This grand theme music is closer in form to the theme music used in television in one specific way. In general TV theme music eschews musicological originality: such theme songs are intentionally associative and thus purposefully not 'unique' in the same way as other forms like traditional classical music or contemporary experimental music. As Rodman explains, typically the TV theme consciously "draws upon musical styles that persist in the audience's collective memory and perhaps even borrows material from many other musical sources that preceded it" (2010: 15). Rodman acknowledges that this stylistic legacy has often left critics under-impressed with the form: "scholars may perceive this lack of uniqueness as a weakness in music". But, as he points out, this musical intertextuality is actually crafted very purposefully. "Television producers and directors consider [such derivative forms of music] a strength because this lack of uniqueness taps into a cultural familiarity with viewers" (ibid).

This could easily describe the dispassionate theme music of *Thor* or *A Series of Unfortunate Events*. Arguably, these particular styles in fact created a sense of escapism around their narratives in part by not referring

to any actual place, tradition or cultural conflict and instead connote only
other films or TV shows. Heard this way, their derivative connotations are
not necessarily a reflection of a composer's lack of talent but in fact are a
purposeful promise: they announce that these shows will safely grant the
viewer a familiar escape from daily concerns and strife that will not leave
her with any lingering discomforting, memorable conflicts.

15. Dedicated to Gabrielle Kelly.

BIBLIOGRAPHY

Alighieri, Dante. 2006. *The Divine Comedy*, trans. and ed. Robin Kirkpatrick. London: Penguin.

Aristotle. 1986. *Poetics*, trans. S. Halliwell. Chapel Hill, NC: University of North Carolina Press.

Burnett, Francis Hodgson. 1961. *The Secret Garden*. London: William Heinemann.

Dickens, Charles. 2002. *Great Expectations*. London: Penguin Classics.

Hauge, Michael. 1991. *Writing Screenplays that Sell (reprint)*. New York: Collins Reference.

Rodman, Ron. 2009. *Tuning in: American Narrative Television Music*. Oxford: Oxford Music/Media.

Ruskin, John. 1856. Of the Pathetic Fallacy. In *Modern Painters*, vol. III, part 4.

Shonfield, Katherine. 2000a. The Use of Fiction to Interpret Architecture and Urban Space. *Journal of Architecture* 5 (4): 369–389.

Shonfield, Katherine. 2000b. *Walls have Feelings: Architecture, Film, and the City*. London and New York: Routledge.

Virgil. 1990. *The Aeneid*, trans. Robert Fitzgerald. New York: Vintage Classics.

Wallace, Lee. 2011. *Lesbianism, Cinema, Space: The Sexual Life of Apartments*. London and New York: Routledge.

PART II

Boundaries Visible and Broken: Empathy from Shade Space to Showcase Space

The Library of All Stories: Purgatory, Therapy and Character Arcs in Dante and in *Great Expectations, One Hour Photo, The Third Man* and *Sunrise,* in Camus' Novel *The Fall,* and in Edgar Allen's Poe's Short Stories

For a moment let's ignore the religious intent of Dante's *Divine Comedy* and see his massive phantasmagoric construction in a different, purely secular light. Picture his three linked zones not as a real place but instead as a meta-dramatic edifice that we might call The Library of All Stories Ever Lived and That Will Ever Be Lived. Since Dante has designed this grand metaphysical machine to accept and sort all lives that will ever be lived, it can organize and hold all possible human stories. And because it can evaluate people's lived stories and thus slot them into spatial planes with many concentric zones of overlapping actions and appropriate punishments, Dante's construction claims to be meta-narrative: by claiming to properly archive all dramatic life stories, it also claims to reveal the building-codes that determine the dramas of life. All "shelved" inhabitants of a zone are grouped there by their specific type of character arc, and this arc determines the kinds of spaces to be found within that "library" zone and that decides what stories arrive there. In other words, because it is designed as a kind of walkable grand library that will organize and hold all human tales, with their specificity preserved but all properly arranged, linked and shelved by common themes and story arcs, his *Divine Comedy* is a massive architectural construct that aspires to contain all narrative space.

We see this most directly in Hell's city of Dis, which is both an early instance of centralized city planning and also an infinite city: we may

© The Author(s) 2018
A. D'Adamo, *Empathetic Space on Screen*,
https://doi.org/10.1007/978-3-319-66772-0_5

meet the exemplar of a ring's neighborhood, the pedagogically-shaped spokesperson for a specific bad behavior and hellish suburb, but really the land runs off infinitely behind them, always ready to hold more. In each of Dante's three zones there is space to hold billions because it is actually *story* space, an empty plot zoned and deeded and waiting for you to build your own lot in life.

In this chapter we take Dante's building-codes secularly and yet seriously. In fact we will argue that after Dante there are three basic zoning laws to Western narratives, three main forms of story arc for characters: hellish, purgatorial, and heavenly. Each form of arc corresponds to one of Dante's spatial zones, which means that his Hell, Purgatory and Heaven reflect certain building-codes of narrative that we will need to better understand our topology of story space. Here we will examine hellish arcs and stories, while later chapters of Part II focus on purgatorial stories. In Part III we examine heavenly arcs and stories. Again, the intent is to lay bare some of the dramatic building-codes that undergird so many Western narratives today, to show in a sense how his Hell, Purgatory and Heaven, shorn of their claims to an afterlife, exist in story and also make claims on our real lived lives.

ARCS THAT BEND TOWARDS HELL, HEAVEN AND PURGATORY

First, a tour of Hell. As we have noted already, every single one of Hell's characters is in a specific geography in Hell because his or her life story contains an arc that is simply Hell-bent on its completion.[1] But it is also important to notice another aspect of their situation: no-one Dante meets in Hell is going anywhere. No matter how long they suffer, this is where they stay because dramatically their stories are over. Hell is final.

A similar dramatic finality, an inertia of the soul, also settles on the occupants of Heaven. Unlike the gods of the ancient Greeks who seem to live lives full of fascinating and world-changing adventures, the characters in Dante's Heaven are easily the least dramatic of *The Divine Comedy*. Even their life-stories are far less interesting than those of the other two zones: it seems as if these characters have all dodged the slings and arrows of misfortune to arrive here unsullied, ready to take their place in a flat, unremarkable place unmarked, unburned and unbent by her or his particular character history.

However, by contrast to the closed fates of both hellish and heavenly inhabitants, each of the characters in Purgatory, that distinct zone linking Heaven and Hell, has a chance to escape, a second act, a dramatic possibility to undo the mistakes committed in life and then rise to Heaven. Some carry stones for an age before ascending, others must come to some great revelation or insight before they can move on, others must simply pay the price of their sins in pain. But in all cases, the arcs of the inhabitants of purgatorial space are dramatically still alive. His Purgatory introduced a new form of story arc that was only primitively realized before Dante—the purgatorial arc, which we discuss in the following chapters of Part II.

To round out our overview of these character-arc zones, it might be useful to revisit the concept of the character arc itself. Earlier we defined a character arc as a change in, or a final failure to change, one's core tendencies. In a dramatic character arc the outcome of the arc will directly affect the character's possibility for happiness, and possibly the lives and happiness of others. As the writer and narrative theorist Charles Baxter notes so crisply (Baxter 2012), our dramas tend to focus on arcs like that of Lady Macbeth, who says in the penultimate moment in her character arc that "What is done cannot be undone." Baxter asks us to imagine a door that, once we walk through it we cannot go back to where we were; this, he suggests, is the defining quality of dramatic moments where a character arc becomes fixed and cannot be changed. Many examples of this exist in life, ranging from losing one's virginity to committing a murder.

In Dante's world, all the characters in Hell and Heaven have already walked through such doors in life. Now those doors are solidified *"Lasciate ogni speranze, voi ch'entrate*: Abandon all hope, you who enter" is written on the archway into Hell: it implies not only the tortures ahead but that your own story and your character arc are now coming to a fixed conclusion. While smoldering dramas may lie ahead, any further changes in your character do not: you have already walked through all of your dramatic doors in life.

ACTIVE AND PASSIVE HELLS

If this were their only building-code, Dante's zones would be clear and simple. But there is another dramatic wrinkle in his plan, a wrinkle that carries over to all of our stories. In Hell we run into many unchanging dramas, but they fall into two kinds: passive and active.

On the one hand, many of the characters in his hellish spaces have given themselves up to their new fates. Think of Farinata, or of the characters in the sullen ooze: these are people who now lie supine or defeated in their imprisoning space, knowing and accepting their fate while suffering through it. They have all become what writers would call passive characters, characters without an active objective. Lacking any goal to struggle towards, seeing no escape and no alternative to their fate, they simply suffer, doing nothing to resist their suffering. We meet such people in life and literature.

CAMUS' NOVEL *THE FALL*

Consider for example Clamence, the protagonist of Camus' novel *The Fall*. Clamence is a famous lawyer who at first leads a very active life fighting for the poor and the oppressed. But one night, coming home after visiting his mistress and crossing the Pont Royal bridge—which spans the Seine where it flows like a giant canal through the heart of Paris—Clamence sees a woman dressed in black standing on the bridge's edge. He knows just what the woman is about to do, yet he walks on. He reaches the street at the other side of the bridge before he hears the sound of the splash and the scream behind him. He does nothing but listen, frozen to the spot as she drowns. This moral and physical immobility becomes the Dantean moment for our main character, and is the turning-point of *The Fall*.

Years later he is passing near the same spot one evening when he hears laughter. And now his suppressed memory returns with a vengeance: though rationally recognizing that the laugh must have come from some passing pair of friends, he cannot escape the conviction: "I could still hear it distinctly behind me, coming from nowhere unless from the water."

And with this the anonymous dead woman in black becomes not just a ghost but a shade that comes to inhabit him and change his perceptions and his career, locale and life. His spirit crushed under the weight of this moral crime, our successful, highly-respected lawyer now quits his practice and leaves Paris to live in foggy London. Then after years of ironic stances and itinerant moral clowning he finally comes to rest in Amsterdam, drawn to its constant existence under sea level, to its dark foggy nights and its reputation for unsavory urban squalor, becoming not only an habitué but a fixture of its Inferno-like ring of canals and of the bar *Mexico City* in its infamous red-light district. Without work, he is now a connoisseur of the depths of depravity, a night-walking flâneur and a debauched, self-immolating character straight out of Dostoevski, a self-abasing Stavrogin, a man who has dived not only underground but under sea level, drifting listlessly through the canals and gutters of a wet nocturnal Amsterdam as if hoping to find some Mack the Knife character who will put him out of his misery.

It is a moody and sometimes gothic novel, a cross between Henry Miller and *The Third Man*. It is also a classic example of a Dantean space: a city becomes a visual, sensual and even aural projection of a specific Dantean moment that our main character cannot get beyond. It is a Hell in the classical Dantean sense not only because of its specific visual and sensual references, overtly drawn in the novel itself, but because it uses the same deep architecture of Ugolino: it expresses the inner conflict, turmoil and guilt of a paralyzed main character. Here Amsterdam is not an active space: our narrator is not pursuing any specific goals or overarching external objectives. Nor is it in any way a purgatorial space: our narrator is going nowhere and will never overcome his crime of immobility on the Pont Royal. This paralysis may explain why the novel has never been made into a film: once Clamence walks away from the suicidal woman he becomes passive, a metaphor for a paralyzed Europe after the Holocaust.

Other stories have a similar self-abasement arc but use different spatial strategies: think of *Barfly* (1987) which constructs grotesque Dantean spaces that are smeared and caked theatrically with grime and cracks to reflect the self-abasement of the committed alcoholic Bukowski. Contrast that film with *Leaving Las Vegas* (1995) which, while also featuring a similarly self-abasing alcoholic protagonist, instead remains in unheightened dramatic spaces as we watch the character drink himself to death. The spaces in *Barfly* are a reflection of the inner life of the character, while *Leaving Las Vegas*'s are indifferent backdrops that convey little emotional information (Figs. 5.1 and 5.2).

Figs. 5.1 and 5.2   The Dantean space of *Barfly (1987)* vs. the dramatic space of *Leaving Las Vegas (1995)*

How to Stay Active in Hell

But it's important to note that not *all* characters in Hell are as passive as these examples from *The Fall, Barfly* and *Leaving Las Vegas*. Many do not simply accept their fate: some struggle fiercely against it. They are like Ugolino, who never gives up his drive and his goal: in a sense he is quite excited to finish telling Dante his short tale so he can get back to gnawing at the skull of the archbishop. He is still seized by rage, by a burning sense of revenge, still maddened by his own desperate guilt and grief. Though he may not understand how defeated he is, Ugolino is very dramatically active. In fact his activity is a fundamental part of his hellish trap. Like Capaneus, his emotions still construct and are the burning energy of his architected space. Characters do not only make and be their own Hell: they can at the same time constantly generate it all around them, constantly feeding it with their fierce energies, constantly trapped like Sisyphus in a loop they themselves make and yet cannot step out of or recognize.

Often in our dramas this is a problem of Self-cognition. *We* know Ugolino is in Hell, but does he? It is an open question. We can easily imagine that if he did himself understand he is in Hell then he might in this moment of revelation give up his struggle and lie there sobbing next to the archbishop. Perhaps some part of his mind knows this and drives him on: to stop gnawing on the archbishop's skull would be to face the death of his children and so to face himself. Perhaps he knows that would be a level of Hell that he cannot move to without becoming permanently shattered and incoherent. And besides, who would then punish the archbishop? Better to continue the vengeful relationship between them, better to have an objective. And so as often happens, revenge holds the vengeful together, becoming a shield against overwhelming grief and the fear of psychic destruction.

Inferno Arcs: Are You Stuck in Hell? Would You Know If You Were?

Now we visit some Dantean characters that are already in Hell when we first meet them in a story.

Consider Miss Havisham in her many cinematic realizations (1946, 1998, 2012): she has no desire to leave her gothic Dantean space. She could simply walk out into the sunshine at any time but, she stays a social isolate in her house, like Ugolino unable to confront her situation, the passing of time in the world and her own shame at being abandoned, instead fixating on taking revenge against men. Like Ugolino, she has both a fierce shame *and* an activating passion that glue her to her space. But unlike him, who has his enemy trapped in front of him, Miss Havisham cannot ever find her jilting suitor, and so she has instead decided to inflict pain on all men. The novel's main character, young Pip then stands in for her suitor: as object of her vengeance Pip is her latest instantiation of Ugolino's archbishop. Note that while the vengeful Miss Havisham is active in the story, she is like Ugolino nevertheless passive towards her own Dantean space; neither fights to get free of it.

ONE HOUR PHOTO

Other characters in empathetic Dantean spaces are actually trapped there and have only a passive relationship to it even if, like Miss Havisham, they have quite an active role in the plot of their stories. This describes Norman, the protagonist of *Psycho,* but it also applies to the story of Sy, the protagonist of the thriller *One Hour Photo* (2002). This is the story of a clerk who runs the one-hour photo lab at a drugstore, who discovers through a family's photos that the husband is having an affair. Sy tries to insert himself into the family, then violently intervenes in the family's life, punishing the father and his lover by forcing them to pose for naked photos. Sy is then arrested and interrogated.

As an adult Sy is a highly controlling person. We know this largely because of how he is framed, and this sense of control is violated both psychologically and spatially as he begins to crack up and confuse his own past with the truth of the family he is obsessively observing. As his psychic pressure builds and he enters psychological spaces that convey his sense of danger, he feels compelled to force his own sense of right onto this unsuspecting family in an attempt to rewrite his own memories.

We learn at the film's end with the investigating cops that Sy's father abused him as a child, forcing him to pose naked for pictures. Knowing about this Dantean moment, we begin to see that Sy has been confusing the history of his own horrible childhood with the present story of the family that he happens to meet: Sy, we realize, has like Ugolino been living in two periods at once. Even though we now recognize how this has made him a danger to those around him, we nevertheless find him empathetic: in fact, all of the empathetic machinery of Dantean space is invoked in *One*

Hour Photo. We realize that Sy, while wanting to care for others and while needing a family of his own, will always be lonely. Because we see no character arc for him, no change in how he relates to the world, no self-reflection on his actions, no way out of his childhood trauma, we know that his future efforts to help others will also only alienate them from him. And yet we realize his motives are actually rather admirable—he was actually trying to save the family—and we also realize he deserves our pity. Sy is on his own in a Hell he did not make and cannot escape. He is in the end rather like a less dangerous version of Norman at the end of *Psycho*.

As the example of Sy shows, a character trapped in Hell can spread his own torture and pain far and wide without ever facing his condition, yet if we are granted access to his Dantean space we can still find him empathetic. But this film also shows something else: it illustrates how the frame is used in unique ways to take us into the Dantean space of a character. To see how, we should first discuss the use of the frame in cinema and television in some depth.

SPACE AS EXPRESSED THROUGH MIS-EN-SCÈNE AND THE FRAME

First, in any moment of empathetic reaction we experience in a narrative we might ask ourselves the following question: what is triggering my empathy here? Am I empathizing with the situation or with the character? With the moment and the spectacle or with the underlying themes? With the music? With the production design? With the framing? And how do these elements all work to make me cry or cheer?

In this book we have proposed some tools for revealing the roles of empathy, character and emotion in story. But is it right to ask broadly about the machinery of empathy in story, or is this too broad a question? Do film and television differ fundamentally from myths, epic poems and novels in their use of emotional machinery? Does the nature of a visual medium separate it permanently from space in spoken and written story? This question is deeply connected with another: what is the role of the filmic mis-en-scène—of the framing, sound design and music—in creating our empathy?

Let us for example consider some categories of space that are useful for teaching cinematographers and production designers, categories that don't obviously appear in spoken and written story, though they may appear in static form in the set-design of plays. Below are seven spatial oppositions that can help describe most mis-en-scène.[2]

A frame can be described as a matrix of:

1. Balanced vs. unbalanced.
2. Chaotic vs. organized.
3. Open vs. closed.
4. Flat vs. deep.
   (Shallow vs. deep VOLUMES)
5. Wide vs. long.
   (Shallow vs. deep FOCUS)
6. Centered masses vs. distributed masses.
7. Foregrounded materials vs. a clean foreground.

We can look at a few examples here. Take two that represent psychic disorder and violence. *Apocalypse Now* (Fig. 5.3) tends to use unbalanced, open, chaotic, deep and wide frames, with its masses distributed, while *One Hour Photo* (Fig. 5.4) uses closed, organized frames with centered masses.

Take two other films that are both high in tone: *Amelie* tends towards organized, closed, flat and often deep frames with distributed masses, while *Raising Arizona* (Fig. 5.5), which imitates the cartoons of Wiley Coyote, uses an often-distorted open frame with centered masses and the deep volume of a distant horizon.

These categories *can* carry specific tropes with them: for example, consider neurotic characters like Sy, who often are too committed to reality and try to control it, as opposed to psychotic characters, who are often lost in their own world where their emotions stalk with freedom.

Figs. 5.3 and 5.4 A chaotic open frame vs. an organized closed frame = *Apocalypse Now* vs. *One House Photo*

Fig. 5.5 *Raising Arizona* uses spatial categories, landscape and performance tropes reminiscent of the comedy WB cartoon *Road Runner*

It is often true that the spatial representation of neurotic characters tends to use balanced, organized, closed frames, indicating their own need to control their worlds, while psychotic characters are often represented by a kind of chaos intruding into the world's order. We actually see this equation of balanced with control in many of the neurotic characters and spaces we will discuss in this book, such as *Star Wars, One Hour Photo, 50 Shades of Grey, Pleasantville, Mad Men* and, arguably, *The Graduate*. And we will see the equation of psychosis with chaos in *Apocalypse Now*, most Bond movies and in the documentaries *Tarnation* (2003) and *Waltz with Bashir* (2008). But still this is not by any means an incipient meaning of the frame: the same categories of balanced and organized frames are used by contrast to represent safety and life in *Aliens* and in *Hiroshima Mon Amour*, for example. It is the underlying character that determines the meaning of these deployments of frame and not vice versa.

To think of another example, an open frame can represent freedom (a trope of Westerns) or poverty (a trope of some neorealist films) or danger or the future or an infinite number of other associations, and these associations are largely determined by the demands of plot and by the history of the characters as well as by genre tropes. Like a color palette, these categories carry many and often contradictory histories and associations, but can also be determined by vivid backstories and personal histories, and so these frame categories do not reduce to a code of dramatic meanings independent of specific stories. In fact, their meanings are best understood by seeing when and how they grow as we follow the development of a film from idea to treatment to script to rewrites to visualization.

The visualization and the visual book usually comes into being only once the project has been funded and the cinematographer and production designer join the team, which usually happens after months if not years of hard work crafting a character and the oppositions and alliances that character finds in a world. Frame choices almost always come quite late in the conceptual process of filmmaking and so we will treat the process as largely determined by a story's character and plot, categories that are usually determined much earlier in any story's fashioning.

The crucial point is that character links frame and space: once a menu of framing devices becomes linked to an emotional state of a character, this empathetic linkage then allows for other frames in the story to hark back to this moment or to these emotions. Different scenes with similar or clearly-opposing spaces then become linked and defined by these emotional associations. In many films, e.g. *Amelie*, these categories link the overall look to create a specific emotionally-charged world, while in others these linkages shift precisely because they track and inform us about the changing story and character arc of the film's protagonist.

EMPATHETIC LINKAGE OF DANTEAN FRAMES

This brings us back to *One Hour Photo*: this film illustrates how a Dantean sequence in an otherwise realistic-seeming film can have clear residual effects: Sy's Dantean dream, which comes well into the film, makes other scenes and framing suddenly resonate emotionally. A quiet set of gridded lines in the background of an earlier ordinary shot now feel like Sy's attempt to control his world's chaos. The attributes of mis-en-scène that this frightening dream highlights—a balanced frame, plain white and blue surfaces, receding perspective lines, and a total lack of the earth tones given to the family's life—have been seen in the film from the start, but after Sy's nightmare they acquire significance. Now we know they express Sy's attempts to keep control of his inner demons by seeing the world as devoid of disturbing, messy human relationships. That suspicion is confirmed in the final scene by his joy over his final stack of photos, quotidien pictures of the clean objects and white walls of his hotel room. This tactic is also there in *Batman Begins,* where a set of umbrellas at Bruce's parents' funeral suddenly announce themselves as echoes of his childhood run-in with the bats in the scene that opened the film. In such films we are turned into emotional detectives, looking for clues and then linking residual emotional signals among otherwise realistic settings. (As we will see, the film *The Third Man* also has something of this residual framing effect in its final shot, which harks quietly back to the earlier sequence in the sewers to imply that Holly is, in some psychological and moral sense, still trapped in that murky environment.)[3]

One Hour Photo becomes alternately more balanced *and* more chaotic as Sy wrestles with his demons. Thus the spatial frame in a film, although it can be relatively unchanging, can also be harnessed to the development of the character's sensibility, fears, hopes and situation so that it dynamically expresses character conflicts and changes. In empathetic spaces framing tends to become more baroque and non-realistic, often in order to both announce that we are entering the experiential point of view of a character and to convey something about how this character is under psychic stress. These changes, usually married to a change in sound effects and in music, often intentionally break from the earlier pattern set in the film, and set a series of visual flags for the viewer in subsequent scenes, creating an empathetic linkage.

This is seen and felt in Sy's dream in the middle of *One Hour Photo* (Fig. 5.4). This non-realistic scene brings us into his sensibility, which in turn gives a new meaning to some of the film's location, situation, sound, music, color and framing. But note that Sy is not in conflict with his space: even if he is active he cannot change, and so this is a passive Hell, one he was thrust into long ago as a child and will never leave. He is dangerously active in his story but passive towards his Dantean space.

SPACE IN THE MAKING: HOW TO BUILD
YOUR OWN DANTEAN SPACE

"She may be going to Hell, of course, but at least she isn't standing still." This great line by E.E. Cummings[4] gets to a core question at the heart of the films we look at in this and the next four chapters. In this remark there is an admiration for characters who refuse convention, who fight against something, who dare, but it also has traces of the sentiment that people create their own hell by choice and decisions, a sentiment that Dante shared.

Consider examples of characters that aren't standing still and suffering passively in their own Hell but are running towards it. We begin by considering stories that use Dantean space to make this journey empathetic. In many of these stories a character's Dantean space is created before our eyes, usually because we witness them constructing their own Dantean moment and then experience it in increasing sensory and acoustic detail as it settles into them and seals their character arc, freezing their character in place.

DANTEAN SPACE IN EDGAR ALLEN POE

Edgar Allen Poe has two short stories that show a character meditating on committing a murder, then committing it and covering up, and then being haunted by the killing in a powerful spatial and aural way that leads to their conviction. These stories are very reminiscent of Dante, of course, in part for their clear and grotesque pedagogical horror.

In *The Black Cat* a husband who develops a hatred for his wife's cat blinds the animal and then murders his wife. He hides her dead body by putting it up against the wall and covering it with a new concealing stone wall. But then as the days go by, a horrible keening scream begins to come from the wall. He can hardly believe it, but neighbors too hear it and start to tear down the wall, to find not only the dead wife's body but also the blinded yowling black cat perched on her head.

In a similar short story, *The Tell-tale Heart*, the protagonist kills a man and then hides him under the floor in his house. And now over the course of days he begins to hear the beating heart of the dead man. Finally, when the neighbors convene in the room to discuss what to do about the disappearance of the man, the sound of the beating heart grows so loud in the mind of our protagonist that he finally pulls up the floor in desperation, thus revealing the corpse and condemning himself to death.

Both stories use their spaces to project guilt, rather like Camus used Amsterdam in *The Fall*. Guilt is a highly cognitive emotion that is the force behind so many hauntings in life and drama, and it plays this role because guilt marks a break in the self-perceived character arc of an individual. In these stories by Poe guilt is married to a Dantean moment in the life of the protagonist: the action of murder and concealment of the dead body is such a strong experience that it returns in sensorial and aural form, interpenetrating all later experiences, becoming the unvanquishable aural and visual evidence of this character's deed, and finally making life so unbearable that it leads to the revelation of the crime and punishment of its perpetrator.[5] These characters actually wrestle with their own Dantean spaces as they struggle with their own murderous actions.

Racing Towards Hell Only to Avoid it at the Last Minute: Murnau's *Sunrise*

We can compare the two Poe short stories we discussed above, which feature characters living in a dread of their own making, with the protagonist of Murnau's *Sunrise* (1927).

Here too we have a protagonist living under a cloud of guilt: he plans to murder his loving, innocent wife. But here guilt is working very differently: reflecting yet another aspect of its deeply cognitive nature, the guilt in *this* film is not looking backwards to a crime committed but rather looks forwards, to a crime imagined and planned in some detail but not *yet* committed. This is the narrative space of dread: here our protagonist has not yet done anything wrong but is literally bent under the weight of his plans to murder his wife, abandon his child and run away with another woman.

This heavy cloud of guilt is heard from the moment the music starts under the opening titles; when we meet him our main character is already living in the shade of his coming Dantean moment. He knows what lies ahead and yet he runs towards it anyway, but the knowledge of what will happen has already turned his world dark, strange, tense and fearful. His plan twists his face and clouds his vision, darkening the world and the music that beats in his ears. By embodying his own dread and guilt, this space foreshadows the moral disaster he is knowingly propelling himself towards.[6] In a sense he is like the people Dante meets in Hell: like them he is full of moral knowledge of his deed even if, unlike them, he hasn't yet committed it. And so this man rows onwards towards his own Dantean moment, against the current of his wife's long-suffering understanding and love, even while knowing that his intended action will break his life in two. So this film and its revolutionary, thickened air of psychological space is about a Dantean moment; though that moment lies ahead his future fallen state is already vividly imagined by our protagonist, creating the taut noir tension by threatening repeatedly to hove into view and settle permanently in his mind.

With this film we can see how different guilt is from other self-generating emotions that envelope the spaces we will discuss.

In life and drama, guilt is a deeply cognitive emotion because it is about planning and self-judgement. Its side-effect is to make us feel uncomfortable in our own skin and come to hate ourselves and seek for a way out. Because guilt involves us in judgements about our planning and our actions, guilt in drama about one's external objective is a strong foreshadowing force, as the tension of Murnau's *Sunrise* makes very clear.

Guilt, in both life and drama, is usually resolved only by either rejecting some planned action that intends to cause someone harm, or by somehow paying for or undoing the damage of an accomplished harm, even in cases when the protagonist didn't fully intend the harm he caused. When the guilt is about an accomplished action, the protagonist must engage in a kind of balanced erasure of the event, a kind of penance or redemption, a purgatorial event of some kind, as we see in Dante's Purgatory, and in stories from *Lord Jim* to *Jaws* to *Spider Man* to *Toy Story* and *Gran Torino*. And when the guilt is laced with a strong intention, when it results from a plan to do someone harm, as in *Sunrise*, the guilty protagonist must reject and fully deliver himself from the plan. Only then can he deliver himself and his wife from this Hell: only then can the sun finally rise again.[7]

We can make a few further useful distinctions now about the different kinds of relationships a character can have with her space. In stories like *Amelie* the space is an expression of the character's best side, of hope and dream and joy: we might call these inviting spaces. But for Poe's two murderers and the character in *Sunrise*, their Dantean space becomes an expression of the antagonist they are struggling against. We might call such places abrasive spaces, spaces that rub against the character to provoke pain.

There are also hellish spaces that are not abrasive, exactly. For example, the hero of *The Fall* and the Bukowski character in *Barfly* seem comfortable in their Hell: in fact these protagonists have engineered or sought out this particular space and now treat it as a kind of nest that they do not want to leave. We might call these clearly unpleasant yet sought-out spaces self-abasing spaces. These are a kind of mirror of what the character feels he deserves, or has become, a willingly-chosen space of self-judgement. Our next example shows how a character comes to actively and knowingly devise his own hellish self-abasing space.

THE THIRD MAN

The Third Man (1949) is the tale of a man who knowingly heads into his own Hell; once again we witness a man who constructs his own Dantean space before our eyes. Here our protagonist experiences a Dantean moment by causing the death of his friend and thus condemns himself to an existential Dantean space for the rest of his life.

When we first meet Holly Martins he is not in Hell nor is he entertaining the idea. A breezy winsome innocent American with no real understanding of the recent holocausts that have swept Europe, Holly arrives in post-war Vienna at the behest of his hero and childhood friend Harry Lime. In short order he learns Harry is dead, falls in love with Harry's grieving girlfriend Anna, learns Harry faked his death, and finally that Harry is a sociopathic crook, responsible for the murder and maiming of children and a stand-in for the destroyers of Europe.

As these external events unfold they produce a major inner change in Holly. We learn at the start that Harry is dedicated to his friends and to a morality as simple as the dime-store westerns that he writes for a living. But by the end of Holly's story (shown so powerfully in the famous long last shot of the film) we realize that from now on Holly's life will be quite different, that it has been broken into two parts. The innocent life of that rather jokey carefree Holly who loved and idolized his friend Harry is over, replaced now by this lonely, knowing life that began when he lured Harry to his death in the sewers under Vienna.

Again this break comes thanks to a Dantean space that is made before our eyes. A cloud of guilt hangs over Holly after he betrays Harry to the police in the sewers of Vienna: this becomes a traumatic Dantean moment. After all, by even his own simple childhood morality Holly has violated the code of the West and killed his friend, and even if he has done this for the right reasons, he can never be sure if his jealousy over Anna (who is still in love with Harry) was also a factor in this choice. From now on our protagonist will move through the world in a thicket of the emotional space of Harry's killing in the sewers. Harry is now a shade that will never leave Holly's side.

We feel the shade of the sewers in the film's famous last shot in the graveyard, that minutes-long shot of the long lines of the broken trees in which Anna approaches Holly as if from the end of a long tunnel and then walks past him as if he too were dead. Now she is gone forever and he is here forever: in a sense Holly will never get out of those sewer tunnels. This is Hell in the post-war existential era, where people do the right thing under the shadow of vast evil yet are nevertheless unable to escape its shade.

We can compare the glow of the ending of *Sunrise* to the harsh light and broken trees of this final graveyard setting in *The Third Man*.

Coming only twenty years later, *The Third Man* clearly takes place after the vast moral earthquake of the Holocaust and World War II. In the far simpler morality tale of *Sunrise*, good and evil are fixed oppositions and our protagonist neatly sidesteps the abyss of evil and steps back to his wife and into the sunlight. But in *The Third Man* by contrast the simple oppositions of good and evil are echoes of our childhood, will-o-the-wisps, tricky lures that conspire to pull us into a bottomless gap, illusions that only the protagonist still clings to. Holly is not the film's moral center: unlike the domestic drama of *Sunrise* which features only one man's moral wrestling, Vienna's rubble-filled landscape is peopled by Giacometti-like survivors and the ghosts of hundreds of millions of dead and dying. The children that Harry Lyme has crippled and killed reveal the real landscape of a desperate Vienna that grounds the film.

As a result there is a metalyptic difference between the placeless location of *Sunrise* and the real location of post-war Vienna of *The Third Man*, which is so geographically, historically, socially and morally anchored in a specific world-historical place and time. As we will see, crafting a Dantean space with such elements can lead to real-world effects on viewers and a transposition and deep characterization of those spaces in the popular imaginary.

Now we open the gate to Purgatory, a different story realm from Hell, a place where some very different demands of closure come to shape an arc. This next zone is easily the most storied zone of our culture today. But as we leave Hell and enter Purgatory, we only point out how Dante's Christian spatial zones and their associated dramatic rules and arcs have become so ingrained by the consumers of Western story structure that they remain invisible by being so assumed and naturalized. Hopefully the realm of Purgatory and its distinctive purgatorial arcs, spaces and stories might help to reveal some of these tenacious structures that have become so instinctual.[8]

NOTES

1. Dante's Hell is not only populated by Dantean spaces. In Dantean spaces, this Hell-bent action then actually bends Hell into his own special, personal shape, but many other parts of Hell—fiery lakes, swampy devil-filled zones—are highly populated and not architected by any individual sinners: their occupants have ended up there for simple shared sins such as theft or counterfeiting.

2. This is a non-exhaustive list drawn from various books on cinematography and painting, and I often use them in class to sharpen the conversation and clarify the visual book as well as help to determine the storyboard designs. (Note these categories can also help in the design and depiction of the *acoustics* of a space: some in fact can also be used to describe the music or the mix desired in a scene.)

3. By contrast there is no such Dantean empathetic linkage with the protagonist of *Young Adult* because Mavis never receives Dantean mis-en-scène: her subjective inner life is not expressed in the frame or the sound design but comes through in the disjunctions between her dialogue and others, between her sharp cutting affect and their casual calm. While *Young Adult's* Mavis is a Dantean character in a dramatic space, Sy is a Dantean character in a Dantean spaces of varying intensities and self-protective alienation.

4. Cummings (1958, p. 98).

5. Poe's marriage of psychological realism and Dantean technique, where guilt is a specter of hallucination, ghosts and shades, soon became a trope of horror fiction, of detective stories and eventually of noir films. These influences are seen in for example in Victor Hugo's naturalistic and Dantean novel *Thérèse Raquin* (1867), which, thanks to its many atmospheric aural and visual dimensions, was also turned into a successful play in 1873.

6. The use of cinema space to echo his tension is everywhere—note the suddenly—intruding silhouetted horsehead at 18:01 married to an emotional startle in the soundtracks of a short, muted cymbal clash. The repeating theme here too is used emotionally to express the antagonist, a repeating, low-note two-tone heart-beating melody on brass and strings that is so reminiscent today of the iconic, similarly-repeating two-tone cello-bass melody on *Jaws* and the low repeating beat-melody that announces the antagonist of the *Terminator* films. He suffers from a psychomachia-like version of the evil woman, who at minute 22 appears in ghost form to tempt him and propel him back to his murderous objective.

7. As Miss Havisham's example shows, some secondary characters through their hellish or heavenly state are physicalized, foreshadowing warnings for the story's other characters. Sometime, however, a character is trapped in a passive Dantean space in order to be rescued by the protagonist: think for example of the overt Dantean example of *What Dreams May Come* (1998), where the Orphic task of the protagonist Chris is to rescue his wife from her personal hellish mental trap.

8. Dedicated to Andy Beinen.

Bibliography

Alighieri, Dante. 2006. *The Divine Comedy*, trans. and ed. Robin Kirkpatrick. London: Penguin.

Aristotle. 1986. *Poetics*, trans. S. Halliwell. Chapel Hill, NC: University of North Carolina Press.

Baxter, Charles. 2012. Undoings: An Essay in Three Parts. *Colorado Review* 39 (1): 96–110.

Camus, Albert. 1991. *The Fall*. New York: Vintage.

Cummings, E.E. 1958. *A Miscellany*, ed. George Firmage. New York: Liveright.

Dickens, Charles. 2002. *Great Expectations*. Penguin Classics.

Dostoevski, Fyodor. 2003. *The Brothers Karamazov*. London: Penguin Classics.

Dostoevski, Fyodor. 2004. *The Idiot*. Washington: Penguin Classics.

Egri, Lajos. 2005. *The Art of Dramatic Writing*. New York: Bantam-Dell.

Field, Syd. 2005. *Screenplay: The Foundations of Screenwriting*, rev. ed. Delta Press. New York: Bantam-Dell.

Shakespeare, William. 2003. *Macbeth*. Washington: Folger Shakespeare Library.

CHAPTER 6

Ghosts and Shades and Place: Empathetic Hauntology in *Gravity, Lars and the Real Girl,* and *Hiroshima Mon Amour*

Nor mouth had, no nor mind, expressed
What heart heard of, ghost guessed.
—from *Spring and Fall*, by G.M. Hopkins.

THE LAND OF GHOSTS AND SHADES

In this chapter we examine the ways the dead walk among us in drama, how they are purgatorial burdens, emotionalized landscapes that are often deeply loved but that we must face and work through to achieve purgatorial or therapeutic freedom.

Our exploration will also distinguish ghosts from shades, comparing these two very different dramatic manifestations of the dead. Ghosts are very common devices in drama: they are essentially characters with desires and memories of their own who haunt a place or person and occasionally take corporeal form. Sometimes they also have the ability to do things: to move pencils, distract characters, or even kill people. Ghosts can also make requests of a main character that can lead to their destruction or salvation: think of Hamlet's father's ghost who tells him to kill his uncle.[1] Usually we see the faces of ghosts.

Shades, however, have a very different force and presence: they are not seen in the present but instead hold the power to make the living see the world in a certain way. In that way they are often spatial presences, especially when we enter the point of view of a character who is herself possessed by a shade: via that sideways step we see the world through

© The Author(s) 2018
A. D'Adamo, *Empathetic Space on Screen,*
https://doi.org/10.1007/978-3-319-66772-0_6

129

that shade. This is why it is a bit of linguistic luck that the slang word for sunglasses is shades: though we easily forget we are wearing them, shades can change perception and emotional life, obscuring some facts, emotions, people, colors and corners while highlighting others, all the while without themselves being directly seen. As a result, a shade can have a power just as dangerous or as liberatory as any ghost.

We now look at three very different films which are, however, all built upon similar Dantean moments: all three feature the presence of a loved one who has died, an empathy-evoking hauntological shade.

Gravity

The science fiction film *Gravity* (2013) features both a ghost and a shade. The ghost comes forth briefly in the affable form of the dead astronaut Kowalski, while the shade, present throughout most of the film, is the main protagonist's dead daughter, who has died before the story starts and who is herself never directly present or even seen in any photograph or memory.

The film revolves around Dr. Ryan Stone, a scientist on a space mission to repair the Hubble telescope. Ryan clearly does not fit comfortably into the team: she has trouble getting along with others. Soon we learn why she is so sharp and self-isolating: she is still in grief from the recent death of her little girl. It turns out that Ryan received the news of her daughter's death while driving her car at night: afterwards, feeling lost and bereft, she took many aimless nighttime drives.

Once again we meet a character trapped in a specific Dantean moment in her past, a moment of huge consequences that she cannot overcome and that took place in a specific environment—she was driving alone in her car at night—that has in a sense taken over her perception of everything (Fig. 6.1).

As Ryan tries to fix the satellite, the story's inciting incident literally hits: because of a missile strike on another satellite, they are suddenly assaulted by a fierce storm of metal shards and everyone but Dr. Ryan and the astronaut Kowalski are killed. He saves her and they sail out into the dark to rendezvous with the International Space Station. They find it abandoned, then both barely escape when it is almost destroyed by another storm of debris.

Unfortunately, thanks to some technical complications, only one of them can survive and so before Ryan can stop him Kowalski selflessly

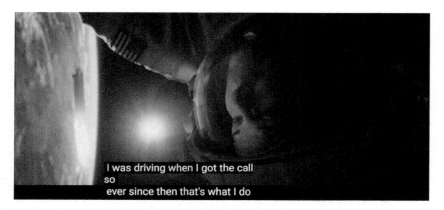

I was driving when I got the call
so
ever since then that's what I do

Fig. 6.1 Dr. Ryan lost in her grieving memory, *Gravity* (2015)

cuts himself loose to save her and floats away into the darkness of space. Left alone in the small capsule, Ryan struggles to direct it to re-enter earth's atmosphere but fails. She gives up and turns off the capsule's life support, then sits in silence waiting for death.

And now a tapping comes from outside the capsule: it is, miraculously, Kowalski. He comes inside, having somehow saved himself, and now gives her the hard talking-to she needs to save them both. But once she gets the capsule working, she realizes this manifestation of Kowalski was not real. After a fiery re-entry into the atmosphere, she crash-lands on earth, swims from the capsule, and in a scene of rebirth she finally stands up on the shore in the sunlight.

In this case we have a story with both a ghost and a shade. Kowalski in his ghost form is easy to understand and appreciate: he is a character with objectives and opinions. You can often argue with a ghost and, ever since the film *The Sixth Sense* (1999), ghosts themselves often have their own character arcs. These figures, which are sometimes manifestations of guilt or love or desire, almost always carry some real role in the plot but they differ in obvious ways from shades.

A shade does not take physical shape: instead it occupies your body and mind, as in the case of Ryan's dead daughter. In *Gravity*, for example, here in the present Ryan is still stuck in the car she was driving when her phone rang and she suddenly heard of her daughter's death. For Ryan, the shade of her dead daughter has turned the space vehicle into the car so that Ryan is in a sense still driving through the dark, beset on all sides by sudden killing blows that sweep others away, leaving her alone in deathly silence and the emptiest of nights.

One clue that there is a shade in a story is that the audience will know someone important to a main character has died but will see nothing or very little of the face of the dead. Denied our own access to their physical form, we see and experience only their effects on the protagonist. Compare *Gravity* with *The Official Story*, discussed in Chap. 3. In the pivotal scene of the playhouse, it is the vivid *absence* of the adopted daughter's real parents that rushes into the room, the house and the mind of our main protagonist when her adopted daughter relives her original, hidden and off-screen trauma. We see nothing of little Gaby's dead parents, nothing directly of their invaded, shattered house: instead we feel their presence, their inhabiting of the playhouse, their inhabiting of the lives and minds of Alicia and Gaby.

Shades can control an entire narrative space: in *Gravity* the dead daughter occupies not only Ryan's mind, mood and suicidal drift, but outer space itself. To finally escape the shade's world, Ryan must leave the blackness of night and fall through fire to water, to crawl back onto land and into air and sun and life.

In a sense outer space has become a kind of transference object for Ryan: just as the dollhouse hosts the shades of the dead parents in *The Official Story*, so black space hosts the shade of the dead daughter in *Gravity*. In a way *Gravity*'s grief-laced space is a kind of dark inversion of the shade-laced sky in the film *Up*: in that film the shade of the main character's joyful, adventurous dead wife has colored the sky with a sense of joy, relief and escape. Both *Gravity* and *Up* offer a therapeutic Dantean space, a space that serves as a lathe on which the protagonist, by external or internal effort or both, can resolve conflict and grief and be born again in a new space. Like a character completing a purgatorial task in Dante's *Purgatory*, Dr. Ryan works through her grief: escaping space is escaping that car of doom and death, a difficult, cathartic graduation out of a traumatic memory and into health.

PURGATORIAL VS. THERAPEUTIC ARCS AND CHARACTERS

Let's now put Ryan's escape from her isolation, loss and guilt into some context. We have claimed that after Dante, Western stories generally represent arcs and spaces of three kinds: hellish, purgatorial and heavenly.

With *Gravity* we have moved from Hell and Hell-bent arcs to Purgatory and purgatorial arcs.

There are many examples of purgatorial arcs: the thriller film *Jaws* (1975), for example, has this classic structure. A girl is killed by a shark in a small seaside town. Afraid of losing his job, the town's sheriff gives into the pressures of shopkeepers in town who are scared that the news will keep tourists from coming to their beach: he agrees to say that the girl might have been killed by a passing boat. As a result, unsuspecting people flood the beach and then the shark kills a small boy. Now the sheriff has a death on his conscience. To erase this crime the sheriff must overcome his inner conflict, his fear of the water, and then risk his life to go out and kill his external antagonist, the shark. It is not an easy task.

We have already talked in Chap. 3 about Buzz Lightyear in *Toy Story*, but here it is worth noting that while Buzz has a therapy arc in the film, Woody actually has a purgatorial arc. He is responsible for pushing Buzz out the second-floor window out of jealousy and envy. To undo his unjust action Woody must leave the house and go find Buzz, then save him, rebuild his shattered sense of self and then bring Buzz back home. This kind of balancing of action, doing some hard purgatorial task to undo a mistake or a crime, is very common in stories.

Often both therapeutic and purgatorial arcs are mixed together. Consider, for example, the story of Detective "Rust" Cole, the protagonist of the first season of HBO's *True Detective* (2014). Across the first season Rust must experience a therapy arc to overcome the death of his daughter in a car crash, but at the same time he is also responsible for destroying his partner and friend's marriage and for killing a number of suspects in the course of his work. By the end of the series—which goes into Dantean space in increasing stretches as the tension of the season rises—our protagonist has passed through a wide range of tortures and wracking pain in his efforts to find the serial killer. In the series' final cathartic and highly empathetic moments Rust finally passes through a personal transformation, crying about his dead daughter and regaining a sense of hope as he stares up at the night sky with his forgiving partner. While throughout the season it has been hard to distinguish the character's therapeutic struggles from his purgatorial suffering, the viewer's strong empathetic reacton and release in this scene comes from sensing that both arcs are finally complete.

Gravity also illustrates a therapy arc that at times seems purgatorial, as though Ryan somehow feels responsible for the death of her daughter or for the team of astronauts that have been killed. We might offer the following simple distinction between the two arcs and then give an explanation for how they are linked.

A purgatorial arc features a character making some big mistake, recognizing it and then pursuing a known goal in order to pay for or erase that mistake: this describes the sheriff from *Jaws*, Colonel Nicholson from *The Bridge over the River Kwai* and Woody from *Toy Story*. By contrast, a therapy arc features a character unaware in some way of the forces that control and impel his character and who, through struggles, becomes aware of his emotional problem and then either faces it or fails to overcome it. This describes both Rust and Dr. Ryan. (It also describes Lars of *Lars and the Real Girl* and the female protagonist of *Hiroshima Mon Amour*, the protagonists of our next two examples.)

Often the two arcs are mixed: many therapy stories are full of painful purgatorial actions because both are marked by a difficult unworking and forgetting of traumatic memories. In Dante's *Purgatorio* the sinners who work through their symbolic actions and come to fully grasp their sinful actions then wash in the River Lethe, the river of forgetting, and with this bath they finally wash away their guilty memories: then and only then are they able to walk out of Purgatory. This three-step struggle—of grasping some painful event in the past, then working to change the character tendencies that relate to that traumatic event, and then at last forgetting the painful event (through a washing-away or a burial) also undergirds a successful therapy. Both *True Detective* and *Gravity* take advantage of this parallel to create violent spectacles that only later, on reflection, are revealed to be part of a long, painful trail towards self-insight. These characters' violent spaces serve to emotionally release traumatic memories, apparently necessary steps in the uprooting of a shade. But of course a drama needn't conflate the two arcs: the character of Lars in our next example show a non-purgatorial example of a therapy arc, where space remains quiet and gentle throughout.

We can briefly compare *Gravity*'s big-budget, spectacular Dantean space with a low-budget non-spectacular film, *Lars and the Real Girl* (2007), which also features a successful therapy arc in which the main protagonist manages to bury the past and move forwards into a new life. However, while *Gravity* stayed largely within the shaded space of Ryan's grieving perspective, this next story instead stands outside its shaded Dantean character, Lars, and stays entirely within dramatic space.

On the Rich and Strange Sea Change of the Dead: The Wide Gamut of Hauntings

"Full fathom five thy father lies:
Of his bones are coral made:
Those are pearls that were his eyes:
Nothing of him that doth fade,
But doth suffer a sea-change
Into something rich and strange."

Shakespeare, *The Tempest*, Act 1, Scene 2

Lars and the Real Girl

Lars and the Real Girl (2007) is a low-budget drama set in a small town. When we first meet the film's main protagonist Lars, he is a social isolate, a neurotic who cannot touch people. Lars lives with his brother Gus and is scarred by a series of Dantean moments in his past: his mother died when he was born and his father abused him when Gus left home. So far Lars has held these scarring moments in abeyance, but that changes one evening when his brother Gus announces that Gus's wife is about to have a child. Disturbed by this, Lars has something like a psychotic break that, as Gus and his wife slowly realize, is powered by Lars' reawakened guilt about his mother's death, his fears of being abandoned again by Gus and replaced by this baby, as well as Lars' newly-triggered desire to have, like his brother, a partner of his own. This last desire is a particular problem since Lars is so phobic about people that he wears white gloves to keep from touching anyone.

Lars' solution is simple: he purchases a life-sized sex doll that he orders on the internet, names it Bianca, and then starts a romantic but non-sexual relationship with the doll, squiring her about town and bringing her to dinner parties. While the viewer stays at a dramatic distance from Lars' perceptions, we do see that the sex doll has in a sense become inhabited with the shade of Lars' dead mother, becoming both a realized physical ghost and, as his conversations show, also a shade that lives only in his mind. For most of the film Lars then psychotically explores his deepening non-physical relationship with the doll, caring for her by bringing her to doctor checkups (Fig. 6.2), helping her to bed and so forth.

Fig. 6.2 A Dantean character in a dramatic space, *Lars and the Real Girl* (2007)

And now Lars' healing begins. After he meets a local woman and starts a friendship, he slowly becomes convinced that Bianca is sick and then that she is dying. He puts her in a wheelchair and starts taking loving care of her, and eventually becomes convinced that she is dying of a terminal disease. In a highly-empathetic last act, the entire town comes to sympathetically recognize that Lars is actually working through some very deep issues: they begin to facilitate his fantasy in many caring ways, and with their help when Bianca 'dies' Lars can finally bury her, freeing himself of the shade of his dead mother and then finally beginning a real relationship with a local woman whom he can touch.

This film is a drama and stays within dramatic space. The locations are unobtrusive settings of low spectacle, like those of *Little Miss Sunshine* and *Young Adult*, staged in ordinary, lower-middle-class places that do not intrude in on the drama being played out among the characters. And like those other two films, the camera and sound design observe all the usual boundaries of realism: we never enter into the protagonist's own distorted perceptions of his world. But in this film we rarely lose sight of Bianca: her silent, comically-awkward presence always reminds us that part of Lars is somewhere else, somewhere we cannot go, and that he is trying to free himself from a terrible and abusive childhood. And so, although we stay outside his perceptions, this becomes a very empathetic film that exhibits both compassionate and communal empathy: at first we come to understand what he has been through and how it has affected him, and then we see his childlike solution, that the doll is not a sex doll but really a doll of transference, of re-enacting his missing relationship with his mom and modeling the marriage of his brother. With this insight we gain compassionate empathy for Lars. Then as we see him taking such care of the 'dying' sex doll, we respond to him personally with communal empathy, increasing our empathetic investment in him. And then when the entire town begins helping him through his transition and through his need to bury 'Bianca,' we also feel a great sense of communal empathy for everyone.

Again, as we saw in the film *Young Adult*, this is a Dantean character acting out in a dramatic space: given no access to Lars' inner experience and staying in realistic and unspectacular settings, we can only imagine his inner storms from his behavior. However, our next examples show how as we increasingly enter into a character's subjectivity the story's space can grow increasingly Dantean: as a story enters this pressured, torqued emotional perspective, its realistic boundaries begin to break down, bending under the weight of the character's guilt and hope and grief-wracked memories.

Hiroshima Mon Amour

In *Hiroshima Mon Amour*, Duras and the director Alain Resnais do something very remarkable: they turn the world of Hiroshima and its erased radioactive past into a dance of space. This tour-de-force of transference features two lovers with similar Dantean moments in their pasts, both possessed by shades of beloveds horribly killed in the war. But it also manages to treat each character differently, granting Dantean space to the French woman and dramatic space to the Japanese man in the same film, and often even in the same spaces. Though we gain only oblique glimpses of their dead beloveds, never seeing the face of her dead lover and never seeing anything of his dead family, we nevertheless feel the controlling power of these shades in every frame.

The story barely has a plot in the ordinary sense. A French actress, who is only identified as "she" but who is our main protagonist, is in Hiroshima in the late 1950s to be part of a film about the city's atomic bombing in 1945. As the film opens she is in the midst of a one-night affair with a Japanese architect, only identified as "he," who is native to Hiroshima.

But soon the film reveals two entirely other levels because both the lovers carry specific traumas from the war. Hers took place fourteen years earlier in her native Nevers, a town in France, when she was just 17. She fell in love with a German soldier who was part of the occupying force in the town. The two became lovers and the world changed for her—it was suddenly full of joy and hope. But when her lover was killed as the war ended she was punished as a collaborator, having her hair shorn off and being locked in a cellar while mad with grief. Finally, her parents essentially abandoned her, putting her on a bicycle at night and telling her to bike to Paris. She rode off and, it seems, has never looked back. In all the flashbacks that she narrates in the present in her confessions to the Japanese man, we never see the face of the German.

We learn less of the Japanese man's personal experience: he tells her he was away fighting when his family was killed by the bomb in 1945, but we never see his family and never enter his own memories. However, we do gain a grounded if impersonal sense of the utter horrors they must have gone through after that fateful day of the American bombing through seeing the French actress's research—her walks in the city's museum—and through the film's use of harrowing documentary footage of the bombing and its effects on the survivors.

Though both she and he are casual at first in mentioning details about their past, it gradually grows clear that both war-experiences, which took place 14 years earlier at roughly the same time, were Dantean moments. And after they begin exchanging vague, oddly rhetorical confidences while in each other's arms, each finds in their increasingly intimate revelations that the dead are growing stronger. For her he becomes a mirror of her genuine suffering, a chance to glimpse how empty and shaded her life has been since the war, while he himself gains a sense of how lost he is.

Pulling each other into their pasts, they slide rather hopelessly towards full confessions to each other, and by the middle of the film she is speaking honestly about her horrors for the first time in her life and to a man she has known for only a few days. At first the dead German is not supplanted by the living Japanese lover, who though he strives to connect with her is largely locked into the role of confessor. But then in a long confessional scene[2] she starts pouring out her terrible memories. The challenge of this is that she is still enamored and committed to her dead beloved, even as he is now both powerfully evoked and beginning to fade: as a result she feels she is betraying and losing her dead German beloved by speaking of him for the first time. And now, in the grip of memory she actually conflates the two men, beginning to address the Japanese man as if he were her dead German, producing an eerie performance that shifts from affected to neurotic to authentic as it elides and slides between the present Hiroshima and the past of Nevers in 1944.

Meanwhile the Japanese man finds that his own memories of the bombing are evoked by her story. Like her, his memories cannot be effaced by the rebuilt city's present, by its modernist sunlit streets and clean-swept plazas: instead that dead city of ashes affects everything he sees and senses, including her white body. As they confess these emotions they are drawn closer to each other and yet also repelled by their own allegiances to their dead loves, and this begins a dance of attraction and flight that crosses the city's bars and streets all night long.

The film's most memorable sequence is by itself such an apparently simple and undramatic scene in which nothing is resolved or argued over. Coming in the third act, it is the minutes of her walking down Hiroshima's neon-lit streets at night as he follows her (Fig. 6.3).[3] Dollies of Hiroshima's streets are jump-cut into dollies of streets in her native Nevers. And gradually the viewer understands why this apparently prosaic scene is so haunting. As she walks she is being followed by her own specter: that is, she sees in this living man the shade of her dead German lover, and in this city the ghost of her own lost Nevers. He meanwhile seems to sense that she alone can understand what he has lost, how he too is split between that banished shameful past and this sterile present. In a very real sense while we stay in the film's neorealist present, seeing an ordinary street while gaining no cinematic access to their own churning emotions and memories, we also realize that they are both in the other's psychomachia, each wanting to be lovers but each thrust into the role of a past grief-soaked love: while we watch him follow her through a night in 1957 Hiroshima, we know that she is walking down the streets of a long-ago Nevers with the dead German man. Meanwhile the German's shade has a clear stand-in in the Japanese man, who himself is walking through a night vibrating with the ghost of the destroyed Hiroshima where his family was killed along with hundreds of thousands of others.

And so three different spaces are joined—1944 Nevers, 1945 Hiroshima and present-day 1957 Hiroshima, creating what we might call a neorealist haunting of the defeated dead. A Dantean space is created

Fig. 6.3   A space that is Dantean for her and dramatic for him, *Hiroshima Mon Amour*

using the strict palette and techniques of neorealism of actual locations and the tropes of realism and traditional documentary, all glued together by personal and historical memory. This is character haunting but wedded to the history of a world at war. As these two adulterers drift through the seemingly-illusory streets of a rebuilt present that now carries little mark of what terrors happened here, they carry on their shoulders the story of an entire generation still shell-shocked and damaged by war.

The only redemption in the film, and it is honest and true, comes in a small dramatic repetition. It begins in the bar in the middle of the film: after she confesses her truth, her pain and her fear of losing this memory to him, he asks her if she has ever told this story to anyone. When she says no, that this is the first time, he grasps her wrists in joy. Though shocked at his ecstatic reaction, she also smiles brightly, though the reason for her smile is not very clear: has she fallen back into her actor's role? In the film's final moment he again seizes her wrists, and she again reacts with a bewildered joy and surprise, but now it seems genuine, as if he has snatched her back from some dangerous ledge.

The repeated tableau seems to mean that despite the erasure of memory, of lovers by bullets, of families and cities by nuclear weapons, of love by time, death still does not have complete dominion in the world. In fact real true joy comes from authentic actual intimate human contact and the sharing of grief and the consoling of injuries, even if only in a casual affair had by two people who are too scathed by memories to have real anchored relationships in their present living life.

One way to experience this film is to feel its lush romanticism. This too seems to owe something to Dante, though in a way we've not yet discussed. There is something of her condemned situation that resembles the condemned-soul architecture of Dante's Francesca and her own linked and wandering lover. Like Francesca, our protagonist has chosen to go against the social and political norms in loving the wrong man. And like Francesca, we can see both sides of her curse. And like Francesca, she seems sometimes frightened that the Japanese lover might yank her down out of the air and back into life, yet at other moments she seems to blow about the land with him, unable to leave her German-Japanese Paolo.

At least, this is one interpretation of the protagonist's motives. But we see a productive ambiguity over the motives of a main character: Duras has provided a rich and obscure layering of motive here. The main character grows increasingly fascinating because even as she painfully spills out her tragic backstory, her motives and feelings for the Japanese man grow not more clear but rather more opaque and hard to grasp. We can't tell how much of her motivations are about her desire to be released from the German lover's ghost, how much is a hatred for the Japanese lover for doing this, how much she wishes she were with the Japanese man, how much she wants to be punished as the French punished her for sleeping with the enemy, how much she has internalized that social view of her. Finally, looking for motive, we wonder, are these two simply overcome by survivor guilt?

Repeatedly she expresses the following lines of self-abasement: "Who are you? You destroy me. I was hungry. Hungry for infidelity, for adultery, for lies, hungry to die. I always have been." Has she internalized the punishments of the angry French who shaved away her hair? Is she longing to be punished for loving? For surviving? Is she simply longing for death? Her motives remain opaque to us: all of these impulses might be jostling within her. Without knowing this, we cannot quite be sure of what her character arc is really about, or of what her final bright smile means. Does it signify that she is now released from her shade. Is she committing to a relationship with this man? Is she simply trying to end things on a higher note, or is she just showing a certain French jouissance? We think of the adage of showing and not telling, or of the biblical point that "you will know them more by what they do than by what they say," but here these characters do so little and muse so much that their psychology is largely closed off to us. As a result of our prismatic glimpse of her chaotic emotions, Hiroshima seems by turns a longed-for, inviting space, an abrasive space, a judgmental space, a tryst space and a space of self-abasement.

In part this happens because of her growing ambiguity, which so vividly dramatizes the human problem of self-knowledge and self-deception: she shows how even when we are earnest and not engaged in presenting ourselves well or in outright lying, we are still not the best reporters on our own desires. Our own actions often surprise us, revealing ourselves to ourselves as well as to others. Despite her marked penchant for brooding, she is obscure to herself, indecisive in the truest meaning of ambivalent in having very strong desires to do quite opposite things.

Duras' scenario notes describe the protagonist as wrestling with the fact that she survived the death of her love, but it is not entirely clear if this is guilt: though unclear in the script, it seems more clearly to be grief in the performance. But yet we ask ourselves questions as we watch her: we wonder why she has never told this story—the core event of her life that she wrestles with every waking moment—to her husband, the man she is happy with and has had children with and is apparently happy to return to. We answer this question for ourselves: perhaps this is because he would not understand, having never been through anything similar, while the Japanese man has lost his family in the bombing of Hiroshima. And having been in the Japanese army in the war, he won't judge her for having been involved with a German soldier. Is she thinking simply that she has found a tragic twin in him: is that the source of their antipathy and bond?

And so she confesses it all to the Japanese man, further forgetting it even as she tells it, hating him for asking her to tell him yet needing to tell. Losing her old love and finding a new one, she is helpless before both. She becomes the protagonist of a kind of anti-therapy movie where, like Ugolino, she fights to keep certain painful tragic-romantic memories alive, fights to remain within her own psychic torture out of love for the lost beloved. Like Francesca, she cannot give up her pain because it is too anchored in her love. And like Ugolino she cannot strive for her own therapy and healing: when it threatens to arrive at the end of the film, she is terrified and lost.

Simultaneously Resnais and Duras are using another divide to obscure motive and character, another device to create meaningful ambiguity, to give us a sense of glimpsing some multiplicity of meaning. These two do not act out scenes in the ordinary way of dramatic films: instead they are staged in odd frozen tableaus, among dissonant montages and documentary footage. Most striking of all, they continually lapse into a polished, precise and often artificially-declarative delivery with each other in which they take turns speaking without any of the usual impulse to interrupt or speak over each other, becoming respectful in an almost incantatory style. With a few exceptions, their arguments are abstract and formally presented, as in the long opening argument of the film about whether she truly did see Hiroshima. In an early example of identity politics it is a fight over conceptual schemes and emotive truth. She thinks she understands something of what happens but he denies this, saying she never can understand or even see the real Hiroshima. Her reactions to his accusations comes only in long blocks, so that rather than composing a scene their speech feels more like a Platonic dialogue or like court testimony recorded separately from two witnesses. And so the status of the entire first sequence is unclear, are we hearing thoughts or testimony or confessions or dialogue? All of this becomes even more abstract as we realize these lovers who have so much to say never address each other with any names, nicknames or endearments. At times we wonder, can these two characters even hear each other?

This ambivalence is heightened by a non-realistic form of blocking: in general they stand very still as they speak, always carefully blocked in their actions and gestures so that personal particulars of spontaneous movement are erased. This lack of spontaneity in people who are well-trained actors is heard even in their laughter which feels forced and uncomfortable.[4] And while they discuss intimate memories, outside of her painful memories of Nevers there are no particulars—we know nearly nothing else specific about either of them. They often parrot facts about the war and other non personal issues: at one point, while she has her face in his caressing hands, she begins to sound like an almanac as she talks about the Loire river. Their performance slides between a smiling nonchalance and a brooding inner contemplation of their memories. So much seems intended to slide past each other and not land, conveying a world of banalities and indifference where people cannot communicate emotionally.

In contrast, we see small authentic details and moments of performance only as she recounts her traumatic memories. Usually these memories are seen playing out in visual flashback with no sourced sound—the sound stays with her voice and contains the backgrounds of the setting where she recounts them, giving a defamiliarizing distance.[5] And yet the empathetic romantic bonds between these two are continually broken in the film, only slowly and somewhat bitterly reforming again as she repeatedly but almost unwillingly seeks out some contact. And this is complicated further by apparent breaks in the dramatic frame that seem to pull them apart even when they are together.[6] These moments with their specific details and strongly relayed emotional memories pop the actors out from the film's cold backgrounds with visceral force. While the Japanese lover's focus on her and his need for her is sometimes total and absorbed, it is quickly followed by his odd and cruel comment to her that "in years ahead when I have forgotten you and had many other adventures like this out of habit, I will remember you as a symbol of forgetting." And this poetic declaration does seem to land on her with a cruel force he doesn't himself recognize or see. While we are unsure if he knows he has even said it out loud, the comment seems to launch her away from him and so to trigger his long drawn-out pursuit of her through the neon-lit cityscape.

All of these tactics combine to produce a unique marriage of a highly charged romantic empathetic bond between two highly alienated characters. Compare the nature of the drama here to the more conventional ones of, say, the dynamic central to films that have a surface similarity like *Before Sunrise* (1995) or *Wings of Desire* (1987), which both feature a couple moving through a city in search of each other while having intellectual and poetic conversations about the state of the world and the nature of romance. As these two characters shift so fast, what is this shift, exactly? Are they shifting psychologically in reaction to each other? Or is this a dramatic aside, a technique taken from Eugene O'Neil's play *Strange Interlude*, in which he speaks his inner thoughts out loud but we are to understand she cannot hear them?[7] Or are we still inside realism and these two are actually struggling hard to invent and to give advice to

each other? Has a simple affair turned inadvertently into this paired tragedy, and now they are struggling through it to understand their own suffering, to come to grips with the nature of love after war, working hard
to come to insights for themselves and for each other as a form of con-
solation, and perhaps of healing? Or are they simply trying to be cruel
to each other, pushing each other away when they feel rejected or out of
an underlying anger at the foreigner, the newcomer to their own care-
fully-fenced inner terrain of vulnerability: are we seeing a familiar trope
of romance dramas, the dance of repulsion and attraction? Is she angry
with him for his abstract talk? When she leaves him now is she punishing
him? As she then wanders through the streets, staying just yards ahead of
him, is she abandoning him? In the eerie scene in the Casablanca bar is
she trying to make him jealous as a punishment for his inadvertent casual cruelty? Or are they both just solitary obsessives, lost in their grief,
whose paths keep crossing in a small, empty city?[8]

It may be impossible to decide what we are seeing: we might plausi-
bly attribute all of these motives to *Hiroshima Mon Amour*. But whatever these jarring shifts are about, their overall aesthetic effect is clear:
these two are not dramatic characters and we are not in a dramatic space
like that of *Before Sunrise*. From the start all of this refusal of ordinary
dramatic conventions transforms our characters into symbols, or anyway
gives them another dimension: through these many carefully deployed
distancing effects, the two become statue-like analogues of meanings,
unwitting stand-ins for ideas and forces and great choral masses of war-
dead that lie beyond their own characters' understanding.

In the final scene they actually name each other by their city's
names. In the face of all this we accept that their motives are obscured
not only because of akrasia or because this is often the human condition—especially for people who have undergone extreme suffering and
loss—but also because these two are trapped in overwhelming culturally-
wide Dantean memories that are themselves crafted by the remorseless
war. And so now as these two walk both together and alone through
Hiroshima, walking through the memories of their own past tragedies
and haunted by their own loved dead and dead loves, they also cast a
million shadows each, the shadows of the millions of dead and the shadows of all those still living who have lost everything that matters.

And now we might comment on the sheer number of distancing
devices in the film. This strange, experimental formalism paradoxically
pushes us away from the typical Hollywood beat-by-beat experience

of the fictional characters' lives. Instead these devices link the characters' ever-present individual suffering to that of their dead shades. And because these shades are described in abstract terms while their situation refers to actual massive historical pain, we find our own empathetic reactions are now linked to a history of suffering that yet reinforces the romantic, emotional pain of the fictional characters. Knowing the leftist commitments and aesthetic experimentalism of both Duras and Resnais, we might say that this film is a rather unique example of how to marry Dantean characters to the very different sensibility of Bertolt Brecht. Though we cannot discuss him in this book, Brecht is perhaps the only other figure in Western narrative history besides Dante who changed the tradition by marrying a new moral sensibility to a large-scale productive re-invention of narrative technique. Perhaps only a Brechtian Dantean space could so romantically combine alienation and exposed pain, distance and empathy, erased individuality and emotional immediacy, catharsis and lingering horror.

This complex mixture is felt acutely in the film's final scene when the space becomes its most placeless, as if they are no longer in Hiroshima or 1945 Nevers but in some white box of modernity. As she finally returns at dawn to her hotel room with him still in tow, a new alienation takes over. She has arrived, indecisive and bleak, in a room whose anonymity reflects her own sense of being lost and bereft of roots and place and certainties, ending up with him in this placeless place so lacking in any detail.

This final room is a non-place of the kind Augé defined (Augé 1992, p. 122). A non-place is one of transience that carries few or no markers of personal history and thus carry a sense of anonymity and even of indifference. We will see a similar use of non-place spread through New Wave cinema to describe utter alienation and dejection: two years later we find it in so much of Olmi's *Il Posto* (1961) and in Antonioni's *The Eclipse* (1962) where Monica Vitta is anxious and torn in another alienating hotel room. And now in this depersonalized, ahistorical emptiness, a place whose ordinariness perhaps emblematize the boredom, rote days and emotional facades that each is returning to in their family lives, now in this place a final emotional reversal takes place. Now he grabs her arms and she smiles and looks at him in some kind of hope. Once again we are unsure what we are seeing, yet it is emotionally compelling and highly empathetic.

We should make some distinctions now between this film and *Gravity*, a discussion that looks ahead to our next chapter's Dantean documentaries. First, the female protagonists of both *Gravity* and of *Hiroshima Mon Amour* are both in some sense resisting their own healing: each of them is still very much in love with the memory of the dead beloved that keeps them frozen in a certain state of grief, and this love conspires to both keep them miserable as it also keeps them from entirely realizing or grasping their own unhappiness. In such stories healing would mean to allow their memory of the dead loved ones to lose some sense of its vividness and closeness, and they are simply not ready for that. But then unlike Ugolino, who is now in a permanent Hell and will never be ready to face his actions, by the end of their stories both of these two women have been able to gain some distance on and control of their grief.

Another point is worth making. Dr. Ryan's Dantean moment came to characterize her sense of space, but we do not feel at the end of *Gravity* that space *itself* has gained any tragic airs. We realize we have been in a subjective tragedy and that space is not itself characterized by the death of Ryan's young daughter—actual outer space itself, we know, has an objective reality uninflected by this fictitious narrative. By contrast, the Dantean spaces of *Hiroshima Mon Amour* are quite different in this sense: they extend out from the film, connecting causally with and deepening our emotional sense of the actual Nevers and Hiroshima. The fictitious protagonist of *Hiroshima Mon Amour* characterizes Nevers because her story of being shorn of her hair and locked up is drawn from the stories of many young women all across France after the war. Her punishment and madness represent real historical forces and events. And Hiroshima is even more deeply emotionalized, because the film links his story (and to a lesser extent hers also) to the powerful forensic evidence of Hiroshima's trauma, revealed in the documentary footage, then visually contrasts it to the present-day *erasure* of that trauma in the rebuilt city. Documentary serves as a bridge between their empathetic space and history, linking their fictitious romance with the real events of the bombing. While *Gravity* was one woman's story and one woman's Space, *Hiroshima Mon Amour* (like *The Third Man* and *The Official Story*) uses Dantean space to bring empathy to actual historical places and events, creating a political hauntology, an actual collective mass shade composed of the war dead.

With this bridge, Dantean space brings alive the real lived history of two actual war-torn places in a very intersubjective and emotionalized way. Like the example of Aeneas in the *Aeneid*, the nature of two cities in wartime are dramatized through the vehicle of a protagonist's traumatic experiences. Just as Aeneas's character and story represents both the fall of Troy and the birth of Rome, this French "she" and Japanese "he" now similarly represent the past and future of whole cities and nations. But unlike the *Aeneid*, here the places become enlivened, their history made empathetic and experienced, through a new aesthetic. Thanks to their own somewhat depersonalized and erased personal stories and abstracted performance styles which lack many of the specifics of realism, their Dantean moments mingle to characterize Hiroshima's destroyers, its victims, and its uneasy anxious present. But their increasingly-emotional affair also points towards a specific future for the cities and places in the story: by enacting a romance in 1958 about a woman who loves a German and a Japanese man (two soldiers who fought long ago for the defeated, scorned countries), their mutual empathic healing and union helps to mark the end of the war's great divisions. In a way this film's break from conventions does not only announce a new cinema but rather a new coming world, a new form of being, and perhaps a new geography. For all of these reasons this film is the first cinematic expression of the new globalism that would come to define the EU project. It also begins a new Aeneas-like tradition of using contested cities to represent both a personal inner crisis and yet express the hopes for a new start to our politics, a theme we will explore more fully when we discuss the film *Amelie* in our last chapters. But for now consider *Wings of Desire, Alice in the Cities* and so many other cinematic and narrative efforts that are laced with the birth and hopes of the European Union. In all these films we find ourselves in a borderless land of the soul where international bonds and character changes can happen that offer a way out, an escape from the dreadful national histories of the protagonists. It's hard to find any comparable project or effort in literature, song or any other branch of European culture: nowhere but in cinema do we really see artists struggling to create a new and specifically *international* identity like this. The lack of that broad project is sorely missed in today's Europe, but perhaps these examples of radical aesthetic invention can point the way towards a new culture and a new synthesis of identities.

Stepping back now from this tour of shades, we see how the shade is a device of Dantean hauntology. Following Derrida (1993) and Fisher

(2009, 2014), we use the term hauntology to identify an ontology of absence, of something that is not present and is in fact in some sense missed: in such narratives not only are we "haunted by futures that failed to happen" (Fisher 2009) but the ontological elements that make up a shaded narrative's world (for example in a film's case the locations, production design and other craft elements) are working differently to connote a loss and lack rather than a presence. A shade is in this sense an empathetic frame of hauntology that takes us inside the sensibility of a character trapped in an overwhelming sense of loss.

The Official Story, *Hirosima Mon Amour* and *Gravity* simply make no sense without us realizing there is a shade at work, and yet that shade has also hidden itself to announce its absence, to highlight how the fabric of existence has been carved, wounded and rent. Just as Ugolino's icy twosome and toothsome revenge are a projection of his missing, murdered, eaten children, so in all these examples a forceful overwhelming memory of loss animates all that is present, though our examples announce their wounds in different ways and for very different dramatic and social purposes.[9]

Few of us has met a ghost in life but anyone who has suffered a moment of grief, who has seen their world darken and echo with loss, has met a shade.

The world is dappled: as Petronius said, there are shipwrecks all around us if we can only train ourselves to see.

NOTES

1. See Baxter (2013).
2. Beginning at minute 45.
3. The walk itself begins as they are passed by a duo of guitar players quietly strumming the snatch of a melody. This source music fades but is soon replaced by a funereal piano in score that then ties together the jump cuts between two dolorous dollies, both moving at the pace of a funeral train, that marry the lonely uninhabited night-time Hiroshima they are walking through to her remembered daytime Nevers of 1944. As she wrestles with the emotional turmoil raised by the Japanese Man behind her, the familiar dissonant score enters again, and we are now with her emotions in score, voiceover and long lonely visuals of them walking. And always her voice intones her quiet confessions in a formal, abstract and poetic register which is nothing like ordinary speech. Mallarmé once said that the job of poetry was "to clean up our word-clogged reality by creating silences around things" (quoted in Sontag 1983, p. 196). This part of the film does create

silence around things, or really silence is laced through whole cities and holocausts, but it then alternates its many quiet meditative shots with long stretches of words and subdued traumatic memories.

4. Throughout this film we see the Nouvelle Vague's commitment to breaking the bonds of naturalism.

5. But there are flashes of realism and performative empathy as well: for example, at one point (48:00) she talks about loving the taste of blood after tasting the blood of her dying German lover, and this is intercut with a jump-cut memory (itself invented as a technique in this film) of her in her cellar scraping her nails bloody on the stones of her cellar room and sucking on them. Though once again this breakage is observed rather coolly and distantly by the film, she is lost in this memory of how the bodily boundary between her dead lover and her was breached in a sensuous way: we see this when now in the present in the Japanese bar, her hand accidentally touches the beer glass with a tiny sound, an ordinary sound that shocks her as it drags her back into the present.

6. This ambivalence is created through directing the actors. Again and again the actors seem to stop communicating with each other and announce their own thoughts, as he does at 1:05:00, saying things that would be cruel if actually said to a new lover after she had made such an intimate confession. Then their performance becomes careful and deliberative in intonation and thoughtful in affect, closer to that of the film's early voice-overs, so that we cannot be sure if they are hearing each other or simply lost in their own deeply depressed thoughts and memories.

   And then there is the constant radical shift from the intensely personal and bonded subjective emotions to a coldly-clinical objective eye. For example, only a minute or two after she was under some strange spell that allowed him to take the place of her dead lover literally before her eyes, and even as she finally throws herself into his arms after her confession (1:04:40), she says "It's so good to be with someone sometimes!" The impersonal nature of this declaration, so detached from him in particular by its double-barrelled generalizations of "someone" and "sometimes", does not land on him in any negative way. In fact, it is oddly underlined by his own smiling acceptance of her suddenly dissipated attention. Once again, his reaction pushes us right out from the expected personal bond of intimacy we expect from most romantic dramatizations: clearly something else is being sought in this film.

7. For a good discussion of this technique, its uses and antecedents, see *Eugene O'Neill: A Playwright's Theatre* by Egil Törnqvist, pp. 159–161.

8. Or is this all wrong? Are we simply experiencing a kind of metalepsis? Is the voice here simply shifting from the characters to that of the writer herself? After all, from the start the writer's voice has never been far away.

9. Dedicated to Anne and Bill Iannone, Aida and Walter Gross, Rose, Lisa and Jason Scarpellino, and Valerie Vail, Layla, Aaron and Lewis Cole.

BIBLIOGRAPHY

Alighieri, Dante. 2006. *The Divine Comedy*, trans. and ed. Robin Kirkpatrick. London: Penguin.

Aristotle. 1986. *Poetics*, trans. S Halliwell. Chapel Hill, NC: University of North Carolina Press.

Baxter, Charles. 2013. The Request Moment. *A craft talk delivered at Warren Wilson MFA Program and at Bread Loaf Writers' Conference.* Excerpted at https://www.graywolfpress.org/blogs/craft-charles-baxter-request-moment. Accessed May 1, 2017.

D'Adamo, Amedeo. 2013. Dantean Space in the Cities of Cinema. In *Media and the City: Urbanism, Technology and Communication*, ed. Simone Tosoni, Matteo Tarantino, and Chiara Giaccardi, 244–260. Newcastle upon Tyne, UK: Cambridge Scholars Press.

D'Erasmus, Stacey. 2013. *The Art of Intimacy*. Minnesotta: Greywolf Press.

Derrida, Jacques. 1993. *Specters of Marx, The State of the Debt, The Work of Mourning, and The New International*, trans. Peggy Kamuf. London and New York: Routledge.

Dostoevski, Fyodor. 2008. *The Demons*. London: Penguin Classics.

Fisher, Mark. 2014. *Ghosts of My Life: Writings on Depression, Hauntology and Lost Futures*. Zero Books. Alresford, UK: John Hunt Publishing.

Shakespeare, William. 2003. *The Tempest*. Washington, DC: Folger Shakespeare Library.

Sontag, Susan. 1983. *A Susan Sontag Reader*. New York : Vintage.

CHAPTER 7

On Collapsing Boundaries Between Protagonist and Antagonist: Dante's Tricks and Others in *La Vie En Rose* and *Apocalypse Now* and in the Documentaries *Tarnation, Elena* and *Waltzing With Bashir*

The last chapter introduced us to the concept of shades that had taken over a character's point of view, and there we contrasted *dramatic* shades with Dantean shades, showing how each is a different form of space. We looked at shades in *dramatic* spaces—the examples of Lars and of the Japanese Man in *Hiroshima Mon Amour*, where the story largely stayed in an empathetic realism outside of their own subjective experiences—and contrasted these with shades in *Dantean* space, where we share the shaded protagonist's point of view—this describes the protagonists of *Gravity, True Detective* and *Hiroshima Mon Amour*. In this chapter we go further into examples that more clearly depart from realism via deploying expressionist uses of sound and picture, taking us into Dantean characters whose perspective is overtly offered to us. This form of story space brings us within the suffering or joyful experience of a protagonist, announced clearly by a far more expressive use of aesthetic form, often marked by the blurring and breaking of established aesthetic boundaries, revealing a Dantean space of overtly-broken borders. This is the realm of immersive Dantean space.

© The Author(s) 2018
A. D'Adamo, *Empathetic Space on Screen*,
https://doi.org/10.1007/978-3-319-66772-0_7

Watching a Tragic Shade Seize Edith Piaf's Throat : The Long Dolly in La Vie En Rose

La Vie en Rose, the 2007 biopic about the life of Edith Piaf that won Marion Cotillard the Oscar for best actress, shows us an immersive Dantean space in the making. In the film's signature sequence, the virtuoso traveling shot that launches us into the final act, we see a ghost become a shade[1] that then takes possession of Piaf's space, mind and voice.

Her possession begins as we fade up from black in an intimate close-up of Piaf waking in bed. She lies there languorous with her lover Marcel, a professional boxer, who smiles and says he must get up (Fig. 7.1), put on his watch and go off on a flight to a professional fight in another city. A radiant Piaf leaps out of bed to bring him breakfast, her buoyant mood in striking contrast to her usual glum meanness, and the camera begins to follow her in what will become a four-minute uninterrupted traveling shot that serpentines through her apartment.

On her way to the kitchen the first disquieting note comes as Piaf passes a servant, a young girl who is inexplicably crying. She snaps at the girl in passing but carries on. As she travels through her apartment in a long dance with the steadicam, more somber servants are revealed, standing silently, half in shadow, and clearly possessed by some depressing reality that the singer doesn't yet share. She begins arguing with these

Fig. 7.1 *La Vie en Rose (2007)*

people as she looks for Marcel's watch and then, after returning to her bedroom, she starts hunting for Marcel himself, who seems to have disappeared. Her friend tries to calm her and to explain that Marcel's plane has crashed and he has died. Now she begins to panic and tries to escape them, her hands wavering in a palsy of grief and shock. She begins to cry (Fig. 10.11) and then to scream, and her staff reach out to her, apparently to calm her. But soon, in a moment reminiscent of Pina Bausch's dance-theater, they are pushing her past the camera which pivots to watch her stumble down a dark corridor. Suddenly beyond her at the end of this corridor the lights rise and we see she is going out, almost staggering, onto a stage. And now we begin a seamless sound transition (a là *Amadeus* (1984)) as we hear her launching into one of her more famous songs. Carried across the cut by the song's power we finally cut (again, a là *Amadeus*) to see her singing the tragic dirge in a grand opera house to a packed and mesmerized crowd.

The dead ghost of Marcel is transmuted by this sequence into the form of a shade of grief: the shade now takes possession of Piaf's sonorous voice and becomes the very nature of her song. The effect is powerfully empathetic: we understand that Piaf took this terrible sudden grief and thrust it into her singing over and over again, night after night, never truly leaving behind or getting over the death of Marcel.

But note how different the shade of Marcel is from those of the previous chapter: here realism is being discarded and inside her sensuous and diced-up temporal point-of-view, as unsure as she is whether the Marcel she woke up next to was real and has just left is a memory, or was in fact just a ghost and has already died. With Marcel's death her grasp and ours of the boundaries of time and space have collapsed, just as they do again at the end of the shot when she finds herself shoved down her apartment's hallway onto a grand stage before an audience. Now, lost and bewildered, she can only sing. Compassionate empathy is created in us with the help of this breaking of space and time and of source and score: this melding-together of memory and present brings us straight into her own mind and heart as she is deranged by grief. And with this an intensely dislikable character becomes hopelessly empathetic while the iconic shot of Piaf on stage is now imbued with a life and character.

Sometimes a character denies her own therapy or purgatorial arc and is in some sense generating and immersed in some long active distraction of self-punishment, and this is often staged in a spatial sense. Ugolino, for example, has a strategy of gnawing with frenzied focus on his enemy's skull, thereby, making him be too busy to be forced to contemplate his actual psychic wounds. Piaf too is not in a therapy arc: we never see her get over this moment, or even really process it in any way. Instead it seems that from this moment onwards the shade of Marcel will always be with her, inflecting her singing voice with tragic timbres for the rest of her days.

Entering the Shade: Crossing Sensuous Boundaries as a Technique of Intensifying Empathetic Space

Note the difference between the external perspective on the shades of the last chapter and the striking sensual envelope of *La Vie en Rose*'s revelation scene: here we feel we are in some sense experiencing the apartment through the shrouded confusion of Piaf herself. The grim lighting, long tracking shot, time-confusions and musical transitions all tell us we are in some sense both outside and also inside Piaf's shattered mind, experiencing her long-term grief, and meeting and feeling the presence of Marcel the shade. A boundary is collapsed: by entering the shade's vision but yet not leaving this present world, the cinema envelope is in two worlds at once.

Amelie also does something similar. First, as in Piaf's scene, it enters the shade's vision. It does this by simply carrying forwards the tropes of an 8-year-old's world into her adult life, and we make the connection between the two periods, seeing the adult Amelie as somehow still as childlike and innocent as she was the moment her mother died. But this film also hides the shade's power rather like the way the realism of *Gravity* hides that shade's power in Ryan's present. At first we do not really see Amelie as being controlled by or stuck in her childhood: the light childish playful tone of the film at first feels simply like a strong style-choice of emphatic and delightful caprice. The fact that its rather unique thoroughness is grounded in the first act's dramatic structure only becomes clear as we enter a second reading, a review of Amelie's motives and character.

Dante's Erasures of the Borders Between Self and World

With these examples we have entered the realm of expressionist technique, so marked by its non-realistic and boundary-breaking form, and these tactics also owe something to Dante's original invention. In *The Divine Comedy* Dante utilized many fascinating tactics of border-breaking that throw further light on the nature of Dantean space, with its urge to break down the wall between past and present, between inner and outer realities, and between reader and story character.

To see how, let's recall that Dante's Hell is not just a bad place to be: it is a place where the traumatic memories of its inhabitants actually generate its architecture. This makes it a highly individualistic, highly personalized place, a teeming necropolis where so many sufferers exist in a singular space that is distinctly theirs, a space architected and made manifest by their specific values, fears, traumas and actions. As a result, their inner emotional experience is made three-dimensional: Farinata's agony wafts out to include Dante and Virgil like the smell and the smoke from his burning sepulcher.

We remember such characters so vividly because their space in Hell is a powerful evocation of both their story in life and their emotional pain being lived in our moment. Their tales are psychologically realistic *and* their past trauma is alive and breathing all around them and us. To achieve this Dante deployed space in many interesting ways: we have already explored how he used a traumatic memory to architect a current space, but now we can briefly mention four other aesthetic tactics separate that reinforce this double-visioning.

One trick was to continually conflate the different grammatical forms of the word 'in' (*dentro*), so that Dante's characters could poetically combine the external, physical sense of being immersed *in* the water or being *inside* the house with the inner psychological sense of being *in* love or *in* sorrow or *in* pain. He uses this repeatedly. Consider again Canto 7, line 123, where one regretful prisoner describes his mistake in life—harboring resentment inside himself—as essentially incubating his current imprisonment in hellish muck: "(In life) we ... nursed in ourselves sullen fumes, and (thus) come to misery in this black ooze." By bridging being 'in' the realm of thoughts and emotions to an external realm of ooze, he extends a sense of one's responsibility for cultivating the self to a form of environmental architecture. One's resentment and guilt about that resentment then somehow produces an actual ooze in which one is immersed.

This passage also shows another trick of Dante's—to reveal people immersed in water, mud, fire, ice, blood, or other enveloping environs that phenomenologically connect the body to a place. That immersive substance was often described in realistic detail in terms of how it caused continual agonies in the tortured. In the frozen lake of Caina Dante takes this even further: near Ugolino two murderers are glued together and to the ice-lake by their tears which pour from their eyes and then freeze, further erasing the boundary between their prison and their body.

We can mention one last brilliant trick of Dante's for collapsing the boundary between the body and the emotional realm. At one point while locked in the tower Ugolino has a dreadful foreshadowing that he will ingest his children. It comes as they beseech him to eat them: he looks into their faces and "sees his own face" reflected there. This thought both reminds us all that one's children are "of one's flesh" while also foreshadowing his hungry cannibalization of their bodies. It is a powerful way to convey both Ugolino's fatherhood and his own intense horror of his coming dark marriage with their flesh.

All of these tricks deepen Dantean space in that they help erase the border between person, body, crime, emotion and hellish punishing environment. Cinema has taken up this same border-crossing, time-collapsing project, and it is especially clear in films with Dantean space. In fact perhaps it is actually *because* these stories require the cinematic elaboration of Dantean space that they are among the best examples in our tradition of 'total cinema,' that form of filmmaking where all of the craft departments are being employed in groundbreaking ways. Leaving the frame of standardized Hollywood realism, they can mine Romantic, Expressionistic, Gothic and other aesthetics to express the emotional conflict in their particular realm, opening a rich expressive range of craft-choices. After all, Dantean space offers a powerful art form of *subjectivity*, a way out of mimetic realism, a form of storytelling based on the character's point of view, one where we enter the sensual, emotional point of view of the main protagonist and 'see through their eyes,' 'walk in their shoes' and 'enter their heart, mind and imagination.' Such films can construct not just a plausible setting but rather any setting that reflects the character's inner dramatic tension, and this can take any form that the protagonist's imagination can lend it. And so the range of possible aesthetics are sharply expanded in stories expressing Dantean space.

For this reason cinema is often at its most powerful when it is expressing Dantean space. Cinema is always married to spectacle, but when spectacle is also a deep dramatic expression, the expression of the intimate inner conflicts, hopes and dreams of the main characters, then cinema is raised to a new level of intensity. A film then becomes a specifically *Dantean* spectacle, one serving a narrative drive, much more powerful than conventional cinema's spectacle where the mis-en-scène generally serves only as a beautiful backdrop (in the film industry this form of production design is called 'eye-candy') or as the quiet and unobtrusive arena of the drama—places of mere dramatized space.

COME BE TRAPPED IN MY FAMILY AND MY MIND: DANTEAN SPACE IN DOCUMENTARIES

Dantean space that takes advantage of these empathetic tropes of emotional breakdown is also powerfully realized in certain documentaries that are structured around traumatic personal and social memories. We think here of the examples of *Tarnation (2004)*, *Waltz with Bashir (2008)* and *Elena (2014)*. These three documentaries utilize the same dramatic machinery of traumatic event, Dantean characters, therapy arc and the elaboration of shaded space that we have been detailing: in fact these films often also use some of the same editing, soundtrack and music techniques we have described in earlier chapters to suture the viewer into the character's shifting memories as well as to create similar ghost and shade effects.

Tarnation

Tarnation is about a young gay man's investigation into the causes and effects of his mother's psychological breakdown. His journey leads him back into his own past, a childhood where he and his mother Renée both are extensively recorded performing for the camera, and his investigation eventually exposes the event that drove his mother mad: Renée was abused by his grandfather. He then journeys to Texas and takes his mother out of his grandparents' house and brings her to New York to care for her.

Elena

Elena is about the actual and psychological search by Petra for her older sister Elena who disappeared two decades ago when Petra was a child. Elena left Brazil during the dictatorship years to become an actress in New York, where she disappeared without a trace. Now two decades later Petra too goes to New York to become an actress, and there she is filled with the saudade-like memories of her lost sister, growing closer to her own ghost until she cannot tell herself from her own sister.

Tarnation and *Elena* have some striking parallels: both investigate some fundamental, mysterious and radically disjunctive moment in a family's life, and both have access to diaries and to large bodies of family material made not simply to document events but originally created as performances, including very expressionistic moments of dance, symbolism and grotesque emotional overacting. This material, and the way it is re-contextualized and reprocessed by the filmmakers, then links the past fantasies, hopes and projections of family members and of the filmmaker with present fears and reflections. By creating layers of re-editing that use slowed-down and sped-up footage, added voice-over, subjective and defamiliarizing sound effects, color effects and layered musical scores, a rich cinematic space is created in which not only mood but also character and family arcs are revealed. Through this frame we are given glimpses into the inner life of these families, particularly at moments of charged family history that triggered some mysterious twisting of everyone's life, and then the effects of that twisting are again felt in the form of personal emotional spectacle. And as the protagonist investigates these memories and the present, slowly the mysterious force behind this twisting is revealed, allowing the protagonist (and perhaps other members of the family) to finally heal.

Waltz with Bashir

Waltz with Bashir is also interested in breaking out of traditional documentary form in many of the same ways, and it too slides frequently between sequences that claim objectivity and those anchored in the main character's subjectivity. Similarly, it also distrusts some specific established story that involved the main subject. In addition, its investigation to discover the truth also veers between reality, dream and nightmare. It too uses highly empathetic spaces that are anchored in a character's perceptions and are crafted Dantean spaces where the past keeps leaking into the present. And it too veers often between realistic and heightened and expressionistic uses of sound and sound effects that meld us to his sensibility.

However, the film's formal approach is different in two ways. First, it is entirely done in cartoon and cartoon-like rotoscope. And second, it is more overtly a therapy tale—in fact the story is framed by therapy sessions in a therapist's office—and it singularly investigates the suppressed memories of the main character, the events around an actual historical massacre of Palestinians that he was involved with as an Israeli soldier during the invasion of Lebanon in 1982. With the therapist's and with friends' help he is able to recall the trauma of the war and eventually of his own suppressed role in the massacre, and finally he can come to grips with his own feelings of guilt and responsibility that made him suppress the memory of this whole period of his life. Signifying this psychological breakthrough, the film's final images are real footage of the aftermath of the massacre.

Dantean Docs

All three of these very personal documentaries are empathetic Dantean documentaries, using the same mechanism of memory and machinery of empathy that we have been discussing to create spaces that reflect the tortured and torn psyche of their protagonists, revealing a subjectivity that is suspended between different times and environments. All three films are also mystery stories, with that form utilized in a specific way. Those forms are used to allow the protagonist to be an emotional detective of sorts, whose journey is overtly intended to be understood as a therapy story. To construct this journey, Dantean space is used to dramatize and delineate the changing personal stages of innocence, of corrupted and disturbed time, of recognition and investigation, and finally of freedom and a new start.

And all three films violate the usual boundaries of documentary film by using techniques of expressing subjective emotional states that are taken from narrative film. *Waltz with Bashir* does this through expressionistic sound design and graphic-novel-style cartoon versions of real footage, often cut in the style of a music video and sometimes overlain with the voiceover of a narrator remembering past events. *Tarnation* achieves this through radical music cuts married to complex editing cuts that often feature multiple screens, by radical post-production processing of images and by a richly-layered sound design, very unusual for documentary at the time: all of these techniques create a Dantean space where we enter first the mind of his electroshocked mother and then later into the filmmaker's own puzzled, anxious tortured memories and show them carried over into his anxious, tortured present. *Elena* uses most of the same techniques to break the border between realism and the subjective experience of trauma, but instead of mimicking *Tarnation*'s harsh confrontational aesthetic of anxiety and psychosis that seems at times like that of a slasher horror film, *Elena* strives to create a floating aesthetic of drift and lost souls, an echoey expanse that we might find in a romantic ghost story. All three create the loss of borders of dream-states, but *Waltz with Bashir's* and *Tarnation's* is closer to nightmare. And in all three films we are convinced by the Dantean spaces, which repeatedly border on chaos, that the protagonists might lose their minds, sucked into the land of shades and ghosts.

LIVING IN A COLLAPSING DANTEAN MOMENT: *APOCALYPSE NOW*

To look for the origins of some of these expressionistic techniques, one film in the canon suggests itself: Francis Ford Coppola's *Apocalypse Now* (1979), which is justly famous for its groundbreaking use of space, music, sound and its marriage of subjectivity and spectacle. And while Coppola himself acknowledges that the film is a flawed masterpiece, rightly locating the failures in a sagging and comparatively unchallenging third act, there are so many moments of true greatness in the first two acts that cinema history has forgiven the film its flaws. Nevertheless, it is useful to understand both the film's great power and its failures. We use our terminology to examine the linkages among its three iconic scenes: its mesmerizing opening, the famous Ride of the Valkyries set-piece which launches the film's dramatic action, and the attack on the DuLong bridge, a sequence which ends film's second act and launches it into its third act.

Though based somewhat loosely on Joseph Conrad's novel *Heart of Darkness*, the film transposes that novel's portraits of the Dutch colonial horrors being visited on the Congolese into the American military's horrors and misadventures being visited upon the people of Vietnam and Cambodia. In both versions of events the narration remains on the side of the oppressors, showing how their unfettered power in an apocalyptic landscape becomes a slow poison that destroys their souls and minds: the film focuses not on the effects of the war on the enemy but rather on a range of American soldiers and officers, and particularly on the inner struggles and character-arcs of the film's main character, special intelligence agent Benjamin Willard.

Willard is given his external objective in the film's first sequence where he is told by army and CIA officers that Kurtz has "gone insane" and must be "terminated with extreme prejudice". To kill Kurtz Willard must first navigate up a long river through Vietnam and then continue on into Cambodia to the jungle where, he is told, Kurtz romps viciously and with apparent moral abandon.

Willard's external objective is the first major departure from the novel. In Conrad's original story the main character travels upriver not to kill but to rescue Kurtz. The role of that narrator is like Dante's in the *Inferno*: a traveling observer of a series of personae, each with his own history and goal and each singularly warped by the many soul-destroying pressures of the land. In the film, Willard retains some of this observer role but with two major differences. Willard's external objective of killing the errant guerrilla leader Kurtz aligns Willard more closely with his intended target, allowing him to be a kind of stand-in, surrogate and echo of Kurtz. It also aligns him with the murderous and increasingly-crazed soldiers he meets as he heads up-river. In addition, in the film Willard gains a much clearer character arc and struggle than the novel's narrator because his adventures along the way push him to question his goal. The river becomes a path into his own interiority: he says the river "snaked through the war like a main circuit cable plugged right into Kurtz."[2] Willard's striving to get "upriver" through the war, and the conflict each episode presents to his external goal, can then compose his journey into his own heart of darkness. The film will end quietly (and, many feel, unsatisfyingly) as a redemption tale when Willard, after having brutally murdered Kurtz, throws down his sword and leads his surrogate son Lance through the enemy camp and out of the madness. As he passes through Kurtz's army, everyone throws down their weapons, apparently inspired by Willard's act to practice war no more.

Paralleling this journey is a shift in form that is announced even in the brief introduction (which serves as a kind of short overture): as Willard moves further up the river the film moves from an objective form of adrenalynic spectacle common to a dispassionate thriller to a Dantean form that mirrors Willard's own growing inner conflict and guilt. And in this journey through elaborate and emotional forms of spectacle, the film combines space with music and sound design in two very distinct ways to magnify and realize Willard's changing character.

This play with form and the breaking of sensual boundaries is announced right away in the condensed overture of the film's opening minutes. When we first meet Willard he is already in his own Inferno: he seems to be having flashbacks of a helicopter-led jungle airstrike from a previous mission, but it might be drugged-out visions or perhaps flash-forwards to later events in the film. If it is a flash-forwards these explosions might be from either the Valkyries episode from the middle of the film or from the final airstrike that ended some edits of the film.[3] And so immediately we are in an uncertain space: is this a real event? A memory? A psychological metaphor?

The questions deepen because right from the opening frames we experience a collapse of music, practical sound effects and manufactured sound effects: The Door's song "The End", which is itself nearly boundary-less in its noodling drug-like dreamy guitar solos that follow no clear musical time, is here marvelously deployed over dissolves of the jungle and of Willard's meditative face.[4] Originally written by the errant son of a navy admiral[5] about a romantic break-up, here the song plays as a love song to death, telling us that Willard is both in some sense addicted to ending the lives of others (we will learn he has already assassinated six people on earlier missions) and that he is suicidal himself. The song also sets up a pattern of paradoxically embedding the music of well-known anti-war bands—the Doors, the Stones, CCR, Hendrix—in this war film's soundscape, a device which continually complicates our sense of the characters' identities and torqued allegiances.

On the technical side "The End" is also a very early example of music that doubles as an acoustic bed, that is, an almost environmental set of sound that makes no or very slow and gentle melodic progression. As beds often do, this lulling, boundariless quality grants this opening a dreamy mood that stands outside of cinema time, a function quite different from the film's atonal, dissonant Moog-based main score that announces the film's growing psychological and plot tensions at the end of every sequence.

The song functions on a number of levels. A well-known pop song after its release in 1967, it places us in the film's Vietnam-era period.[6] More forcefully it serves as antagonist expression by introducing death, the film's antagonist. But it also subtly positions death as a friend, a welcome and familiar presence for the protagonist, which sets up the paradox of Willard's character. The music also sets genre-tone here—its disquieting quality and marriage to spectacular bombing gets our adrenaline going and announces this film will have real thriller episodes, but with dissolves to Willard in close-up staring straight at the audience, it also associates this spectacular violence with Willard's own altered, drunken and stoned mental state. Possibly, the lyrics suggest, this violence will be a tool or aspect of a spiritual journey.

The music also depends on an exoticism in its tonal choices: the guitar has a vague hint of orientalist place thanks to its vaguely-raga-like formal nature and its high-pitched twangs played in the high tonal range in the neighborhood of a sitar or a Chinese pipa. This plays problematically into the colonialist-era concepts of the film's source-material, which mapped the colonized zones as a 'dark zone,' a murky exotic land of dissipation, simultaneously borderless, foreign and all-too-free of moral restraints, a place where white men escape civilization and rationality in a liminal zone of otherness where they can practice animalistic self-discovery and a personal spiritual journey. Finally, the song also quietly announces the film's own sympathy with the counter-cultural, anti-war movement, an allegiance that will not become completely clear until all the weapons are thrown down in the film's last moments.

These qualities of the Doors' song are emphasized by the very first trick by the film's sound designer Walter Murch. A drum-like percussive bed of processed synth sounds introduces the song over black—it is a beat of chopper-like noises resembling and layered into the Door's own processed guitar notes because both have long echoed sustains and a growing warbled rhythm of changing time, though the chopping sounds start with a dreamy breath and then end with sharp attack, similar to some reversed-sound footage. This sound effect, produced on a synthesizer, is placed in a very present score, yet it anticipates the approach of a slow-motion passing helicopter, shown first passing across a slow-mo shot of verdant green palm trees, announced by orange wisps of smoke and then passing in the extreme foreground, fragmented while in swooping attack mode. And dramatically, cued by Morrison's first sung line of lyrics, announcing "This is the End, Beautiful Friend," the entire tree-line explodes in slow motion, with orange flames from a massive napalm attack dominating the entire frame.

Note the borderlessness that has been achieved even in this first montage: already by collapsing the roles of music and sound effects, score and source, environment and space, and while showing deep backgrounds with surprising intrusions of extremely-close interrupting elements, Murch establishes a collapse of the subjective and objective. Our frame, sliding dreamily from balanced, calm, long volumes with a clean foreground to unbalanced and exploding volumes with continual and chaotic foregrounded intrusions, only adds to the effect.

From here we will dissolve and crossfade through at least three realities: the subjective brooding shots of Willard which give this all the feeling of memories without any specific place in time, with shots of Willard staring at his ceiling fan in a hotel room, both crossfaded with shots of the violent orgy of the airstrike's hellish destruction and aftermath. Willard stares directly into the camera in close-up, and then a cut to a ceiling fan re-attributes the helicopter sound effects to Willard's mental filtering of memory and his present. The opening music montage ends with a dolly to the hotel window and the shifting sound perspective on a source helicopter sound, followed by the first placed sourced sound effect: Willard's disembodied hand lifts the blinds to see an ordinary Saigon street far from the front lines.

Right away with Willard's confessional voiceover, recorded with a confident and intimate presence and affect, we learn we are taking this trip through his eyes, that our narrator is wrestling with guilt and combat PTSD, has divorced his wife and that he is reflecting on the coming journey from some placeless and never-revealed future moment of revelation. But the sequence's acoustic unreality continues, if in a subtle form: underneath this next montage of him alone in the hotel room, where we dissolve dreamily through scenes of Willard engaged in acts of self-abasement and dissipation, there is a quiet, trilling and hissing bed of exterior jungle environment playing throughout. Again the border between self and surroundings is unstable.

All of these tricks of the sliding nature of sound, music and space become a rhythm that will announce and punctuate the film's next four sequences. For example, we see them again in the famous "Ride of the Valkyries" scene that completes the film's set-up and launches the story's action. Willard and his boat crew are to be led to the mouth of the river by the Ninth Air Cavalry, itself commanded by Lieutenant Colonel Bill Kilgore, who sports a cowboy hat and a mildly Texan accent. Suddenly Kilgore has a capricious idea: hearing off-handedly from a soldier who surfs that near the river's mouth is a wonderful point-break for surfing, Kilgore decides to attack the Vietcong village so that they can surf the point. Suddenly the crew finds itself in a flying V of military helicopters, swooping in spectacularly from the sea on an unnecessary bomber strike on a village and a children's school to clear the beach for surfing.

For many viewers this iconic moment has indelibly wed Wagner's overture to the film. In this scene Willard serves as an observer of Kilgore and his infectious ethos which ripples out among his crew. First, the scene makes it clear that there is no military objective in attacking the village: the captain chooses to do this simply because he admires surfing and there is a perfect point-break off-shore. By this brilliant step the entire external objective of this action leaps away from the expected plot-logic of winning the war, being instead the passing caprice of this demented figure who loves war simply for its adrenalynic spectacle.

Similarly, the use of the music in the attack takes us into Kilgore's joy and passion, wedding us to his own vision of what this war is about. Kilgore, devoid of empathy, is part of the dispassionate male culture we described in Chap. 2: in this early scene we stay visually and aurally with his sense of war, following the firing of the bullets and the missiles, dwelling only on their spectacular operatic arrival and never seeing or hearing the actual pain or agony they inflict. This carefully-curated suturing introduces us to the addictive joys of war: only slowly as the film unfolds do we slide over to the receiving end of violence.

Many kinds of music would help this effort, but the screenwriter John Milius proposed this Wagner overture, chosen in the story by Kilgore. And now we see how music can create an operatic space that characterizes a layered character, deepening the resonance and spectacle that the character then provokes. This overture brings powerful historical associations: it evokes both the fantasies of the Overman sketched by Nietzsche, Wagner's friend and fan, and also the deeds and alluring darkness of the Nazis, who raised Wagner to state-cult status. The effect here is to ground Kilgore in—and force us to identify with—a European high culture sophistication of a Nietzschean bent joined to colonial and racist endeavors of the darkest kind.

Like the use in *Clockwork Orange* of European classical music to bond us to the violent character of Alex, here too we are unwillingly bonded to the joy of a violent protagonist, but with one difference. Here we see this character through the mediating presence of our narrator Willard who, while sensing all this dark joy, remains skeptical of Kilgore, somewhat like the narrator in the *Inferno* who observes and sometimes comments on the many sinners he meets. But we have also begun the journey of Willard's own inner emotional character arc: while his disapproving observation of the surreal madness of Kilgore both grants us a critical distance from it while also making Willard empathetic, it also reminds us of the explosions that opened the film, which seemed linked to Willard's own demons. It seems as if the same infectious and addictive power of this war's violence might be playing out within Willard as well.

Second, this scene's mixture of surfing and warfare, one of its many ironic mixes of Western war machine and recreation (itself quietly implicit in the very idea of a Hollywood war film), collapses another boundary that the music's introjection underlines. And yet even as we collapse so many boundaries, we also gain a new boundary in the form of a basic gender distinction: in contrast to the highly over-masculinized Kilgore and his all-male army, the village has a school with many young girls and many of the communist soldiers are women. As a result the screaming voices of the Valkyries, initially identified with the attack helicopters, will become more placeless as the attack unfolds, coming to stand in for the rage and screams of the women being shot and killed and who are striking back as the attack unfolds but who are always held at arms-length in long-shot so we do not empathize directly with them.

And now we can see the many dramatic and Dantean layers at work in the use of *The Ride of the Valkyries*. First, this specific act of psychological warfare is a deep and fascinating expression of Kilgore's past, hinting at a fascist personal ideology along with a specific aestheticization of the adrenalynic violence that the war gives him the opportunity to explore, at high cost to many others. By invoking our codified high–low culture distinctions, Kilgore's love of this song suggests too that despite his quotidian Texan brogue and cowboy affectations he is educated and from an upper-class American family and therefore has a far-more knowing understanding of this entire experience than his cavalry soldiers. And suddenly with this new identity glimpsed, a cultural, social and colonial hierarchy maps onto the military machine that Kilgore rides like a bronco.

Meanwhile Kilgore's addiction to this adrenalynic violence, akin to his love for surfing, is underlined by his wonderful final line in the scene: "Someday this war's gonna end", delivered sadly as he exits. In this moment we and Willard gain a glimpse of Kilgore's desperate future and are left wondering, where will Kilgore get his fix when the war ends? What will he do to engage his own operatic fantasies of power once he no longer commands the air cavalry like this? Will he be as lost as Willard was in the film's opening when he had no mission? And with this question we not only begin to meet the obscure Kurtz but also begin to see Willard becoming both more self-conscious and also more clearly implicated in a Kilgore-like addiction to the beautified violence of the film's opening montage.

Now Willard travels on upriver, approaching the land of Kurtz, and finds himself unwillingly in the riveting boat scene. Here Willard finally sloughs off his observer role: after the drugged-out young American crew botches a simple stop-and-search of an innocent Vietnamese family's boat, killing two and injuring their young daughter, Willard cold-bloodedly executes the injured girl to prevent them from stopping to find her medical help. After killing the girl on the boat, Willard muses in voiceover that he is beginning to understand Kurtz's ruthless and murderous methods of total war: in this landscape, pragmatic instrumental logic of war feels much cleaner than trying to be compassionate, which he tells himself can only be a lie.

And after these insights and events, the boat arrives by night (the first night in the film) at the DuLong bridge. Willard tells us this is a charged boundary, the geographic border between Vietnam and Cambodia, the political line between a quasi-legal war and an illegal, undeclared and secret one. And this is the last outpost of Americans, the gateway to enter the realm of Kurtz.

The spectacle quickly grows very intense with desperate soldiers trying to swim out to the boat to escape, with bombs exploding and flames roaring, and strings of Christmas lights swaying along the bridge's wires. The shifting volumes of space are lit by moving beds of light and darkness, all periodically lit up or backlit by explosive fireballs on the bridge. In the earlier Valkyrie sequence we experienced the exhilaration and power of firing bullets and bombs. Here we are on the receiving end, experiencing the long-term effects of being bombed. We learn this hellscape is oddly a static and permanent state of affairs: the bridge is destroyed every night and then rebuilt every day, a sisyphian waste of lives and effort, done simply so that the American generals can claim the road is still open. Willard now leaves the boat to find the person in command here who should have further orders, and now Willard is joined by the soldier Lance, who has just dropped acid. As they set off together into this new hellscape Lance has a parallel with Kilgore in the Valkyries scene: once again Willard is in the company of someone having an intense experience that is in a real sense leaking out into his own perception.

And now the sound and cinematic boundaries begin to collapse. As Willard hunts through the amorphous compound, three forms of music play: the drunken circus merry-go-round strains that seem to be score, the cacophonic tinny Hendrix guitar-solos that are sourced off the cheap tape-deck of a soldier (but often feel score) and the plucked cable twangs that seem to be the cable-bridge snapping but might be score horror sounds from some experimental composer. (In 1979 they would also carry a fresh sense of science fiction warfare for their marked similarity to the laser cannon and blaster sound effects in *Star Wars IV: A New Hope* (1977).) The circus music that plays here is warbled, like so much sound in this film, and then slides into groaning rhythms as if it is the voice of the American war-machine itself, trapped and floundering here in the mud.

Meanwhile a masterful mixing of sounds unfold that are hard or impossible to source, making a new demand on the viewer to make sense of this place. A shrill bed of crickets subtly rises and falls to help mix and dislocate the screams and shouts and snatches of dialogue from many different soldiers, which is never blended into hubbub and so makes constant demands on us to integrate it into the unfolding story. At one point a disembodied voice screams at us to "listen to the music!" Gradually this command seems to be placed: it seems to have been shouted by a barely-glimpsed soldier, briefly encountered by Willard, who is grappling with another desperate, possibly insane soldier, in the mud of a trench: maybe he is trying to get the screaming soldier to concentrate on the sound of some distant music in order to calm him. The conflict and emotions of this wrestling pair are in stark contrast to others that Willard passes just meters away, who lie passively, laconic and seemingly bored. Then there is one whole short dialogue: "Goddamn it nigger you stepped on my face!" "I thought you were dead." "Well you thought wrong!" We are unsure if the speaker is Lance because this takes place with absolutely no clear visual clue of who is speaking. Marking a trope of subjective Dantean space, all clear answers and attributions are carefully erased, as are the borders between source and score, environment and sound effect, music and bed.

And now the Hendrix can be heard, cut across by a percussive machine-gun fire as Willard approaches the army bunker. Adding to the confusion, for a dramatic stretch both sounds dominate this space without having any apparent source, then finally are revealed to be coming from the bunker. The Hendrix is akin to an earlier use of other pop songs in helping us appreciate the soldiers' access to energetic, anti-war, pro-drug protest music. But the density of the shifting soundscape is emphasized again by swirling search-lights that keep changing the visual volume and contours of scenes, almost as if we are inside an accordion. Sometimes the cuts are hidden inside the drops to blackness so that when the swirling search-light returns we suddenly find ourselves inside a new shot.

Willard now meets a panicked soldier firing wildly into the darkness at a lone Vietcong soldier who we are told is 'inside the wire' and can be heard cursing out the Americans. An inexplicable red light starts flashing in the background—easy to miss among the pyrotechnics—and a character called "The Roach" comes out, triggering a terrific acoustic reversal. Now the tape-deck playing the guitar is clicked off and a new quiet rushes in: all score and most source sounds fade as the Roach listens to and tries to echo-locate the screaming Vietnamese soldier. Everyone else stares at the Roach, listening with focus like him, wondering if and how he can do this. As his voodoo necklaces rattle and his large eyes stare vacantly, a calm, laconic affect comes out in his voice and movements, a relaxed centeredness similar to Willard's relaxed, intimate voiceover. In the quietest dramatic moment in the entire film (a charged taut silence that creates its own new tension paralleled only with Kurtz's moment of death and release which will mark the end of the drama) a massive shift in acoustical presence takes place: after all the cacophony of machine-gun fire, competing music, the bursting of bombs and the wreckage of the bridge, we now hear only crickets and the tiny rustle of the Roach's voodoo necklace. Listening, the Roach says, "He's close, man: *real close.*"—a line which then becomes Willard's own line minutes later in the voiceover as he senses the closeness of Kurtz. In this way it is as if Willard and his crew never fully leave this unreal zone of the bridge behind.

Finally, the Roach fires and kills the unseen soldier. And when this pregnant silence ends a change will have happened in the central goals of the film: Willard has crossed over into Cambodia and, we begin to think as the boat heads into the land of Kurtz, he has also stepped across into some new metaphysical state of being. And like the sequences of the Valkyrie attack and the killing on the boat, this remarkable sequence also ends with a cut-line that hangs in the air. When the Roach is asked by Willard "Soldier, do you know who's in command here?" the Roach answers simply "Yeah." And then turns away. The answer floats in the dark, disembodied and unseen like so much else here. With Willard we wonder, who *is* in charge here? No-one? The Devil? Kurtz? Willard himself? We saw a red flag of a Black Power fist briefly in the background where the Roach lives. Is white hegemony in charge here? The filmmakers' carefully-designed glimpses of many answers ends our scene without giving a clear, fixed conclusion.

The overall envelope of cinematic effect, with its carefully-engineered demands and glimpses that force us to interpret space and information as best we can from scraps and fragments, is arguably the subjective, sensual, acoustic and cinematic highlight of the film. On one level we feel this break is the natural dramatic conclusion of the past hour and a half of the story: it is as if Willard's own rhythm of meeting many different condemned American men has accelerated, as if he has here reached a low circle of hell where the tightly-set concentric circles of the damned are packed more closely together. Or perhaps this scene shows the weight on Willard of his own assassinations, such as his recent killing of the innocent girl on the boat. Perhaps Willard has now entered his own purgatorial space and is facing his shades. Or perhaps his mind is simply breaking down.

Perhaps all of these interpretations work here, but one cinematic change is clear. With all of this new technique, subjective intensity and work demanded of the viewer to try to make sense of what is unfolding, we no longer stand apart from the war as Willard has done for the first hour. This space is very unlike our Kilgore-like perspective in the Valkyrie scene, and completely different from the cold realistic objectivity of the moment when Willard killed the young girl on the boat. The chaos of the bridge scene is so direct and personally experienced that we and Willard are both demanded to make sense of all this madness.

And so, like the film's opening, this scene creates a form of protagonist bonding that transforms the adrenalynic spectacle of the war, granting it a personal and emotional force. When the Dulong bridge becomes a Dantean space for Willard, our own confusion over the collapse of the usual boundaries between source and score and between music, sound effects and environmental sound beds, serves another purpose beyond illustrating Willard's situation: it also draws us much more closely into his point of view and conflicted emotional journey.

Meanwhile the careful sound-mixing in this scene, the way that source and score begin to bleed into each other, reminds us of similar techniques used when we first meet Willard. Here too sounds shift us from the dispassionate space we enjoyed in the Valkyries sequence to a Dantean space expressing Willard's character and arc.

On Prismatic Characters : Is There a Shade in This Story? Is This Dispassionate, Dramatic or Dantean Space? Is Willard a Dramatic or a Dantean Character?

When Ugolino looked into the faces of his children whom he knew he would soon eat, he saw his own face looking back at him. Already he is losing his mind: even as he sees his paternity there his imagination is already flash-forwarding to when they will be part of his own flesh. Shades can have all sorts of warping temporal and sensual effects on a protagonist, as we have seen in this journey from *The Divine Comedy* to the Dulong bridge. However, while nearly all the stories examined in the last two chapters feature the death of a person who then shapes the present-day vision and actions of the main character, there are other stories that *can be read* as shade tales but do not need to be read this way. In fact, it is not clear they should be.

Apocalypse Now has this quality. We cannot tell if Willard, the protagonist of *Apocalypse Now*, is a Dantean character with a Dantean moment in his past, or if he is a dramatic character who is simply executing his orders as he wends his way through an insane world. The problem is a lack of knowledge: we are unsure if the situation is insane or if *he* is insane and, if he is the source of this sensual chaos, why exactly that is happening. Part of the problem is that we can never tell at any point in the film if Willard's mental breakdown that opens the film is a result of taking drugs and alcohol while being recently divorced or if it is caused by the fact that he had already killed six others before this story even starts. We never see anything about those earlier killings: we only know with his opening voiceover that something that has happened here in Vietnam has caused his divorce and his breakdown and prevents him from going back home to the USA. He says he was given the mission to find Kurtz "for my sins", but we cannot tell if he is being ironic or confessional or both.

We also cannot tell if he is in any way marked by his assassination of the girl on the boat, and if that is in any way responsible for the Hell he is then tipped into from the DuLong Bridge onwards. Is Willard suffering from a shade? Perhaps: we can't tell. And so, as we see in other films, we cannot be sure in the end of Willard's final character arc. As a result his arc, and simultaneously the major cinematic spaces of the film, can be read two ways because Willis is a prismatic character: he can be read to have two distinctly different inner lives, creating a cognitively shifting and shimmering character.

There are many prismatic characters in our tradition. Take painting in particular. *The Absinth Drinker* of Degas, for example, vibrates brilliantly between two forms of portraiture. At first glance we see the woman and the setting, a neorealist portraiture of a haggard woman caught in a moment of complete despondency. She sits at a table in a café, ignored by the man seated next to her. But then we notice other details. First, where is the support for the table? Degas has made the tabletop seem to float. And the odd fluorescence of the lighting, the complex contrasts of the surfaces, which show both deep scores and a diaphanous glow, are both harshly real and dreamily softened. All of this makes us begin to suspect we too are seeing this world through the absinthe-blurred eyes of the woman. This is the same erasure of the boundary between realism and a subjective expressionism that we saw in *Apocalypse Now*. And, as in that film, we cannot tell if this is a Dantean space or just a drugged-out dramatic space of a subjective point-of-view: with this painfully sympathetic absinth drinker we are given no biographical information to tell what we are seeing.

A somewhat similar case exists with the twisted faces and worlds of Francis Bacon. These characters seem to be wrestling psychically with their condition, but are they? Are they snapshots of moments of crisis? Are they portraits of permanent states of affairs? And if so, are they self-aware or are we alone alert to their condition? This question takes us back to Dante: does Ugolino realize he is in Hell? Does any of us? As we have seen, the problem with being in a Dantean space is gaining a place to stand outside of its shaded vision. Like the most powerful of shades, such spaces often hide from us either behind the shield of akrasia or because they are so much a part of our self they cannot be separated enough from our perceptions to be clearly seen for themselves.

A similar prismatic problem of interpretation is encountered with Lee, the protagonist of *Secretary*, whose deep motives have also been erased from our view. By the film's end we see her happy, but we never actually learn why she likes to pee in her wedding dress and be debased by Edward. At one early point we see that she self-injures: a series of cuts she makes to her thigh hint at some kind of past abuse, but we are given no access to this, and so we cannot be sure if by the story's end she has landed in her own Heaven or Hell. Her man Edward can even seem like a kind of hero: he does, after all command her to never again harm herself, thereby invoking a communal empathy. But if on the other hand we think there are long dark fingers extending from some abusive events in Lee's past that are puppeting her into this abusive relationship with Edward (which is not at all an odd assumption in view of the many bandaids on her leg), then we see Lee as a Dantean character trapped in goals and desires not entirely her own, a version of Lee that lies closer to the original protagonist in the short story by Mary Gaitskill.

As usual we depend on the film's music to give us emotional and character clues, but here too Angelo Badalamenti's score does its best to cover Lee's tracks. The theme-song gives no hint of real dangers or darkness: instead we are cued to think of tango, games, ironic comedy, fantasies, and possible references to erotic films, but nothing tells us about Lee's need to be dominated and debased. Lee's own theme, "Broken Blossoms", grants her fantasies some comically-broad sardonic tones (conveyed by the faintly rubber-banding bass which is cross-faded with a friendly strip-tease-like guitar riff). The filmmakers' erasure of all clues to Lee's past, along with the gamification of her abasement and the moon-faced seemingly genuine grins of Maggie Gyllenhaal, lets us feel she has finally found the one man who can make her happy. But this conclusion results from an act of erasure: rather than giving a genuine account of a BDSM character the filmmakers have made a deliberate decision to hide Lee's motive.

This refusal to explicate the character or reveal her backstory carries from the script across to the performance and the soundtrack, creating an ambiguous, prismatic and titillating narrative. In the end we are left wondering, is Lee now enslaved or enlightened? As the film's tag-line directs, we have to "assume the position:" we have to assume something about Lee to decide just what her own arc is, what we and she are enjoying, and what the meaning of the space of the office really amounts to. Is it an echo of places where she was abused? Is it a safe space where she can finally express her true self? Or is it just a strange realistic space? We might call this kind of cognitively shifting character a prismatic character. For the same reason, the spaces such characters generate also shimmer with a productive, provocative uncertainty, and so we might call both Lee's office and Willard's Dulong bridge prismatic spaces.[7,8]

NOTES

1. The shot itself seems clearly inspired by the great moment late in the film *Amadeus* when a sick, weary and debt-ridden Mozart comes home to his apartment to find his wife and child gone. He is then lectured by his mother-in-law for being a useless philandering drunkard. Mozart has a revelation as she stands over him raving on and on: the film cuts from her to a heavyset female actor singing curses in a lovely high-pitched voice. We dolly out and find ourselves at Mozart's grinning enthusiastic conducting of his new opera. The edit illustrates his genius at transmuting a screeching complaint into a moment of beauty in a famous opera: in a great dramatic reversal (marking a complete change in his fortunes), Mozart is directing with ecstatic energy and the crowd is cheering, just as his mother-in-law's grating voice served to dramatize his own hung-over misery, its lovely slide into the rising source sounds of the performance, and then of the cheering of the crowds, serves as an emotional envelope reflecting Mozart's emotional transition into joy. This marvelous sequence does not utilize Dantean space but is simply a dramatic entrance into the point of view of an artist in a moment of inspiration.
   LVER takes this core idea of dramatizing a reversal through musical performance. And yet it transforms it in two ways. First, the film adopts a signature trick of the filmmaker Emir Kusturica of using the continuous shot of a traveling camera to move away from a place and then return to it later to see a magical change. This camera shot appears repeatedly in his

films but the best use is perhaps in the lime-making kiln scene in *Time of the Gypsies*. (I may be wrong to attribute the shot to my old teacher: however I haven't been able to locate this trick in other filmmakers before him.)

Second, this moment for Piaf, while being about how a singer puts her experiences into her music, is not a temporary moment of joy as in *Amadeus*, but a scarring and permanent moment of trauma that, we infer, marked a new, tragic and permanent inflection of her singing.

2. *Apocalypse Now*, 9: 45.
3. The version in the film has been remixed from the original source tapes by Walter Murch.
4. James (1981).
5. At least, so far in the film this seems to be what is happening. The problem of the film comes as Willard finds Kurtz. Now despite our expectations, there is no clear moments of penance or self-insight or release for Willard: we have nothing of the power of, for example, Ripley's great face-off with the Mother alien. Willard is able to kill Kurtz and then simply walk away. Perhaps we are to understand he has killed his demon, but the sequence lacks any sense of struggle and the cinematic control here lacks the operatic and Dantean power of the earlier descents into Hell. Lacking the subjective intensities of the opening and of the Dulong Bridge, without the operatic power of the Valkyrian attack or even the adrenalynic surprise of the boat killing, and uninformed by any of the moral complexity of the boat scene, this last sequence disappoints. Moreover, its comparative lack of emotional spectacle fails to mark the true release of Willard from his Dantean space.
6. For more on the connection between American music, politics and popular culture in this period see D'Adamo (2015, 2017).
7. See particularly *In the Metro* (Marc 2002).
8. Dedicated to Francesco Casetti and John Hare.

Bibliography

Alighieri, Dante. 2006. *The Divine Comedy*, trans. and ed. Robin Kirkpatrick. London: Penguin.

Aristotle. 1986. *Poetics*, trans. S. Halliwell. Chapel Hill, NC: University of North Carolina Press.

Conrad, Joseph. 2005. *Heart of Darkness*. New York: W.W. Norton.

D'Adamo, Amedeo. 2015. Ain't There One Damn Flag That Can Make Me Break Down and Cry? The Formal, Performative and Emotional Tactics of Bowie's Singular Critical Anthem Young Americans. In *Enchanting David Bowie*, ed. Toija Cinque, Christopher Moore, and Sean Redmond. New York: Bloomsbury Academic Press.

D'Adamo, Amedeo. 2017. *"That Junky Funky Vibe: Quincy Jones' title theme for the sitcom Sanford and Son."* In Music in Comedy Television, ed. Liz Giuffre, and Philip Hayword. New York and London: Routledge.
James, Lizze (1981). *Jim Morrison: Ten Years Gone.* Detroit: Creem Magazine.

CHAPTER 8

Alienated Spaces: DeathStarchitecture in *Star Wars*, Bleached Space and Dialogue in *The Graduate*, Showroom Space in *Pleasantville* and *Mad Men*, and the Dantean Homes of *Homeland*

DeathStarchitecture: The Non-Place Destined to Be Blown Up

The Death Star floats large in our collective imagination, an iconic presence as forceful as any produced by the dispassionate *Star Wars* franchise. But what exactly is this kind of space: are there underlying reasons why it plays such a central role in not one but three of the franchise's installments? Here we argue that yes, this realm and expression of a specifically *mechanical* and *technical* evil introduces a very persuasive form of story space and at the same time defines the film's other spaces by its oppositions to them. Once we begin to grasp the odd inhabitation and oppositions that the Death Star is composed of, we see that DeathStarchitecture is a rather pure example of what Augé calls the ideo-logic: that is, an inner logic of representation that the Star Wars universe uses to explain itself to itself.

The most striking aspect of these giant entities is how little effort has gone into making these spaces realistically functional in any actual sense. For example, despite their size and role, the Death Star does not feature habitation of any discernible kind: though in all three films the

© The Author(s) 2018
A. D'Adamo, *Empathetic Space on Screen*,
https://doi.org/10.1007/978-3-319-66772-0_8

agents of the Rebellion have crisscrossed this constructed landscape they have never once burst into some kind of living quarters or even passed a bathroom. Deathstarchitecture never caters to human pleasures: it offers no amenities for its thousands of troops and technicians, no shops, bars or restaurants, no leisure-quarters or gyms or recreational centers, no barracks and no schools. There are also no children, and, it seems, no women. Furthermore, most of the stormtroopers who walk in military time through its corridors actually lack faces.

This is no oversight: in fact it is central to how this space is working empathetically in this world's dispassionate universe. Deathstarchitecture is actually a planet-sized elaboration of that form of space that Augé calls non-place, the zone of malls, elevators and maintenance corridors.[1] Specific places in DeathStarchitecture are hard to remember: it is an unusually blurred space offering our memory little geographic detail or logic, exhibiting what Augé calls the oblivion and aberration of memory—akin to our blurred memories of giant, generic hotels, that lack their own architectural identities and all personal marks or decor,[2] instrumental places we have to get through to get somewhere else, all of which further undercut our sense of belonging. It is perhaps not surprising that the rebel intruders always need the help of androids to map, navigate or make sense of it. All of these tropes of inorganic, inhuman architecture makes DeathStarchitecture a form of alienated space, itself a trope of science fiction used by Lucas in his 1971 film *THX 1138* and which lies like a shadow behind Deathstarchitecture. That earlier SF film's trope of over-rationalized clean white sterile space and inhuman sounds feels contiguous here, thanks to the inhumanity, the synth acoustics and the overall lack of orientation, even if Deathstarchitecture clads itself inside and out with an elaborate extrusion of technical and physical infrastructure that have assumed but opaque purpose.

Note this alienated space's clear oppositional role in the Star Wars universe: with simple Manichean logic this environment helps show by direct contrasts what the Rebellion represents, why it is so important and why we ought to feel empathy only for the rebels. By contrast to Deathstarchitecture, the Rebellion's spaces are authentic, multicultural, communal, lived-in, unstandardized and largely unrationalized, have a multiplicity of histories, and carry the traces of generations. They also offer strange and exciting social spaces like anarchic dive-bars, bustling marketplaces, unregulated Casbah-like zones and many other realms where social classes mix, interact and relax. None of the production design attributes or spatial cues of Deathstarchitecture—its slick surfaces, rational codes, restricted color palates, alienated, unmarked surfaces and modernist designs—are found in rebel zones, which are marked by aged, lived-in, rough and marked surfaces, a deeply-inscribed sense of historical place, ornament and habitation opposite to the Empire's preferred placeless, ahistorical globalized Modernism. Consider how the appeal of the Millennial Falcon's idiosyncratically cobbled-together, grimy interior contrasts to the Empire's austere, well-run zone: however fallible and comically suspect, those signs of the personal history of Solo and Chewbacka make this ship homey. In short, the spaces of the Rebellion are alive in all the ways DeathStarchitecture is dead.

Moreover, if we use another elaboration of space, Third Space theory of Ray Oldenburg (1989, 1999), we see another level to the designed alienation of Deathstarchitecture. Third Space theory argues that most spaces in contemporary life fall into Work spaces, Home spaces, and then all the common public spaces that make up the Third Space. It is not as if such categories are never observed in a spaceship: think of the chess-playing scene on the Millennium Falcon in *Star Wars: A New Hope*. As the architect Michael Silver once commented, the USS Enterprise in *Star Trek* may resemble a giant office-building flying through space and may never have any of the personalized, taped—together charm of a Millennial Falcon or a Firefly Serenity but it nevertheless has home zones, dining areas and living quarters that though they are certainly denatured (these are after all military spaces on loan to personnel) yet still have distinctly non-military design flourishes and colors, and the walls and shelves usually feature items of personalization that reveal the history and character of the inhabitant. Like the similarly divided space-station setting of the franchise's *Deep Space Nine* (1993–1997), the *Enterprise* also features Third Space common zones like the bar and the cafeteria, where people are 'at ease' in both the military and the physical sense.[3]

As spatial theorists like Oldenburg argue, the balance between these three forms of place tell us a lot about how democratic and caring a culture is: cultures that grant a flourishing life usually offer a balance of the three distinct realms of home life, the workplace, and inclusive sociable places. Instead, the rebels who sneak onto the Death Star find themselves in a uniform work space that mixes corporate and military tropes: communicating erratically with their droids to find a path through this maze, they seem lost in some giant office building's maintenance sector peppered with air-ducts, occasionally meeting some controlling work-desk run by a military secretary.

There is a very clear dispassionate and spectacular emotional logic behind this marriage of sterile institution, opaque rational instrumental purpose, corporate maze and pure work space: we long to destroy such places. And so a Deathstar's fiery destruction offers a perfectly calculated final spectacle for these franchise's dispassionate films.[4] Unlike DeathStarchitecture's own vivid destruction of lived organic worlds, there is nothing, no-one, no history or social realm and no ground to empathize with when such a gigantic corporatized work-space is spectacularly blown up. Good riddance to all that alienation.

Tropes of Spatial Alienation

The spatial alienation techniques and tropes found in DeathStarchitecture include:

1. Crafting non-place, a hard to remember place of no specificity or landmark.
2. Creating a rigidly rationalistic space of vague but dominant instrumental logic, removing all aspects of present-at-handness, so that all is a ready-to-hand tool.
3. Staging sets that use surfaces that have little or no mark of time, history, or variation of architectural vernacular. This trope of rootlessness seems to spring from Modernist architecture and design, which celebrated light, clean lines and aseptic surfaces.
4. Erasing home and the third space and making all a contiguous work space, erasing all marks of individual inhabitance, of homeyness and of community.

This spatial critique (which also shaped Lucas's *THX 1138*), descends from a broad counter-cultural critique of modernism in America that had many sources: it was informed by existential critiques of social and personal alienation inspired by European novelists and philosophers such as Camus and Sartre. It was also backed by sociological explications of alienation in modern life in the 1950s (Reisman et al.) and then in the 1960s became engaged with a Marxist and Situationist understanding of the concept of hegemony[5] and the phantasmagorical nature of city space, as well as new critiques from the budding New Left and others of the psychological controls of large institutions and of capitalism (Marcuse; Foucault).

In this broad post-war cultural front, authenticity was identified with rebelliousness, messiness, informality, recycling, Nature, the aging and impoverished inner city, cultural and ethnic otherness, marginal ice and the breaking of borders and other cultural markers and privileged certain forms of music marked by spontaneity and lack of polish. By contrast alienation was marked by social hierarchy, practiced precision of speech and behavior, uniforms, social scripts, the tropes of militarism, consumerism and of traditional conservative white culture, where social niceties were equated with social control, rule-following and the organized settings of American suburban homes, modernist corporate environments and white hegemony. Our earlier examples (the moments of alienation that we traced in *Hiroshima Mon Amour* (1959), *Il Posto* (1961) and *L'Ecclisse* (1962)) reflected how the 1960s codified this space of inauthenticity and alienation: other examples include the film *Playtime* (1967) by Jacques Tati, but it also found spatial realization in later American films like *The Graduate* (1967) to *One Flew Over The Cuckoo's Nest* (1975) and others.

The sets of such films are contiguous with the American examples we will be discussing in a number of ways. One is a shared reaction to the new post-war skyscraper environs and to the construction of suburban tract housing, both of which implemented the modernist, Bauhaus-inspired use of non-organic building materials and celebrated the artifice of these new materials. This then inspired a trope of their deployment that gradually came to represent the alienation of modern life, an oppressive, over-machined, mechanistic break with the personal and cultural past.

And so Deathstarchitecture and Rebel space can in this sense be seen as a minor and late expression of a widespread, codified meta-critique of space and power that was used to target many cultural antagonists. For example, the same deployment through space, surface treatments and architectural cues of spaces that abrade on our sensibility, that seem wrong and cold in ways that often express the story's antagonist and that also often pop the characters out from their lifeless background, becomes in some films (e.g. *Pleasantville, American Psycho*) specifically a critique of Whiteness.[6] This wide range of use is possible because the very same techniques that in *Star Wars* function simply to heighten the difference between good and bad guys, work at entirely different levels in stories of dramatic and Dantean characters and space. Married to a layered character, the same tactics form complex empathetic machinery to show *inner* disjunction, oppression, abrasiveness and lack: by becoming personalized, they express a specific character's situation, history and oppression. And with this distinction we begin to see not only the complex nature of *dramatic* alienation but perhaps we can begin to see how dispassionate and dramatic forms represent fundamentally different stances towards life. This is a theme we will explore further in Chaps. 10 and 11.

And so as we move from the dispassionate *Star Wars* into a range of dramatic narratives—*Playtime* (1967), *The Graduate* (1967), *Pleasantville* (1998), *One Hour Photo* (2002), *Mad Men* (Lionsgate TV, 2007–2015) and *Homeland* (HBO, 2011)—we see how they deploy such spaces to reveal an *inner* alienation of a main character with inner goals who can find no place or home in their alienated world, a dramatic inner emotional lack, emptiness and longing, an erosion, erasure or full destruction of the protagonist's inner space. One interesting psychological aspect of this dramatic alienated space is that though the *viewer* feels the alienation and connects it to what is wrong in the story, usually the story's protagonists do not notice it. Like a fish who cannot see the water it swims in, they cannot realize or understand even by the end of the drama that these spaces are antagonistic and abrasive.

"Ladies and Gentlemen We are Beginning Our Descent into Los Angeles": Alienated Characters, Dialogue and Spaces in *The Graduate*

The Graduate (1967) actually begins by conflating airports and homes that are all largely free of decoration and are painted an austere white. Again we find spaces with no clear sign of habitation, no clear memories, no messy record of daily events, a world where homes and hotel rooms blend into and could double for each other. We cannot easily distinguish Mrs. Robinson's house from Benjamin's own or from the hotel room where they meet for their trysts, a spatial erasure which heightens not only his sense of bewilderment and ours but heightens the feeling of Oedipal drama. The film will even play with this in a famous montage of hidden geographic edits: when the affair between Benjamin and Mrs. Robinson gets rolling, we have a series of cuts that seem to be in one place but reveal a time and space jump-cut joining room to hotel room, pool to bed and back, giving us Benjamin's sense of bored repetitive sex over weeks as well as his feeling of being trapped in a small world of sameness and meaninglessness in this world. Only his bedroom and Elaine's have any personalized walls, any accretion of personal items, cluttered surfaces and a lived-in look, a realism that heightens their future connection with each other.

Paralleling this austere, antiseptic production design is a use of what we might call bleached dialogue: characters speak lines of dialogue that are so bereft of character, history, backstory and voice that they can be easily traded among many of the secondary characters. This alienation technique in dialogue is achieved in much the same way as the spatial alienation in the film: by purposefully emptying the characterological manifold of meaning in order to create an abrasive alienation effect, to convey that "something is very wrong here."

To appreciate this, consider that rich narrative dialogue has at least some of the following six dimensions of meaning implicit in it. In fact most dialogue in narratives has more than one layer of dramatic meaning at any one time, and as scripts, novels and plays are rewritten there is almost always a deepening and enrichment of levels of meaning in the evolving dialogue.

Being another expression of the characterological manifold, dialogue can:

1. Reveal the past.
2. Move the story in the present (usually through revealing some-one's objectives).
3. Foreshadow the future.
4. Reveal character.
5. Reveal relationships.
6. Entertain or engage us.

Consider the many amusingly-empty lines in *The Graduate*, such as the voluminous advice Benjamin gets, all the empty gushing praise that he flees from in the opening party, and the famous line where Mr. Maguire asks Benjamin to "think about one thing: Plastics." This iconic line also powerfully expresses the film's deep antagonist of empti-ness by expressing nearly none of the work of our six dramatic dimensions, ironically bringing up the film's theme of the fake and synthetic. In that way it resembles the social script of the pilot that opens the film: "Ladies and Gentlemen we are beginning our descent into Los Angeles," like the canned recordings then playing at the airport about the airport's white zones, like the many clichés mouthed by Benjamin's parents. At his most nervous Benjamin too hollowly echoes such lines with unpracticed adolescent clumsiness. Like a room decorated to impress visitors but which expresses nothing about one's history or tendencies, this regulated and socially-required dialogue is empty dialogue lacking clues to character.[7]

In fact, the first real person to say anything real and intimate in the film comes at minute 11 when Mrs. Robinson confesses to Benjamin that she is an alcoholic. Like her realistic acting, this reveal comes as a shock that Benjamin cannot handle: he has, after all, been barely able to master the pleasant scripts that have been parroted by everyone else for the last ten minutes, bleached dialogue that has had between none and two dimensions of meaning. By contrast Mrs. Robinson's admission embodies the first five dimensions of meaning and so lands with real force on him. The line is worth noticing and absorbing, as are her reasons for this revelation, triggering his comic recoil from her opened circle of intimacy even as it anchors her as a real character with real intentions and a real past. Moreover, as Benjamin notes, by admitting such a vulnerability she is not only the first person in the film to show a glimpse of interiority but is inviting him into an inner circle of intimacy, a prelude to seduction. Thankfully her strategic admission does not mark the end of the film's amusing bleached dialogue: just a few minutes later her husband will give Benjamin more heaps of generic advice, even sincerely confiding that "I've watched you grow up and sometimes I think of you as my own son," only to rather hilariously forget Benjamin's name just seconds later.

Because others are speaking with bleached dialogue where lines lack all the standard meanings of dramatic speech, and because the spaces are similarly marked by an absence of levels of meaning as well as exhibiting the tropes of alienation, Mrs. Robinson stands out because in many ways she alone is real. Against their sunny empty singsongy affects, hers is black and brooding, her demeanor bored and sophisticated, her voice low and suggestive. And yet this voice carries direct action and force, backed by commands, because her confidence is assured and total. All this dramatic power both lures and intimidates the uncertain, virginal Benjamin, who is himself searching for a center, for a compass, for a gyroscope that can guide him forwards into his future. In the view of Benjamin, hungrily searching for authenticity and the real in this empty LA suburb, only this older woman who says and does the unexpected can mentor him.

For her part Mrs. Robinson is something of a master psychologist. She seems to sense that for Benjamin his virginity is not innocence but ignorance: unsure of himself, trying to hide his inexperience, he is sure that all these older suburban adults have some access to certainties and clarities that he lacks, and she takes full advantage of this. For forty-five minutes of the film she is the cat and he the mouse: her objectives drive every single scene. Finally his own sense of purposelessness and alienation reaches a height in the aural and physical alienation of the pool scene when he is forced to don a scuba suit and float in humiliation in the pool. It is only after this apogee of sensory alienation and social powerlessness that Mrs. Robinson can finally puppet him into bed. And then it is only after Benjamin can finally peek behind the curtain, or rather under the sheets, and sees no real answers there, no purpose or happiness, that he can at last take some power back in their relationship: the moment comes in the film's center-piece "Let's have a conversation" scene when she begins to reveal her own weaknesses and intimacies. Now he yanks the sheet off the bed, revealing her nakedness and forcing her to apologize. Now he has power in the relationship, but that just means that he too will now be inducted into the bitterness of suburban American life.

BITTERNESS EXAMINED

And why else does Mrs. Robinson seem so grounded, so real? Because she is so obviously bitter.

In fact, this film is a study of bitterness: Mrs. Robinson's bitterness seems to grant her both reality and wisdom in this empty world of platitudes. Sadly for Benjamin, he cannot see the sources of this bitterness in her: when she half-confesses it he lacks the experience to hear her tragedy and her truth and so to have an actual intimate relationship with her, to have conversations of care and complicity that might reflect balance and shared fears and consoling.

We have discussed guilt in Part I and will discuss innocence in Part III: here bitterness serves us well as a bridge. After all, bitterness is, like guilt, a cognitive emotional state that comes from certain forms of experience and reveals character and history. The sunny positive attitude of Benjamin's parents' friends is a socially-dictated affectation that reveals nothing about a person's past or real emotions. By contrast, bitterness in a person usually implies two quite different things about that person's past. First, this bitter person once had hopes and perhaps even ideals: she once saw the world as a positive place that offered some long-term worthwhile pursuits. Second, this person then experienced a betrayal of some kind that she has not gotten over, a moment when the world— perhaps in the form of parents, a jilting lover, a failed social movement, a hypocritical political or religious leader, an oppressing ruling class or a surprisingly indifferent God—betrayed her trust in those ideals. The person, though unable to forget the old promise, then gave up on those pursuits and now is left with a dead version of that idealism and hope, left with a mouth sucked tight by the dusty taste of some poor substitute that cannot sustain her hope.

We are given a window onto this side of Mrs. Robinson: while turned away from him in the "conversation" scene, she admits to her dead idealism, though Benjamin tragically misses this real opening. In a moment where her normal hard mask drops, she reveals that her bitterness springs from the scarring experience of getting pregnant with Elaine, being forced to drop out of college and then finding herself in a loveless marriage and an undemanding, flat life. By her own admission she became a neurotic: she turned herself into a blighted survivor of sorts, her eyes now open, her wits about her, her hopes deemed illusions and jettisoned as such. And as if we were viewing a character in *The Divine Comedy* we now see the condition of the embittered: in the embittering there is often a feeling that the 'scales have fallen from your eyes' so that the old dreams suddenly look childish, quaint and embarrassing, and with this comes the seemingly wiser embittered sight. Having lost the open eyes of the innocent, the embittered now gains a sharp tongue, sharp eyes and sharpened features. And usually the bitter gain a sharp impatience for the innocent.

For Benjamin's part, just as he realizes that his parents and all their friends from Tarzana are too fake for him, he realizes that Mrs. Robinson is too real. But Benjamin doesn't simply give up: still lacking any direction or plan, he now stumbles comically into a relationship with Mrs. Robinson's daughter Elaine: it seems that Elaine, the dreamy innocent, promises the very hope and dream and worth that Mrs. Robinson has lost. And now Mrs. Robinson becomes rather like a starter-girlfriend, or like the sex doll in *Lars and the Real Girl*: she has been turned into a practice run for the protagonist, preparing him for his first real relationship. And after being ordered around by her mother for half the film, Benjamin finds Elaine responsive and reassuringly uncertain, granting him the power of deciding what to do.

Fig. 8.1   *Pleasantville* (1998)

When Benjamin leaves LA to find Elaine at college in Berkeley, California, the nature of the spaces changes. They begin meeting in his Berkeley room, a bedraggled, grungy, real place completely different from the alienated Los Angeles milieus, and for the next twenty minutes as Benjamin pursues Elaine he himself, his clothes and his shiny red sports car will all get grungier and more bedraggled, growing 'more real' in the production design logic of the film. Only at the end, in their iconic moments of being lost on the bus, do we see their dawning realization that neither has the answer for the other. In the end Benjamin himself does not really come to grips with the alienation that surrounds them all.

This is true for most characters that we find in alienated spaces. The reason is simple: born of the state of alienation itself, usually an intangible and undetectable state, alienated space is far easier to observe in others than in yourself. Only rarely, for example in the film *Pleasantville*, do characters actually escape or overcome an alienated space, and there they can do this because, as the proverbial fish out of water, they are tossed into it from another, entirely different space (Fig. 8.1).

Pleasantville

The protagonists of *Pleasantville* are the twins David and Jennifer, two high school students who live in a newly divorced family in a 1990s' version of America where sexual disease and climate change are only two of many frightening signs of change and freedom. While Jennifer revels in the popularity that her extroverted sexuality grants her at school, David longs for safety and security, which he finds by escaping into the solid homilies of an old 50s' television show called *Pleasantville* that is based around a typical clichéed 1950s wasp family.

When the twins are magically transported from the present, which is seen in color, into the black-and-white town of Pleasantville, they first try to fit in and adapt. But soon the free-spirited, sexualized Jennifer brings elements of desire, rebellion and social flourishing to Pleasantville's constricted world. As she inspires its denizens, pushing different characters such as the show's mother to take risks and come to a sense of self—revelation, they move from safe repression to the riskier freedoms of intimacy. But as a character becomes more authentic and more emotionally connected to other people, the change presents itself for everyone to see as they turn selectively into color. This marker of change provokes outrage and punishment in the conservative town which soon demonstrates violently against the liberated 'coloreds.' In one ironic inversion, typical of the film, David helps the family's mother cover up her inner changes by using her makeup to make her look properly self-alienated (Fig. 8.2).

And so into this visually alienated world of black and white, the new opposites of authenticity, spontaneity and beauty all erupt into the space in a very clear way. The spatial alienation of *Pleasantville* follows all the same spatial tropes of inauthenticity as *The Graduate*, which are here made particularly manifest in *Pleasantville*'s period—reference use of cinematography and balanced frames, of cleanly-ordered households and diners filled with non-personal items and shiny unmarked surfaces to capture an imprisoning world of repressive 1950s WASP Americana. It also uses *The Graduate*'s trick of splitting its characters into those who speak denatured, bleached dialogue (social scripts, advice and clichés) and those who speak real dialogue with dimensions of meaning: here too alienated dialogue and alienated space characterize the film's antagonists.

Pleasantville also dramatizes another aspect of both emotion and its spatial realizations: the film shows how contagious the inner conflicts of its characters are. Its shared narrative space illustrates the phenomenon of *emotional contagion,* a real-world phenomenon in which one's mood or affect is communicated to others through social interactions and bonds. Through the device of the TV show it proposes first that neurosis, the impulse to escape alienation and to tightly circumscribe the circle of intimacy are not simple choices limited to the inner self but are in

Fig. 8.2 Staged publicity still for *Homeland* that references Carrie's evidence wall (*Homeland* 2011–)

fact spread and inculcated through media representation, gendered hierarchical structures and social bonds. And then by staging its visual conflict as a duel between two competing cinema spaces, the film then shows how this shared, jointly-internalized space can become more empathetic and rich through social interaction and intervention and by overt social and civic agreement and conflict. This theme, of how the rules of intimacy and of dramatic space are also public and shared projections and how they might be consciously changed to include a richer social and moral vocabulary and more complex and empathetic social bonds, is the subject of our final two chapters in Part III.

Showroom Spaces

These narratives also take a further step beyond DeathStarchitecture by erecting what we will call showroom space for their home—or work-spaces. The specific codification and cues of showroom space are a lack of signs of use of a place's surfaces and objects, their geometric and non-organic arrangement of sight-line and set, and their emphasis on displaying shiny and fresh-minted 'unconsumed' consumer goods. In all of these examples this Showroom space, denatured as it is of human use and personalities, adds to the purposive sense of violation—whether of home and work spaces, of spatial gender assignments, and/or of a character who has become cut off from a personal past and community. Such alienated Showroom spaces can be read as expressions of tight control of the environment by the protagonist (*HomeLand*, *Pleasantville*, *One Hour Photo*), as sought out by the protagonists as a kind of compensation for loneliness and betrayal (*HomeLand*, *One Hour Photo*, *Mad Men*), as an expression of a strong sense of in–out group identity (*Pleasantville*, *Mad Men*), or as a space the protagonist is unwillingly born into and seeks to escape (*The Graduate*, *Playtime*). Moreover, a single Showroom space can indicate numerous internal disjunctions: in *Mad Men* Don Draper is ensconced in Showroom space in part because he lives a false identity, cannot have authentic intimacy with women, is constantly betraying those who love him, is guilty over the abandonment and suicide of his innocent younger brother whom he abandoned, and is anxiously fleeing his lower-class status.[8]

In all of these cases one common thread appears, a thread so pronounced that we can identify Showroom space as a codified body of cinematic signifiers: characters that are found in Showroom spaces lack strong social bonds and, as they slowly come to realize this, the space becomes a fundamental expression of their inner goal, conflict and crisis, their lack of intimacy, of real friends, of authentic social bonds, which are all problems that contribute to their lack of direction and purpose. In *Mad Men* they are both simultaneously quite alluring and yet shout "go live and work anywhere but here!". Through these techniques, Showroom space is thus both a cause and an emblem of a character's moral confusion, and so these Showroom spaces become in their own way a dramatized antagonist in the story, a problem that usually powers the main character to seek out a life and a place of meaning elsewhere, among others who do not seem as shiny and closed and dead as these spaces.

Intimacy Reconsidered

As emblematic of a lack of social connection, social trust and self-awareness, such spaces all indicate a real lack of intimacy in and among characters. Why is there an impulse to withdraw into such closed spaces? What is the impulse to be impervious to vulnerability, to hide one's intimacies, to be alienated in these ways? Why seek out the dull company of the non-intimate?

Because intimacy is dangerous. We have excellent reasons to fear intimacy and to share intimacies only with a very selective, proven, trustworthy few, and only when we are feeling a certain safety with them. You must have reason to feel that they will not use this information against you, as a piece of hurtful gossip at the office, as a weapon in a furious verbal fight, as a bomb that can explode your confidence and reputation. This is the reason for the alienated production design of Benjamin's and Mrs. Robinson's house, which by showing no sign of the past or of individuality also show a refusal to allow intimacy in conversation as well as a neurotic impulse to control the world and evade the chaos of one's personal emotions. This is also why Benjamin in *The Graduate* has to choose between scripts that lack all intimacy and the messy, unbordered, real talks he has and wants to have with Mrs. Robinson, practice-runs of intimacy that then prepare him for the more relaxed and spontaneous intimate talks he can have with her daughter Elaine. At one point when he tries to talk with her, Mrs. Robinson scathingly asks if he is going to share his "college experiences" with her. He hears this fierce rejection as a put-down, not realizing it is a jealous, bitter jibe from someone who never completed college. Elaine, herself in college and not embittered, will not attack him if he talks about his anxieties and worries: Elaine won't laugh at him, and that, as much as anything, makes her his next romantic interest.

Intimacy usually involves risk because it is a revealing of something that a person normally keeps hidden from strangers and acquaintances. It can be small details about the past but it can also be what you reveal by telling those details: chatting about such apparently unimportant details can reveal your sensibility, your own form of noticing, your spirit of living. In an earlier chapter we spoke of how intimacy grows stronger as a bond grows tighter, progressing through a series of concentric circles of trust. We grant more intimacy to a person as he changes from being a stranger to become a neighbor, and then after some caution and coffee together he becomes a friend, and then slowly over months becomes a close friend, and then after a series of awkward and then fun dates he becomes a lover, and then after two years of living together he becomes a partner to the grave. Each step in this relationship allows for the shared facing of tests in life, which if passed then tend to provoke yet more intimate revelations and bonds, each layer of growing intimacy being roughly appropriate to each shrinking circle, each step ideally requiring a greater level of reciprocal risk and so of trust, as each year he becomes a wider and deeper well of your foibles and mistakes and desires and hopes and defeats.

And this is why so much of drama is connected to intimacy: at the center of so many main characters is a cluster of desires, fears and needs alongside a strong impulse to hide it from others. Benjamin's affair is a real and increasingly-problematic secret that increasingly cuts him off from his parents. In *Aliens* Ripley never reveals to anyone her fears about her own body. In *Hiroshima Mon Amour* and our other examples, the dead shades are held so dear by the living because they are the close-held, secret memories that cannot even be revealed to intimates.

And so, while psychologists like Meanes (2000) are right to point out that in life one's trauma often closes off avenues of intimacy with others, that trauma often thrusts one into a lonely world of fear and self-isolation, a very different mechanism happens in the *dramatization* of trauma. Now its aesthetic representation in Dantean space, the space of trauma, is actually experienced as *very* intimate for the viewer or reader, essentially because it takes us straight into the most protected and often secret space of the character, a space we might never have access to even in an intimate relationship with this person. In life Ugolino would likely not tell anyone that he has eaten his own children. Francesca would not talk with a neighbor about her affair, Farinata would not speak about his suicidal impulses to a casual friend. But thanks to this form of mimesis (i.e. the dramatization of trauma), we can go inside and into this secret space of the soul, a space where no-one else in the character's life, including she herself, can go. From this perch we watch or read Madame Bovary's inner thoughts without having a risky affair, taking notes on characterological tendencies and their outcomes without needing to battle through the actual dramas of a friendship or marriage.

THE STRESS OF THE JOB OF THE SEX: GENDER AND THE PURGATORIAL HOMES OF *HOMELAND*

While some Dantean spaces are stronger than the characters they hold, this is not always true. Benjamin never escapes his alienated condition, but Jennifer forever changes Pleasantville. Some characters strive to destroy their Dantean space, while others bravely enter their Dantean space and enact a physical version of their internal struggle before they can heal and finally leave their pasts behind. This is powerfully illustrated in the first season of the television show *Homeland* (HBO, 2011). In the penultimate scenes of the two protagonists, each struggles in and with a Dantean space to break free of their flaws, choices, guilt and mistakes.

And each separately culminates their first season story-arc's trajectory and gender conflict in a dramatically powerful Dantean space. The results in both cases are arguably the most empathy-producing and affecting scenes in the series.

For Carrie this happens at the dramatic end of Episode 11 when her paradoxical efforts to construct a home composed of work comes crashing down as her living-room's large wall of 'borrowed' classified documents is ripped apart and she is fired from the CIA. To unpack the power of this scene, we should first describe the alienated space that is Carrie's home. Throughout the season we see that Carrie's house is not a home but is really more of a workspace for her. Whenever Carrie needs the comforts of home—after for example a long day staring obsessively at Brody's family in his suburban home—she flees to her sister's. By contrast to the 'homey' home of her married sister which is a conventional, child-filled, bustling house where the walls have grown covered with child drawings, where the surfaces are scuffed and marked by a history of use, where objects are placed with the slight randomness of actual home-use, in Carrie's house the glass surfaces tend to be sharply clean and freshly washed, the objects on every table and counter pristine and carefully placed as in a showroom, while the walls are similarly unmarked by scratches or stains. Once again we have Work-house space, a place with no personal history, where Oldenberg's distinction of Work and Home spaces is being combined, a violation which then mirrors a disjunction and an alienation within our protagonist.

So how does the characterological manifold fit the spatial allegiances of these home spaces? Home spaces can:

1. Reveal the past.
2. Advance the story in the present (usually through revealing someone's objectives).
3. Foreshadow the future.
4. Reveal character.
5. Reveal social bonds.
6. Entertain or engage us.

When we revisit the film *Amelie* we see how all of these elements are operating in Amelie's home. But in *Homeland* only Carrie's sister's home is imbued with this 'homeyness': which is to say it is a space with an emotionally supportive environment matched with the physical representations of a rich past that includes social bonds. In Carrie's house, however, none of our six levels of meaning seem to be operating. No wonder she tries to fill her home up with work: it is all the excitement, the social relations and the life she has.

Carrie's need for homeyness is a need to escape the paranoia and distrust generated by her self-assumed work in field counterintelligence. Her lack of homeyness seems to originate in the psychotic break she suffered from in college, which is continually returning and which is represented at the start of every episode in the fearful maze of the show's opening credits. Carrie, we gradually learn, suffered from her big break in her first term at college in the fall of 2001, which the credits reference by news footage of the 9/11 attacks that she somehow feels she might have stopped.

The sense that 9/11 was a Dantean moment for her is deepened by the specific acting techniques of Clare Danes, the actor who plays Carrie. Danes brings a quality of being frozen in an adolescent or pre-adolescent curiosity, vulnerability, innocence and optimism, revealing by turns both an underlying hopefulness that keeps her in the fight through experiences that would embitter others, and also a repeated sudden loss of confidence and urge to cry that attracts our empathy. This quality is often present in a wide-eyed slack—jawed affect as she takes in something without defenses but also lies in her voice's frequent small sudden high-pitched breaks, so well-opposed to the low, husky, knowing sultriness of Brody's sexualized wife even as they hint at both instability and adolescence. In fact Carrie is refreshingly under-sexualized for a romantic lead: while not exactly androgynous she brings a slim, tomboyish physicality to the role that belies the normal sexualizing markers of feminine adulthood. All of this helps support the sense that Carrie is still in some sense frozen in her teens, in the trauma of her psychotic break in the fall of 2001.

These two threads—of her home's alienation and of her underlying instability and paranoia—finally come together in the incident of 'The Wall:' (Fig. 8.2), a large assemblage of stolen CIA documents now covering her living room that if only arranged properly will, she hopes, become a roadmap out of the maze she's built. Hopefully it will reveal the truth of her frantic searches, sexual liaisons and shifting paranoia about Brody, help her distinguish truth from lies, intimacy from functionality, Brody-as-lover from Brody-as-terrorist. It will let her love him or arrest him, and either way will help her return to some kind of stability and certainty and perhaps even to her full job status at the CIA. As the final big scene begins with a ring of her doorbell, Carrie runs from the Wall to her door excited and flushed with the certainty it is Brody, coming there to be her lover and her partner, stabilizing her life and giving it clarity and meaning. Instead, in a dramatic reversal she opens the door onto her boss and his CIA employees: Brody has betrayed her.

Now she has a series of powerful revelations, taking place at many levels. The invasion of this space by antagonistic fellow members of the CIA shows her the impossibility of conflating her work with friendship, sex, love, and family. When the Wall is torn down we see Carrie realize that she is an obsessive, a prying and desperate person with no life or family. This defeat soon leads her to agree to electroshock treatments to erase her present and begin life again away from the CIA. We know of course that while this is all true, her paranoid feelings were also correct and so as we watch her punish herself in true purgatorial fashion through electroshock treatments that erase her memories, we are left with an abrasive sense of injustice and intense empathy that makes Carrie's story feel open-ended and unresolved.

A different dramatic effect, and a different form of Dantean space, is deployed to convey Brody's alienation and violation. Brody's season-long conflict comes to a head in episode 12, the season finale, when he finally enters the bunker to kill the vice-president and complete his mission. Here the writers' overall architecture becomes clear when this space becomes a Dantean cauldron of gendered schizophrenia, the final dramatic collision of Brody's old masculinist American home, his tiny torture cell in Iraq, and his feminizing Arabic home where he played the role of loving wife and mother. Deepening the incipient racism in the show, the Arabic home defines transgression through the violent crossing of homosocial boundaries. In this home the straight Brody is forced to kiss the terrorist and then become a mothering figure for the terrorist's child. Then after bonding with the child, he witnessed this child being killed by a drone authorized by the American vice-president, a trauma that made him commit to the terrorist cause and set out to destroy the vice-president, an emblem of traditional masculinity. Now in the visual and emotional summary of the season, Brody may both lose his mind and set off his hidden explosive vest here in this high-pressure bunker full of male authority figures which echoes with his middle-class home, his torture cell, and the terrorist's domestic home. Only his crying daughter's phone call and her plea that he 'just come home' can save him—he walks out from the bunker, heads home and (temporarily) puts his old world back into balance and his forced choice of allegiances temporarily at bay.

And so a parallel crisis of space reflects our paralleled protagonists. In the melancholy tragedy of our violated Homeland, this masculinized woman has no home at all while this feminized man now has three too many. These penultimate settings bring home the homes of *Homeland*: they are each a Dantean projection of a violated psyche, places where these two characters wrestle with their own shifting desires for non-anxious, non-ethnic, gendered ideals, trapped in half-imagined homes that neither can realize or understand.[9]

This analysis reveals a crucial aspect of Dantean spaces : because they echo with the traumas that originate and power the character's story, and because they often appear in the story when the character can no longer avoid or control her trauma-caused emotions, such spaces are often the site of the unresolved moral, social or gender tensions in a protagonist. This is why they are a powerful tool for dramatists and a useful forensic tool for theorists.

NOTES

1. See particularly *In the Metro* (Augé, 2002).
2. After critiques such as Maximiliano E. Korstanje's, Augé has more recently re-conceived of airports as hyperspaces, places of great consumer and social stimulation, but this older concept is still useful here to describe this form of alienated space in stories.
3. Note that the first five episodes of *Star Trek: Discovery* (CBS, 2017-) features a starship with no Home spaces or Third Spaces and has some of the dark cladding aspects of DeathStarchitecture. This different starship conveys a sense of Work-house space that helps convey the show's sense of a world locked in war. In this way the show resembles Carrie's home in *Homeland*, is a kind of *Star Trek* for the age of the War on Terror. See D'Adamo 2018 (forthcoming) for a social history of spaceships.
4. For a description of dispassionate space in sets see D'Adamo (2013). To see it playing out in contemporaneous music, see D'Adamo (2015b, 2017).
5. For more on this see D'Adamo (2017, pp. 50–51).
6. Some of this critique of whiteness can be traced back to the cultural conflicts over Funk and white and black identity. Consider for example how in her 1972 novel *The Bluest Eye* Morrison defines white environments when describing black girls who have over-assimilated to the hegemonic white culture:
'Wherever it erupts, this Funk, they wipe it away; where it crusts, they dissolve it; wherever it drips, flowers, or clings, they find it and fight it until it dies. They fight this battle all the way to the grave' (Morrison 1972, p. 68). For more on this topic see D'Adamo (2017).

7. Note that while all of these alienated spaces and bleached lines of dialogue are empty in terms of the characterological manifold, this means that they are lacking in character but not in plot. Their character-empty nature is in fact crucially-needed so that the plot, powered by Benjamin's problem and search, can feel urgent and vivid.

8. Some viewers may not relate these internal conflicts to the space and simply admire them as spectacle, even tuning in because they long to be in that world themselves. They have a disPassionate frame of reception towards the show, which means they ignore or overlook or simply cannot see its empathetic linkages. The dispassionate viewer does not link Draper's external objectives of winning every account from the many internal objectives and personal history he is striving so hard to hide in episode after episode. The Dantean viewer instead links all this spectacle of wealth to Draper's deeper reasons for his anxious striving for social status. Once again dispassion is a prioritizing of external objectives over internal ones, while a Dantean reception of Draper requires an empathetic synthesis of character; ie, a grasp of the narrative and mis-en-scene as powered by the characterological manifold. We explore these drames of reception further in Chap. 10.

9. Dedicated to Michael Silver and the Alexandria.

Bibliography

Alighieri, Dante. 2006. *The Divine Comedy*, trans. and ed. Robin Kirkpatrick. London: Penguin.

Aristotle. 1986. *Poetics*, trans. A. Sullivan. Chapel Hill, NC: University of North Carolina Press.

Augé, Marc. 2002. *In the Metro*. Minneapolis: University of Minnesota Press.

———. 2004. *Oblivion*. Minneapolis: University of Minnesota Press.

———. 2016. *Everyone Dies Young: Time Without Age*. New York: Columbia University Press.

Bloom, Harold (ed.). 2009. *Alienation*. USA: Infobase Publishing.

D'Adamo, Amedeo. 2013. Dantean Space in the Cities of Cinema. In *Media and the City: Urbanism, Technology and Communication*, ed. Simone Tosoni, Matteo Tarantino, and Chiara Giaccardi. Newcastle upon Tyne, UK: Cambridge Scholars Press.

D'Adamo, Amedeo. 2015. Ain't There One Damn Flag That Can Make Me Break Down and Cry? The Formal, Performative and Emotional Tactics of Bowie's Singular Critical Anthem Young Americans. In *Enchanting David Bowie*, ed. Toija Cinque, Christopher Moore, and Sean Redmond. New York: Bloomsbury Academic Press.

D'Adamo, Amedeo. 2017. That Junky Funky Vibe: Quincy Jones' Title Theme for the Sitcom *Sanford and Son*. In *Music in Comedy Television*, ed. Liz Giuffre, and Philip Hayword. New York and London: Routledge.

Means, Russel. 2000. *Intimacy and Alienation: Memory, Trauma and Personal Being*. New York, USA: Routledge.

Oldenberg, Ray. 1999. *The Great Good Place*. New York: Marlowe & Company.

How Not to Think like Dante Alighieri: The Social Implications of Dantean Space

How Not to Think Like Dante Alighieri: Guilt, Punishment and the Components of Dantean Space

THE CLASSICAL ROOTS OF DANTEAN SPACE IN EURIPIDES, OVID AND OTHERS

We begin Part III by examining some of Dante's precursors, focusing on stories that use individual elements and devices of Dantean space. Perhaps by first unpacking this aesthetic into the parts that Dante then synthesized to create his powerful aesthetic machinery, we might then better grasp its social and psychic effects. We locate examples of these different elements in certain canonical Greek tragedies such as Aeschylus' *Agamemnon*, Sophocles' *Oedipus Rex* and Euripides' *Bacchae*, while other aspects are similar to the medieval narrative form of the psychomachia.

EMOTIONAL PROJECTION AND THE CHARACTEROLOGICAL MANIFOLD

First, there is what we might consider the kernel of Dantean space, that element of the spatial elaboration of an emotional problem, or in other words the projection of an inner emotional struggle out onto the world of the story where it takes some physical form outside the character and becomes a mirror of that conflict. We actually find this element in flower as early as Aeschylus's play the *Agamemnon*, the oldest extant Greek tragedy. His play presents us with Clytemnestra, the queen of Argos and the wife of King Agamemnon, who is away at Troy leading the Greeks against the Trojans.

© The Author(s) 2018
A. D'Adamo, *Empathetic Space on Screen*,
https://doi.org/10.1007/978-3-319-66772-0_9

The play begins as a guard joyfully sees a distant signal fire in the night: King Agamemnon's ship is finally returning from the war. His wife Clytemnestra has ruled the palace in his absence for ten years, and in all that time her emotions have swirled around one specific Dantean moment: she has never overcome her husband's killing of her favorite daughter, Iphigenia, of whom he made a human sacrifice to keep his army unified as they left for the war Clytemnestra's long-simmering tumult of grief and rage becomes spatially manifest in the play's grand operatic penultimate scene when she invites her returning husband to ascend the palace steps. She tells him that in honor of his accomplishments she has had a blood-red carpet woven just for him, and she now orders this 'celebratory' carpet to be unrolled down the great steps to his feet. Despite his better judgement a flattered Agamemnon is lured onto the red carpet and on up the steps into the palace: there Clytemnestra dismembers him with an ax, completing her revenge and echoing the trauma of Agamemnon's initial bloodying of their house when he killed their daughter.

Aeschylus's idea of the red carpet is powerful not simply because the carpet dramatizes the spider's invitation of the fly into her web. The scene's deeper power comes because this web carries several levels of dramatic meaning. When Agamemnon unwittingly steps onto this large carpet leading up the stairs to the palace, the theatrical space of the palace manifests her simmering rage in many ways because it is simultaneously entangled with their past, present and future. Her fashioned web rings both *historically* with the past—with the remembered blood of the daughter he murdered—and also *foreshadowingly* with his own coming bloody murder. But as the audience knows, this carefully-made red carpet and the treachorous palace it leads up to are also a manifest spatialized presence of his wife's *current* inner emotional storm. In this scene she is like a dramatic character with an external goal and an inner emotional goal, but by creating and deploying the red carpet (itself a kind of tunnel of memory), Clytemnestra's inner goal is projected outwards and shapes the very nature of the space of the story and expresses all of the levels of the characterological manifold.

Writing slightly later, Sophocles then achieves something similar in *Oedipus Rex*. In this play the transgressions of King Oedipus—his murder of his own father and his sexual relations with his mother—are simultaneously cause and externalized and embodied in the plague that is decimating the city he leads. Here the city's plague-strewn streets are somewhat like the red carpeted palace entrance of the *Agamemnon*: in each we have a space that echoes with both a past crime and the current inner conflict of a protagonist. This device again appears in Euripides' play *The Bacchae*: when Pentheus refuses the power and reality of Bacchus, the god of sex and theater, Bacchus is inspired by this king's sexual repressions and youthful prurience to then turn his city-state first into rubble and then into a landscape of violent sexual madness, punishing Pentheus and also presenting him with this wild murderous mirror of the king's own disordered inner state.

This operatic aesthetic of canonical Greek tragedy offers two building blocks of Dantean space. First, these plays all externalize a protagonist's inner conflict and conflictual history by transcribing it onto the space and place of the character in such a way that it drives the plot forwards and marks its completion. Secondly, these stories suggest the idea that the inner desires of a character can also be mirrored in his or her specific *punishment*. All three plays reflect the dramatic logic of the arithmetic or balancing idea that 'the punishment fits the crime.' Such simple ideas have the persuasion of a monetary exchange, in the form of payment or of a measured and meted-out balancing of pain and agony.

But while this dramatic use of punishment embodies important elements of Dante's design, they do not fully constitute it: Narcissus' story, as told by Pausanias (x. 31. § 6) and Eustathius (*ad Hom.* p. 266) offers a new element. Narcissus's story is straightforward: in love with himself and no-one else, he then tries to grasp his own reflection in the water of a well and drowns in it. This story offers an aesthetic compactness that forever defines narcissism—the loved reflection of Narcissus's own image is his downfall. This story elegance offers a new refined dramatic pleasure and economy: the idea that a story's conclusion and a character's punishment can be a direct mimetic attribute or image of the character's desires, flaw or crime. While Oedipus's and Pentheus's own crimes, forbidden desires and inner disorder are vaguely externalized through the punishment of the cities they rule—in the form of a plague for Oedipus and of a band of murderous naked women for Pentheus—Narcissus' fate has no such obscurity: his death by drowning in his self-image literally and overtly mirrors his own character flaw.

While also possessing this aspect of overtly expressing one's crime or flaw, Echo's story goes further, containing an element that will appear again in Dante's stories of Ugolino, Francesca and Capaneus: Echo commits a kind of crime for which she is divinely punished in a very specific way that is not only architected by her crime but is also *an infinite repetition of it.* Like an inhabitant of Dante's *Inferno,* she continues to exist but cannot ever escape from her cursing actions.

Her story can be given in simple outline. Hera comes looking for her husband Zeus who is busy having sex with nymphs, and an unwise Echo tries to cover for him by chattering on and on with Hera to distract her. When Hera realizes what Echo is doing she grows furious and punishes her, denying the nymph's voice and allowing her only to repeat what she has just heard. Echo now experiences a mirror-image of her crime, turning her punishment into an eternal reminder of her defining character moment, and this aspect can also serve as a warning to all who hear her story.

Note that however painful and horrid the punishments visited on Narcissus, Agamemnon, Oedipus and Pentheus, their final fate is not one of suspended animation and torture as Echo's is. But the Greek tradition has other examples of a permanent divine punishment for a crime against the gods, a punishment that should last for all eternity. Think for example of Prometheus's eternal punishment on the cliffs of Tartarus, where his liver will forever be devoured by an eagle. Here, as in Hera's infinite punishment of Echo, there is no balance, no even exchange for a crime: there is instead simply a transgression of the divine that then tips Prometheus (and Echo) into a new existential yet eternal condition. This pedagogical logic—of a punishment architecture married to the character's permanent and enduring struggle with it—is also foundational for Dante's stories.

One final precursor of Dantean space can be noted. This is found in the medieval narrative form of the psychomachia, a form that continues to influence mainstream cinema in films like *Identity* (2003), television shows like *River* (2015), and others. In the psychomachia a series of characters are in fact different manifestations of aspects of one mind. In this form we often have a clear elaboration of an inner conflict, a moment when the dramatic stage becomes nothing more nor less than a mirror of an inner conflict of a protagonist who is struggling to come to some big revelation, insight or decision. (Arguably this form is implicit in some Greek tragedies such as *Oedipus Rex* and *The Bacchae* but these plays are not overt psychomachias.)

In this short survey of Greek tragedy, the Echo myth and the medieval psychomachia, we have identified five of the six main elements of Dantean space.

1. **The spectacular external spatialization of an inner conflict** is found in Aeschylus, Sophocles and Euripedes.
2. **The creation of a dramatic logic between crime and punishment** is also found in Aeschylus, Sophocles and Euripedes.
3. **The construction of an ongoing *eternal* punishment that embodies the character's conflict** is found in the Prometheus myth.
4. **Eternal punishment *and* the invention of a punishment that mirrors the character's crime** are both found in Ovid's story of Echo.
5. **The creation of characters and settings whose struggles and debate are aspects and projections of a protagonist's mind** is found in the medieval Psychomachia.

Given these elements it is not difficult to imagine a character who has landed in some permanent state of spatialized nternal conflict because of a specific event that they are responsible for. We can also easily imagine that that specific event is *mirrored in* the state they are trapped in on some physical or sensual level. But these by themselves do not constitute Dantean space. The one last element that is so prevalent in Dante is the sense that the core conflictual event of a character's story is also a trauma, an inescapable memory from earlier life from which the character cannot escape.

And that brings us back to our first example. Clytemnestra is clearly wrestling with and cannot escape from the traumatic moment that happened ten years before the play starts: the Dantean moment when her husband killed her beloved daughter. When she murders Agamemnon she creates a new Dantean moment, a new murderous trauma, in her own son Orestes, who years later will then himself return to this very scene to murder her and her co-conspirator Aegisthus. And so,

6. **The use of an inciting trauma that then dictates a character's obsessive thought, raging emotions, conflict and objectives** is found in the character of Clytemnestra in Aeschylus's *Agamemnon*.[1]

To see how close Clytemnestra is to the characters in Dante's *Inferno*, we might imagine that her crime were somehow divinely wrought into an eternal mirroring punishment like Echo's. If for example we imagine that Clytemnestra was condemned to relentlessly ax her husband through all eternity we can then easily imagine her as a denizen of Dante's ninth circle of Hell, an intent, eternally-butchering neighbor ensconced within screaming distance of Ugolino.

Judicial Pleasures Versus the Juridical Harmonies of Dantean Spaces: *Reconsidering the Stories of Francesca and Prometheus*

We should distinguish between *judicial* pleasure, the pleasure we take in "rightly" judging someone in real life—be that our child, our partner, our friend or sister or neighbor—and the *juridical* pleasures granted by dramas, that pleasure we gain from feeling a character's fate is a right match for her actions. Judicial pleasure is our own judgement, and our own act of judgement feels right to us when it seems correctly formed and informed by our own construction of events, our moral precepts, history and emotions. These judgments in life embody a sense of power and responsibility. By contrast, the juridical pleasure of *drama* is an appreciation of someone *else's* judgment of people and events, expressed in a fixed way through dramatic form. This dramatic construction of empathies is not spontaneous but is instead composed of symbols, oppositions, rhythms and rhymes and other techniques inherited from thousands of years of story vernacular. However, though it is constructed, Juridical pleasure is not balanced or codified the way our modern legal codes legitimate themselves. Even if the pleasure of perceiving some story 'balance' between an action and a punishment sometimes informs the instincts of our juries and judges, it isn't supposed to: in general we no longer invent punishments but have legal codes that determine what is just.

Justice in *drama* is anchored in an emotion of catharsis tied to a gushing and satisfying feeling of affirmation in the viewer or reader. Dante's *Commedia* is rife with this device: we love Dante's stories because they offer such strange and challenging juridical pleasure. Every case to some degree argues that it is a case of poetic justice, of your crimes coming back to haunt you. As Dante himself uses Dantean space it is always just, giving the impression that Dantean moments only happen to those who deserve it.

We love it when stories have this balance: it provides us with an intense feeling of closure and often of catharsis. But of course this is an aesthetic fiction: however pleasurable and reassuring, this aesthetic is highly powered by a profound ressentiment. In fact in real life Dantean moments are almost never actually just: they are not punishments or the signs of what character work we must now do to become a complete and moral person. In real life, as opposed to so many pedagogical stories, Dantean space is usually inflicted upon us, by an abuser or by random events, and do not befall us by our own actions.

Francesca's story breaks from the juridical pleasures of Dante's other characters. In fact Dante's own uncertainty, emotional anguish, and his fainting spell at the end of Francesca's tale, the only time he faints in *The Divine Comedy*, hints at just this tension in his whole massive edifice. It seems as if Dante finds that Francesca, alone among the denizens of Hell, has her own convincing logic that bears up against his god's. She chose love over propriety, chose love over conventional ideas of the boundaries of marriage, chose love even over her god. To put love first above all else is a moral choice as well as a social one, and she accepts the consequences and is forever with her lover now because at least they are together, ghosts that will forever haunt each other.

Hers is also an empathetic choice, and Dante's own emotional uncertainty in dealing with Francesca's case is the one area where two different moral logics crash together. Her case is like that of Prometheus, chained forever to that rock by the unjust gods: we can see this punishment as motivated by the punisher, as feeling right and satisfying in the eyes of the gods who punish. But the reader can also see it as also very unjust, that there is a great crime happening in this particular Dantean space: we see here that the gods operate by their own rules, that life might in certain intensely dramatic moments have more than one juridical logic. Like Dante, we are unsure if Francesca's fate is truly just. Like certain Greek tragedies, her tale highlights juridical pleasure in a way that fascinates and troubles the reader's own sense of right and wrong.

The uncertainty produced in this example of Francesca fuels the entire Romantic Movement, the first revolt against the law of Moses, against a patriarchal logic, and in favor of stories that have far-less-clear moral lessons, such as fairytales, Greek myths and tragedies and our romantic heritage. In drama we speak about the cut-line, the line that ends a scene and can hang in the air. With Prometheus and Francesca we have a kind of cut-scenario, an ending in a story leaving a character suspended outside of justice, an emotional abrasion left in our consciousness. In this lack of juridical closure we can feel two forms of abrasion: that of identifying empathetically with the character, and thus imagining ourselves left in that nightmarish situation, but we can also ask ourselves if their punishment is just or unjust. We cannot get Francesca out of our minds because she is still there, still floating in that space, still wrongly judged in some sense, and so she stays with us, a story lacking closure and juridical pleasure, a whirlpool of our empathy like Prometheus, deserving rescue like a character left buried underground, eternally trapped in a coffin, alive and beating on the wood.

The Social Isolation of Dantean Space

All of our focus on Dantean spaces in the last seven chapters has ignored one pointed question: does this form of narration teach us to see ourselves and others in a specifically anti-social way? People in Dante's *Divine Comedy* are isolated, trapped within themselves by themselves. Is it a coincidence that Dante's originary landscape is so marked by alienated, atomized and misanthropic characters? Is Dantean space itself implicated in this? Does it as a form somehow carry a certain sense of self that necessarily imposes certain forms of alienation? What are the effects of consuming narratives that deploy Dantean space?

In short, is Dantean space bad for us?

The question seems to break down into two parts. First, though we've largely divorced Dante's form from his thirteenth-century metaphysics and religion, this aesthetic model was originally also a *moral* model, one that welds personal history to responsibility and a code of punishment, and this punitive moral system can still be felt in our stories. And obviously his Hell and Purgatory are both spaces of punishment: both are really prisons, though Purgatory offers time off for good behavior.

Since it is an aesthetic of the self in a form of self-absorption, is it somehow fundamentally opposed to community? Could *that* help explain why *The Divine Comedy* is so alienated and socially dystopic in so many ways? Consider for example the very negative role of community in the poem's hundreds of stories: both in life and death many of its hundreds of characters successfully pull others into Hell or Purgatory, and yet there is hardly a single character in 300 cantos who actually helps another to escape his or her dark fate.

Perhaps this social distrust and alienation is deeply connected to the fact that Dantean space is different from dispassionate and dramatic space in one crucial way. A Dantean space is the emotional space of only one person: it is the singular experience of one injured traumatized heart. Thus it offers only one emotional point-of-view, and it is usually of a heart that, like Dante's, has been made distrustful, bitter, antisocial and misanthropic from the deeply injuring experience, it often drives a person deeper into emotional, social and psychological isolation, to search out some particular isolated pocket of personal Hell. But it needn't: some characters, like Ripley or Amelie, then fight to break out of their isolation to save and to re-enter the community.

SOCIAL IMPLICATIONS OF DANTEAN SPACE

It is time to evaluate the positive and negative social effects of Dantean space on readers and viewers.

On the positive side, there is simply the absolute necessity of having a mimetic representation of Dantean moments to appreciate certain kinds of human experience. This was a powerful and useful invention. Those living a Dantean moment usually do not realize the nature and shape and role it plays in their lives: an external perspective is required to inform them of this condition, and arguably it was Dante as much as any other pioneer of psychology who makes this reflection possible. Before artists began holding this mirror up to us, this entire aspect of human existence was arguably fairly invisible both to Dantean characters themselves and to others. Those of us not experiencing Dantean moments need these representations to recognize this fate in others, and also of course to simply appreciate the true range and nature of what it is to be human. Only these mimetic representations, only journeys into such points of view and experiences can help us understand this.

Once you understand the impacts of Dantean moments on people, you begin to see life differently: you understand that we are all rather like wild bonsai trees caught in a storm: the traumas of the past shape and snap the branches of our character in ways we do not entirely control but which often grant us our singular beauty and brutishness. Dante's characters suggested that our memories of harrowing events stay with us over time, and that some can stretch like taffy into our future. After Dante it was easier to understand that the injuries and buffeting winds of our life, the acidic soils we are born into, and so many other battering forces help shape us into the characters we have and the beauty and darkness we possess, that these forces shape the very ways that some of us hope and desire and live. But the particular mirror he fashioned holds that guilt, punishment and a somewhat primitive definition of responsibility binds the self together, proposing a type of agency and responsibility that to many seems quite wrongheaded and oppressive today.

In addition, the dark side of Dantean moments should give us pause here. After all, despite a few positive examples, Dantean space is by and large a portrait of trauma, of its power to create isolation through negative emotions such as consuming bitterness, obsession, guilt and fear. Dantean space is essentially the portrait of the singular experiences of singularly disaffected human beings. Most Dantean space separates and does not bridge the social realm: it shows people trapped in their own distorted pocket of the world.

Moreover, the human sciences that were invented in subsequent centuries rather convincingly argue that we are not really the architects of our own Hell. In the next chapter we will consider the Dantean space of a rape victim, but only a moment of reflection shows us that life is full of examples where others thrust Hell upon a blameless person. The blinders of this form of individualism, with its attribution of responsibility for pain and suffering, have a very long and suspect history.

These two individualistic aspects of this aesthetic of trauma help explain why the entire *Divine Comedy* is both so alienated and so socially dystopic. Consider, for example, the overwhelmingly-negative role of community in the poem's hundreds of stories. This social distrust and alienation may not bother a modern reader but our urbane response is only a symptom of the way we live now and not a sign of our comparative sophistication. Dante's portrait remains a striking contrast to—and a lightning strike against—the communally grounded sense of self portrayed in Dante's time. Dante's portrait of Florence was certainly drawn from his experience: life there was vicious and unstable for the merchant class and the upper class but there had been few aesthetic representations of life like this. His contemporary readers would almost certainly be far more shocked at the bleak psychological realism of his nether-world than we are because we are far more individualistic and alienated than his first readers were: individualism is of course not a constant in cultures.

We might also speculate that this trailblazing aesthetic of alienation might originate in Dante's own trauma of being betrayed and then banished from his native Florence. This bitter aspect of *The Divine Comedy*—its long passionate and authentic portrait of social atomization, social betrayal and individual responsibility, self-deception and akrasia—can help explain the dramatic impact of Dante's poem on his times. Dante's journey makes a long persuasive argument that the individual is alone, responsible for God's judgements and all-too-often betrayed into

Hell's pits by others. As such, Dante's alarming portrait arguably helped free the individual from the social bonds of the medieval community and thus helped unleash the Renaissance sense of self. But perhaps there is a deeper level of alienation here. Since it is a model that marries memory to responsibility, does it thereby cast guilt as the self's fundamental cement? Also it seems to put suffering memories at the center of so many of its best-drawn characters, and for this reason the empathy that it draws from us is always compassionate empathy: in this chorus of suffering there are no clear voices of powerful communal empathy.

For these reasons and others, it is crucial to understand Dantean space—so deeply connected to the deployment of Dantean characters and story arcs—because it has now spread throughout our world. As we have shown in our examples, we find vivid dimensioned instances today in all forms of storytelling, and this includes other forms of art like paintings, sculpture and video-games that make a commitment to story. In extending our investigation we argue that in whatever genre they appear, spaces animated by this Dantean machinery are not only more powerful and far more enveloping than either disPassionate or dramatic characters, spectacle and space. We argue that such spaces are also more marbled with ideas of the self and of responsibility and thus deserve attention on a sociological and anthropological level.[2]

Lastly, we should return to the point that Dante's examples all create compassionate empathy and lack communal empathy. Dante's system was created almost five centuries before Kant's invention of Deontological ethics, well before Utilitarian ethics, Marx, Weber and Said, and nearly seven centuries before our best philosophers wrought both an ethics of care and an ethics of capabilities. Considering how much of its aesthetic is guilt-based, punitive, connected to juridical pleasures and deeply anchored in subjectivity, Dantean space might not be a good aesthetic for these later ethical systems because it cannot look at the Other in the alert fashion and with the dimensionality that these later moral frames all insist on. Faced with our modern attempts to understand and reveal cruelty and oppression, Dante's ethic and aesthetic seem perhaps a bad match for our contemporary problems.

Ecstatic Space, however, seems a far better fit.

To see this very different form of empathy being married to Dantean space, we have to move forwards three hundred years to the innovations of the architect and sculptor Bernini.

NOTES

1. Arguably, we will see this again when we discuss the myth of Apollo and Daphne in the next chapter.
2. Dedicated to Michael Small, who fashions justice every day.

BIBLIOGRAPHY

Aeschylus. 1971. *Agamemnon, The Orestaia*, trans. Robert Fagles. London : Penguin.

Alighieri, Dante. 2006. *The Divine Comedy*, trans. and ed. Robin Kirkpatrick. London: Penguin.

Aristotle. 1986. *Poetics*, trans. A. Sullivan. Chapel Hill, NC: University of North Carolina Press.

D'Adamo, Amedeo. 2013. Dantean Space in the Cities of Cinema. In *Media and the City: Urbanism, Technology and Communication*, ed. Simone Tosoni, Matteo Tarantino, and Chiara Giaccardi. Newcastle upon Tyne: Cambridge Scholars Press.

Euripides. 2014. *The Bacchae*. New York: Farrar, Straus and Giroux.

Eustathius. 2010. *Eustathii Commentarii ad Homeri Iliadem*. Cambridge: Cambridge Library Collection—Classics, Cambridge University Press.

Kim, Sue. 2013. *On Anger*. Austin: University of Texas Press.

Nussbaum, Martha C. 2011. *Creating Capabilities: The Human Development Approach*. Cambridge, MA: Harvard University Press.

Pausanius. 2014. *Complete Works*. Delphi Classics, Amazon electronic editions.

Sophocles. 1984. *Oedipus Rex*. In *The Three Theban Plays*, trans. Robert Fagles. London: Penguin Classics.

CHAPTER 10

Escaping Dantean Space: On Creating Zones of Care in the Biography of St. Teresa, in Marble and Makeup and through Cinematography

BERNINI AND DANTEAN SPACE

Try for a moment to imagine you are a brilliant and prolific sculptor in Italy in the late Renaissance. You have few rivals in your time, but you are of course well-versed in Dante's poem's brilliant environments (it was then, as it remains, a core text for Italians, acquiring even the imprimatur of a religiously inspired work). With such a vernacular of fascinating figures so present in your culture yet largely missing from sculpture, you might naturally ask yourself the sculptural question: could these kinds of embodied emotional spaces and tableaux be created in the real world? Could narrative space, psychological and emotional space, tableau space and lived space all become joined, mutually embodied as they are in Dante's tale? Could such a space then be realized sculpturally in the real world in such a way as to actually and physically include the viewer within the story's emotional world?

Obviously this is speculation, and obviously the answer we are giving here is yes: we argue that the first glimpse of how such a space might work in the real world comes some three hundred years after Dante, in the next great flowering of Dantean space in the works of the architect and sculptor Gian Lorenzo Bernini. This essay suggests that Bernini took Dante's invention of Dantean space and brilliantly adapted it to create one of his most renown and unique sculptures, his *Ecstasy of St. Teresa* (1647–1652) Fig. 10.1, the work he himself

© The Author(s) 2018
A. D'Adamo, *Empathetic Space on Screen,*
https://doi.org/10.1007/978-3-319-66772-0_10

Fig. 10.1   *Ecstasy of St. Teresa* (1647–1952) by Gian Lorenzo Bernini

describes modestly as "the least bad work" he did. Bernini's singular achievement of sculptural Dantean space unifies a building, natural light and sculpture to create an envelope that brings us into the ecstatic experience of St. Teresa.

This is narrative sculpture: it was commissioned by the followers of the Spanish ecstatic Saint Teresa of Ávila, a mystic and spiritual leader who had died some 65 years earlier. She had left behind a powerful movement and a famous biography that together at the time were making the Catholic Church nervous. Her followers asked Bernini for a sculpture that would convey Teresa's importance.

And so for this piece Bernini chose to dramatize Teresa's famous revelatory transforming moment. Experiencing a period of sickness during which she had been told she had to scourge herself to purge her sin and guilt, Teresa was visited by an angel of mercy (Fig. 10.2) who set her on an entirely new emotional and spiritual path. It was a Dantean moment: she describes this moment vividly in her autobiography as the central experience of her life, the one that would determine the remainder of her efforts, energies and projects as a proselytizer for ecstatic experience.

> Beside me, on the left, appeared an angel in bodily form.... He was not tall but short, and very beautiful: and his face was so aflame that he appeared

Fig. 10.2 Teresa is visited by the angel of mercy, *Ecstasy of St. Teresa*

to be ... all on fire.... In his hands I saw a great golden spear, and at the iron tip ... a point of fire. This he plunged into my heart several times so that it penetrated to my entrails. When he pulled it out I felt that he took them with it, and left me utterly consumed by the great love of God. The pain was so severe that it made me utter several moans. The sweetness caused by this intense pain is so extreme that one cannot possibly wish it to cease, nor is one's soul content with anything but God. This is not a physical but a spiritual pain, though the body has some share in it—even a considerable share.[1]

This is the transformative Dantean moment we walk into when we enter her chapel in Rome.

We can first highlight the uniqueness of Bernini's *Ecstasy*[2]: this is a sculpture that, because it includes its own fixed light-source and takes advantage of the fact that its room is periodically filled with incense, is in some ways best described as a sculptural space or installation designed to project its subject's intense ecstasy outwards as a glow that lights the room's dusty air, including the viewer in a shared space of Teresa's experience.

Teresa's descriptions of her great moment of ecstasy is not unlike the descriptions by Dante's characters of their defining earthly moments. In both, spectacular environments are deployed that also embody emotion, creating empathetic spaces that join the inner experience of the character with the senses of the viewer and allowing him to experience her past memory with marked intensity and immediacy in the present. In addition, the effects of the moment and its intense emotions have endured to deeply shape and guide that person's future life. It is also in the Dantean mode in that her sharing is not just entertaining but serves a pedagogical purpose.

But something new is happening in this particular expression of Dantean space. While Dante's most powerful characters all empathetically share something of their *pain* with us, and so they all serve as warnings, in this sculpture (as in her biography) Teresa shares her *positive* experience of *joy* with us. In other words, most of Dante's characters are describing a space of Hell or Purgatory, and so their spaces are alienating, inhabited by bitter solitary people filled with regrets. By contrast, here the actual Teresa depicts herself as a Dantean character who has tasted Heaven and now tries with all her might to include others in her Dantean space. While Dante's most powerful figures are all about personal alienation and being cut off from friends, community and life, Teresa's is instead an inviting shared and social space: she is not warning us off but luring us in. This aspect is of course also true to her actual historical life and legacy: Teresa founded a practice and attracted a large following of ecstatics.

Moreover, there is something crucial to note about what she is luring us into. While the unknowing viewer is always shocked by its frank sensuality, this is no ordinary erotic statue because it alludes to a very developed form of ecstasy. Teresa was a well-known historical persona: many viewers would know her narrative moment here and would also know she was proselytizing and offering a communion with God and a way to Heaven. So when, unlike Dante's figures, Teresa invites us in to experience and share her joy, this is also both invitation and explanation for us to join the movement, to gain a community and to a joyful access to God's presence. And because she has an incipient ethic of care, an accepting, humble ethic in some ways closer to the cult of the catholic Mother Mary than to Dante, her figure here is in two other ways unlike Dante's world and spaces. First, this empathy is communal and embodies a kind of early ethic of care. And second, it is being offered directly to *us* and not to other narrative characters. And so though Teresa has so much in common with Dante's characters, for these reasons this work also marks a new approach to empathetic space: here we have the seeds of a *social* space that is also a space of *care* and of *innocence*.

If there was an age in the West that was as fascinated by the immersive and the embodied as ours it would probably have to be Bernini's. All Baroque artists—of whom Bernini is a central trailblazing figure— were interested in emotional embodiment: that is, in trying to include or immerse the viewer in a work of art and/or extruding the space of art somehow into life. We see this emotional embodiment realized beautifully here in the extension of Teresa's intense psychological moment out into the actual physical space, including the viewer through many specific cinematic and sensual techniques, sculptural and architectural analogues to Dante's many poetic techniques for collapsing the boundary between a character and an environment.

First, note Bernini's use of the apse of the church. Here he cinematically controls this skylight in a dark, dusky, incense-filled space so that he can elevate both the negative space in and around his tableau *and* the space of the church into an extension of Teresa's dreamy ecstasy. And note how the angel's thrust is echoed in the golden rods of physicalized light extruding down from the walls, rods which also serve to bounce, magnify and golden the light entering down from the apse. And then there is Teresa's face, tilted strategically to bounce the light from the apse towards the viewer. Bernini has controlled the angle of light to take particular advantage of the properties of marble and especially of its subsurface scattering: that is, of the way light goes deeper into marble than into most materials before it is reflected back out, giving the signature glow that made it such a popular and human material. Thanks to the controlled and fixed light source, the marble glow is most powerfully coming from Teresa's face while the unbalanced gape of her mouth and slightly torqued face grant her presence a contrasting realistic instantaneity.

These four dimensions of architecture, sculpture, light and space all work together with the emotional glow of her face and of the flesh-like folds of the drapery to overwhelm and enfold the viewer within Teresa's lifelong Dantean moment. Picture the scenes when the church fills with dust (certainly more common in Bernini's day when the roads outside were unpaved) or the hazy smoke of incense which is used almost daily here in the Catholic Mass and other rites. At such times the air itself—both the direct lighting from above and the bounced light off of her body and face—becomes a visible medium, emanations of her transporting ecstasy that rather magically envelopes the viewer. Note also the sense of suspension of time between the held arrow in the angel's hand and the ecstasy that its penetration will bring to Teresa (or from her possibly-anticipatory expression is already bringing her).

Generally speaking, architecture does not serve any specific narrative purpose and is not harnessed to any specific subjectivity. In this specific way most architecture differs from such memory objects as historical monuments and funerary art. Bernini's many innovations as an architect can obscure the genius and paradigm-breaking idea in this work: here his sculpture married both emotion and character to architecture and even the air around the viewer in a way that any contemporary production designer or video game architect would admire: a Dantean space has been created that for emotional immersion rivals the most immersive 3-D cinematic or video game experience. Bernini's architectural skills are working beyond traditional architecture: his imagination is being bent to serve a story, and more remarkably this is no ordinary monument because these skills are being orchestrated to dramatize a *specific subjectivity* in a *specific emotional state* that in her life Teresa never entirely left, and to do it in a way that immerses *us* in her state.

DAPHNE'S STORY BURIED BY CHARM

Bernini's *Apollo and Daphne* (1622–1625) is, like his *Teresa*, a work which also strives to burst beyond the normal physical and emotional space of sculpture. In another radically daring use of marble as a material, here we find it rather marvelously worked into a vortex of swirling movement and oppositions that strive to fly off and away from the tableau's solid, crudely worked base (Fig. 10.3).

The story being depicted here is simple: the god Apollo, lusting after the nymph Daphne, chases her through the woods. She abhors him and flees. Now as he catches her, she calls out in fear to her father Peneus to turn her into a tree to save her from being raped by Apollo. Her wish is granted and she turns into a laurel tree.

In Bernini's representation of this tale the boundaries of sculpture are again being questioned, creating a statue that uses the oppositions

Fig. 10.3 *Apollo and Daphne* (1622–1625), by Gian Lorenzo Bernini

of male and female to line up other aesthetic oppositions; the tableau is about both movement and stasis, about before and after, about solidity and fragility, the pursuer and the pursued, about the chase and also about how it ends in the immobility of Daphne-as-tree. Note that we can see this same artwork from all three perspectives, dispassionate, dramatic and Dantean, showing how here even the form of our aesthetic is prismatic. We can adopt the handsome graceful Apollo's erotic joy, the dramatic perspective of seeing the pair's conflict unfolding in the moment, or we can enter Daphne's own psyche, her terror and, we will argue, her own Dantean moment of being raped.

First, we can admire the tableau dispassionately, seeing it as an elegant expression of the action of the original story. There is no need to be disturbed by the sculpture when we attribute it the simple external objectives of the original tale: the beautiful Apollo chases a beautiful Daphne, but the girl escapes Apollo and becomes a tree. It is a simple illustrated parable: we appreciate the serenity of Apollo's face and the mastery of marble form, with both personae granted a gloss of elegance and innocence by the glowing, strict austerity of the marble. Viewed in a kind of emotional long-shot, the pair have a delicate tip-toe affect, a kind of ballet-pose that belies the urgency of the situation. In this view, Apollo's handsome innocence and apparent gentleness suggest that this is some young newlywed couple, with the nervous bride having first-night jitters.

A second reading, however, can be a dramatic one. Now we attribute some emotional objectives, an inner conflict, to these characters. On this reading we focus not on Apollo's serenity but on the muted terror in Daphne's face. Now we can appreciate her youth and inexperience, the powerlessness of being a young girl running from a powerful god, and by an act of imagination we might hear her beseeching cry to her father to save her. At the same time we might now be struck by her fierce resistance to Apollo, and with that empathetic act we might note and appreciate the radical emotional torsion of her body, seeing how she is headed in two directions at once as if being torn in two from the point of Apollo's grasp on her hip. Her upper body is rushing up, her hands flung wide in panic like two birds exploding into flight. But below his grasp, her lower half is sinking into the stolid static tree-trunk (Fig. 10.4). This reading is a much more sympathetic understanding of Daphne, and the sculpture is coming alive for us as a snapshot of a quickly rushing drama that has an emotional conflict at its core.

But Bernini is also offering us a third reading, an unusual one in sculpture; he offers us a Dantean perspective. On this reading, the reality and result of Apollo's rape is made clear to us. The psychological effect on Daphne of Apollo's rape is elegantly exteriorized in two contradictory ways, both demonstrating Bernini's subtle understanding of how to work with marble.

First there are the fragile, leafy extrusions from Daphne's fingertips (Fig. 10.5), miracles of delicate marble-work which empathetically dramatize her youth and vulnerability. Here we are in the moments before a rape; at this point she is herself like a young tree in flower, a quality which itself has drawn Apollo's desire. The delicate and innocent nature of Daphne is emphasized by the way the marble has been so thinly worked and the remarkable fragility, even the caution we feel in its presence. (It is hard for the viewer to come close to these wafer-thin leaves without becoming afraid they will somehow break.)

In this portion of the tableau Bernini is also taking advantage of another familiar specific quality of marble; its subsurface scattering of light. There is more translucent light being scattered among the thinly-worked leaves at the top of the sculpture than at the thick marble lower down, creating a hazier, more delicate light from Daphne's fleeing

Fig. 10.4 Daphne detail, *Apollo and Daphne*

section—from her delicately-worked fingertips and from her smoothly-worked arms—than from either Apollo's far-more solid form or from her own bark-encased torso (Fig. 10.6).

Now, descending her body, we jump forwards in the story; just where Apollo touches her, there in the bark starting at her waist, we see his hand triggering her bodily transformation from flesh into an unfeeling, immobilized wooden tree-trunk. Here the marble is not refined: its rough quality gives it more weight and less glow, making it heavy and dead.

We should consider the nature of this static and dulled aspect of Daphne's body. Perhaps Bernini here has intuited the numbed, deadened and insensate emotional and physical state that rape brings to a rape

Fig. 10.5   Leafy extrusions from Daphne's fingertips, *Apollo and Daphne*

victim. In this perspective of understanding Daphne as she "turns into wood", we gain a double-vision: two different emotional moments are captured at once, and the friction between the two moments conveys both the terrifying moment of this girl's rape and the psychological result. For Daphne this moment of violation is a Dantean moment that fixes the rest of her life in a kind of frozen, insensate state.

THE LOST ONES

Notice that we needn't read the statues in this way; in this case our reading is underdetermined and we can choose which of our perspectives to bring to the interpretation. It is a decision to grant subjectivity to Daphne, and what kind we grant her. My own sense that this possibility of multiple readings is part of Bernini's own agenda comes from the strategies he uses in other work, but for now we can propose simply that

Fig. 10.6 Bark encased torso, *Apollo and Daphne*

this tableau is open—a dispassionate, a dramatic or a Dantean perspective can be brought to bear depending on what homologies, subjectivities and form of time the viewer grants to this tableau. It is a decision about which figure and details to pay attention to: this sculpture allows us to in a sense bring close-ups and sound effects to our own reading, allows us to edit the tableau spatially and temporally in ways that open up some points of view and close down others. So far we have avoided a reader-based theory of empathy, but here all three forms of narrative perspective can be brought to bear when experiencing the same narrative work of art; there is some cognitive slippage between these forms of narration and the aesthetic work itself. In some cases, the categories of narrative perspective can be underdetermined in the aesthetic work itself, thus opening it to a multitude of readings. In a sense, this statue is prismatic.

Of course, a work can also overtly determine its own reading in this way. Consider for example a masterful re-presentation of Bernini's sculpture, a recasting of the same story and the same sculptural work by Kate Macdowell that actually informs us of the rape that lies hidden and implicit in Bernini's tableau (Figs. 10.7 and 10.8).

In her *Daphne* (2007) she purposefully closes off the first two forms of interpretation, hewing Apollo entirely out of the tableau. She then shatters Daphne into fragments and scatters only the shards of her face and arms around the base, which now is almost entirely composed of the trunk of the tree that Daphne becomes at the end of the tale. We are clearly now only in one time and one character's experience—Daphne's life after the rape, and we see that this young girl has had her body taken from her. MacDowell here restricts the import of the story to Daphne's emotional perspective, and strictly restricts that further by staging it with the cold, random chaos of a crime-scene.

Note, too, the different material that MacDowell's Daphne is made from and how that changes our grasp of her character and situation: this Daphne is constructed not of marble but of porcelain. This material not only brings in echoes of domesticity by being the stuff of both kitchenware and decorative feminized figurines: it also offers far less subsurface scattering of light than Bernini's marble and shows far more jagged breaks. Thus this Daphne appears to be both a more dead material and a more shatterable one than Bernini's: the deadness shows her innocence has been drained from her by Apollo's violation while the jagged breaks are a record of its felt violence. This too is a sculpture with Dantean space, one that takes us deeper into the emotional disaster of Daphne's rape, but it is much more over determined in its reading: it purposefully forces us to stand inside the subjectivity of the victim after the crime and nowhere else. MacDowell's choice has another effect; because this version shears Daphne's situation of most of the

Figs. 10.7 and 10.8   *Daphne* (2007) and detail, Kate MacDowell

specificity of her individual story, MacDowell's sculpture universalizes the experience to make it all about rape. And yet in this one way both sculptural versions of the story are Dantean moments realized in sculptural forms, capturing Daphne's double-vision, conveying both a specific emotional moment and an entire life that will subsequently be trapped in that intense psychological moment.

This statue now envelopes us only in a compassionate Dantean space: while the original hinted at but elided the rape, this captures the rape as Daphne's past, present and future, displaying the loss of hope and of a certain innocent innerness, capturing the act's immediate physical violence in the breakage as well as the future broken psyche of the raped girl, the sense of her own mind, now fractured and turned solid and stopped. It is not accidental, perhaps, that in the original story Daphne turns into wood; the idea of wood might itself hint at her being in fact unable to escape, since there is a 'wooden' quality that happens to the sensibility of the raped flesh: flesh becoming wood is like marble becoming concrete, capturing in material sensible form something of the deadening that befalls the raped. And though the loss of innocence implied is both problematic (in that the original tale elevates female virginity to some state of preciousness), this is offset by the phenomenological quality of the lost, the loss of boundaries and of one's erotic zones, of will and control, left only with the seeming impossibility of putting one's fractured pieces back together. The raped wants no more human contact, feels betrayed by the skin and the body, is an angry cluster of consciousness that pulls away from the rest of the self, rejecting and distrusting that part that still longs for flirting, for contact, for sex .

And now the raped, not just uncomfortable in her skin but seeing her body as an enemy, a traitorous allure, feels somehow responsible for what happened; the raped has the sense of no longer being made of smooth unified alluring marble but now of broken, dead porcelain, the touch of another married to both a sense of threat and to the loss and lack of her own radiance. The marble of Bernini's Daphne is erotic, curved, plastic, soft, yielding, and intensely alluring. But, this later Daphne might ask herself, who would now reach out to touch such a jagged broken heap, such a pile of smashed dirtied dishes? Who would possibly long for the raped, wonders the raped. And then shies from view and stays broken, hiding among some dense thicket disguised as a tree. Or simply stays in bed with the door locked. Such Dantean space is the space of isolation and the severing of all future sympathetic bonds.

This sculpture makes clear how Bernini's original works so easily as a piece of rape culture: his gives us a smiling handsome Apollo, sinuous and loving in his physical form while backgrounding the access to Daphne's emotions that the *Teresa* so clearly foregrounds. In MacDowell's version, empathy and the memory of male force is provoked by the loss of subsurface scattering of the original and by the violence being made clear, showing the broken-open quality of Daphne, trapped between the male powers of Apollo and her father. Both compassionate empathy and accusation are here in a very Dantean way, revealing by its smoothing and erasure the complex eroticization of the female innocent in the Western male imaginary being expressed in Bernini's sculpture.[3]

What then can we say so far about the political implications of forms of narrative space and perspective? Looking past this shattered Daphne and back at Bernini's masculinist, emotionally obscure version of Daphne, we see how easy it is to elide her traumatic experience even in a story where she was originally the main character. This example shows how the dispassionate perspective is available to those who are not interested in stories that engage us in emotional issues and emotional intelligence. We also see how the nature of the perspective of an aesthetic form may be controlled or left open by the artist or designers of the narrative. But while artists and storytellers can guide an audience's reading, they cannot control it: the choice of narrative perspective can also be renegotiated and redefined by the consumer of the work. It is possible to read a Dantean space as a dramatic or a dispassionate one even if that means denying or radically de-emphasizing or zooming in on some aspect of the underlying narrative itself. Empathy is a cognitive grasp of a situation but it can also be an active imaginative effort: though we have not explored the vagaries of reception here in any depth, clearly readers and viewers bring a broad range of different homologies, identification factors, experiences and empathetic training to the work. Here we have followed the insights of empathetic theorists like Joan Tronto (Tronto 2005), who urge us to bring a training in attentiveness, responsibility, competence and responsiveness to our reception of stories. But this approach takes imaginative effort and training.

The sheer spectacular loveliness of Bernini's Apollo and Daphne lets us enjoy it dispassionately as the story of some joyful chase, but by using Dantean space and foregrounding a form of alternative reading, Macdowell's artwork instructs us on how to re-read Bernini's statue and, by implication, the many barely glimpsed and marginalized stories of women in other canonical works. And that reading begins to reveal the bones of our dispassionate culture. Though we cannot explore this line here, it is easy to imagine dispassion as an ethical and emotive sphincter, a closing off of empathy and of the subjectivities of others. But as thinkers and artists such as Tronto and MacDowell argue, perhaps our dispassionate, dramatic and Dantean frames are better understood as deeply internalized forms of reception, adopted in order to control what kinds of empathy and ethics can affect us and where we look in our own swift flight through our own forests.

THE TACTICS OF INNOCENCE EXAMINED

It is important to notice the category of innocence that we have introduced: while an overt quality of both Apollo and Daphne, innocence is referenced in Teresa through her connection to the Mother Mary cult, a body of representations and tropes where the guilt and the bitterness of Dante's world, sensibility and ethics have been carefully shunted aside. Bernini's Teresa carries echoes of the catholic Immaculate Conception, paralleling her with the innocence, purity and caring tradition of the Mother Mary figure, helping to elevate all three concepts as feminized ethical categories as well as visual and performative tropes.

One form of history that is needed is a history of innocence, a history that is not so innocent itself. While we cannot offer that here, we can at least recognize some iconic visual tropes of innocence that cross over into the tropes of purity, a category used to characterize and cripple women in particular by tying them to childhood.

Think of the innocent women in Renaissance art whose skin is unblemished, whose faces are unembittered, whose bodies are so ignorant of experience that they are free of guilt. While this is not an art-historical account, it seems clear that the continued visual pairing of Mary and her baby Jesus has become an important signifier of innocence, and often this visual unity and an increased feeling of empathy is achieved in this standardized tableau because the glowing innocent skin of baby Jesus is seen in Mary's face as well (Fig. 10.9), creating a bond of radiant, caring emotional union. Of course, these tropes of innocence and empathy are not limited to the mother–child tableau: there seem to be many examples from Bellini and others where the layer of baby-fat existing in babies, children and young teens when grafted onto an adult is one trope of signifying innocence in that adult.[4]

Fig. 10.9 *The Madonna of the Book* (1483), Sandro Botticelli

The distinct reason for this include the lack of lines on a child's face and the nature of subsurface scattering through layers of fat below the skin. A very well-understood fact in modern 3-D graphic rendering, the phenomenon is increased when the face is struck by soft bounced daylight and is undercut by harsh direct light. This reflected glow of bathed and bathing light is why Bernini's smoothed marbled faces convey innocence and inner light. It is also why Audrey Tatou with

Fig. 10.10   Amelie (2001)

make-up emphasizing her similarly-luminous face uncreased by lines of experience, so well-characterizes an Amelie (Fig. 10.10) who feels simultaneously innocent and playfully mischievous: hers is the unseamed face of a child innocent.

This phenomenon is also at work in the terrifying scene in *La Vie en Rose* explored in Chap. 7 where death takes Piaf's lover from her (Fig. 10.11): moving from large bounced light sources to harsher smaller direct light, her face is shown with less and less subsurface light scattering and more and more creases as the scene unfolds. And so losing its rounded relaxed curves, its bounced light and glow of subsurface scattering, and becoming increasingly creased by muscular tension as her revelation of her lover's death becomes inescapable, Piaf's face subtly grows old and stricken before our eyes.

Think here too of other famous innocent female faces: of Isabelle Adjani's face, so good at showing this purity and innocence in the lighting of Néstor Almendros in *The Story of Adele H* (1975). Here the cinematographer's use of soft bounced sunlight (like the light in St. Teresa's chapel) caresses Adjani's own face's uncreased under-layer of baby fat, granting it a glow of subspace scattering that casts her as an innocent, making our empathy flow towards her (Fig. 10.12).

Something like this phenomenon of subsurface light scattering exists not just in paintings from Giotto to Bellini: marble too has played a role in visualizing innocence because it exhibits subsurface light scattering so well while also being workable into an unblemished, evenly finished,

Fig. 10.11 *La Vie en rose (2007)*

Fig. 10.12 Adjani's innocence. *The Story of Adele H* (1975)

creamy surface. And this too brings other associations of purity: the abstract cleanliness of well-worked marble and an alienated erasure of the marks and creases and signs of life then help characterize the pure, innocent woman who has one foot in childhood, exhibiting the ignorance of the world of an infant, and the other in Heaven.

But perhaps innocence holds other potential. In our next chapter we suggest artists have begun using this tradition of innocence to create ecstatic spaces full of active social potential.[5] This is doubtlessly a very positive development, yet their caring innocent protagonists are also all female. When will we see male protagonists who are giving, who are innocent and who create spaces of care and social emotion?

NOTES

1. Chapter XXIX: Part 17, *The Autobiography of Saint Teresa*.
2. Steven F. Ostrow, "Bernini's Voice: From Chantelou's Journal to the *Vite*", in *Bernini's Biographies: Critical Essays*, ed. Maarten Delbeke, Evonne Levy, and Steven F. Ostrow.
3. MacDowell also highlights a collectively selective empathy: while war has been deeply explored in this book and in the culture, today in both the developed and the underdeveloped world we are all far more likely to know victims of rape and sexual assault than victims of war, yet aside from a handful of brilliant examples like this one, we wait for a Dantean treatment of rape in culture that comes anywhere near the expressiveness and emotional violence of an *Apocalypse Now*.
4. Arguably this association is a foundation of so much make-up craft in contemporary Western life and cinema, even as its elevation of white alabaster skin hides a racialized colonial history in plain sight.
5. Dedicated to Anne Christian.

BIBLIOGRAPHY

Alighieri, Dante. 2006. *The Divine Comedy*, trans. and ed. Robin Kirkpatrick. London: Penguin.

Aristotle. 1986. *Poetics*, trans. A. Sullivan. Chapel Hill, NC: University of North Carolina Press.

D'Adamo, Amedeo. 2013. Dantean Space in the Cities of Cinema. In *Media and the City: Urbanism, Technology and Communication*, ed. Simone Tosoni, Matteo Tarantino, and Chiara Giaccardi. Newcastle-on-Tyne: Cambridge Scholars Press.

Gilligan, Carol. 1982. *In a Different Voice: Psychological Theory and Women's Development*. Cambridge, MA: Harvard University Press.

Kim, Sue. 2013. *On Anger*. Austin: University of Texas Press.

St. Teresa of Avila. 2000. *The Autobiograpy of St. Teresa D'Avila*. Dover Publications.

Tronto, Joan C. 2005. An ethic of care. In *Feminist Theory: A Philosophical Anthology*, ed. Ann E. Cudd, and Robin O. Andreasen. Oxford, UK and Malden, MA: Blackwell.

CHAPTER 11

How To Create Ecstatic Space: Zones of Care in the Films *The Secret Garden* and *Amelie*, in the Video Game *Wrath of the White Witch*, and Beyond

In the past few chapters we have begun to broaden out from an analysis of our three aesthetic forms to start considering the viewer's own empathetic prejudices and stances as well as actual history and specific place of setting. Even in minor forays such as our discussions of *The Third Man* (Chap. 5) and *Hiroshima Mon Amour* (Chap. 6) revealed a triangle of interaction of which the three points are the stories, the receivers of stories, and the real world. We have also suggested in a number of places that our three aesthetic forms might also be emotive stances towards the world, as frames of reception embedded in different political, social and ethical. We suggested that these forms also apply to political communication, existing in recruitment videos for military adventurism, and we have suggested that Kilgore in *Apocalypse Now* has some character parallels with the addicts of FPS (first person shooter) video-games. And in Chaps. 9 and 10 we have also suggested there are possibly some detrimental social and political aspects to Dantean space.

But so far suggesting is all we have done: we have not made a real investigation into just how empathetically sphinctered such forms are, nor have we asked ourselves if these should be understood as Geertzian symbolic systems holding together some social and political communities[1] and constructing in/out groups. Nor have we asked ourselves how we might use these insights, whether there are innovative mixtures or

© The Author(s) 2018
A. D'Adamo, *Empathetic Space on Screen*,
https://doi.org/10.1007/978-3-319-66772-0_11

alternatives to these forms in our culture that we might further exploit in order to offer greater social possibilities and new forms of community. That is our goal now: in this chapter we build upon the insights of the *St. Teresa* statue by Bernini as we look for ways to go beyond these limited cultures. Hopefully, however utopian this might sound, as artists and theorists we can now look beyond the social alienations of Dantean characters to find a doorway for escaping the horizon of our own cultural Dantean space.

HEAVEN: CAN ACTIVE CHARACTERS HAVE HEAVENLY ARCS?

In direct contrast to the negative uses and implications of Dantean space discussed in the last six chapters (which focused in turn on guilt, grief, bitterness, pain, alienation and responsibility), we now focus instead on a specific and *positive*, highly social version of narrative space that was invented after Dante by artists and writers and that was designed specifically to battle alienation and create new social cohesion and connection. The films we examine here are *Amelie* and *The Secret Garden* (1911, 1949, 1993, all adapted for film from the 1911 novel by Francis Hodges Burnett). Unlike the many alienated Dantean spaces we have so far considered, which were all hellish or purgatorial, often alienating and all singular expressions of a character, these films promise a very different welcoming heavenly space: in these narratives a protagonist drags others against their will into a new, shared, somewhat magical, enchanted and enchanting space where each character's specific social conflicts, traumas, alienation and loneliness are all resolved. We will call this form of narrative space *Ecstatic space.*

This *ecstatic* space is a phantasmagoric projection of a protagonist's own evolved positive inner space and caring emotions. While the earliest example we have been able to identify is Bernini's statue of St. Teresa, discussed in depth in Chap. 10, we see this welcoming form of space in many modern examples. Consider the end of *Pleasantville*, or the famous barn-raising scene in the film *Witness* (1985).[2] These narratives have a unique ability to enfold others into spaces where they can connect with the protagonist and with each other on a positive emotional and social level.

We propose that this newer form of story space offers fascinating possibilities for the future because it strengthens one's social identity and bonds while simultaneously modeling an expansion of the social in a way that still preserves individual characters. We note that this category is also highly gendered: by contrast to dispassionate characters which skewed male, ecstatic characters are usually women or small children, and in opposition to the practical tasks of invulnerable dispassionate characters, the vulnerability of ecstatic characters drives them to pursue the objectives of creating a space of healing and of constructing a community.

After detailing these examples, this essay connects three investigations. The first asks why ecstatic characters tend to be innocents, and what is the nature of innocence being invoked in all of these stories? How is it like ignorance, how is it about potentiality, how is it about hope, and why does it entangle us empathetically with characters? Secondly, why do we need innocent characters to repair rifts in the social fabric? This relates to the question of the unities among the enchanting atmospheres of Teresa's ecstatic memories, Amelie's Paris, Burnett's secret garden, *Witness's* barn-raising and the video-game *The Wrath of the White Witch.* Here we point out that these narratives all combine the political and social power of re-enchantment that has been detailed by Jane Bennett and others (Bennett 2001; Redmond and Cinque et al. 2015) with the feminist ethics of care identified by Gilligan and explored in some depth by Tronto (Gilligan 1982; Tronto 2005). Lastly, in view of how this form of enchanting space is almost always a projection of an adult female character, we might ask why this form of projected innocence is associated with both male and female children and yet is far more female-gendered with older protagonists?

In the last chapter we briefly detailed the specific codification of cues of these ecstatic spaces in stories, pointing out how the air and atmosphere of innocence has become codified in a certain soft bounced-light lighting style and in the craft-treatment of surfaces, objects and spaces. We have explained how deep subsurface light scattering—the kind that happens with marble and with faces that contain baby-fat—is also usually deployed to convey innocence, while surfaces that have low subsurface scattering—such as concrete and old skin—convey a Bachelardian phantasmagoria of deadness and weight.[3] We pointed out that some of the signifiers here go back to the Western tradition's codification of innocence in the Renaissance, but there are other sources as well. All of these tropes also define the charmed and charming aesthetics of our examples of innocence and ecstatic space in this chapter.

Innocence Reconsidered

Guilt, bitterness and innocence are different cognitive stances towards the world, distinct forms of openness that determines an approach and a way of seeing relationships, morality and possibility. They are forms of discernment, of ourselves and of the Other, leading to marked tendencies of what to expect and what to give in relationships. In these ways they are in a sense different character gyroscopes.

While our culture has many in-depth portraits of guilt and bitterness, we are a long way from understanding innocence. Perhaps at the moment, thanks to a culture that has historically deeply miscast innocence as purity, childishness, or plain old stupidity, we do not see innocence yet for what it is. As a result we now have no ways, means or even reasons to protect or cultivate it. Perhaps that has to change: perhaps these narratives suggest why and how it can be cultured in ourselves and in our social relations. We know instinctually that you must protect innocence when you see it in a child, but perhaps you also have to protect your own innocence. Perhaps this is where the urge to culture the self and the need to create a caring culture both meet.

Furthermore, the innocent is a viral figure of empathy in another way. In the last chapter we spoke of how an empathetic reading sometimes demands attentiveness, responsibility, competence and responsiveness, the training that Joan Tronto (2005) argues lies at the heart of an ethics of care. Of course, these are the very qualities we all instinctually bring when dealing with the innocent. We cannot casually lie, dismiss or be cruel to the innocent. Innocence provokes close reading and our careful and best behavior, and rewarding innocence with care brings us delight in ways that other social relations do not.

Let us look now at the cognitive and character implications of innocence. Unlike guilt and bitterness which seem so knowing and so implicated in ideas of maturity and dramatic arrival, innocence is often conflated with beginnings, with incompleteness, with ignorance and with lack of experience. While guilt creates a continual uncomfortable preoccupation and an urge to hide, and while bitterness is a defensive, sharply-focused form of disparaging attention, innocence is an open attentiveness that while it evaluates does not (yet) judge or distrust. It is also often an active state of character in a story's first act, a decaying state soon to be transformed, swept aside and broken by the conclusion of informative events: think not just of Daphne but for example of *Forbidden Games* (1952), *Los Olvidados* (1952), *Landscapes In The Mist* (1988), *The Official Story* or *Forrest Gump*. Alternatively, innocence is often passively deployed in narrative as it is in *The Pursuit of Happyness* as a form of defenselessness and dreaming. Here the innocent becomes the responsibility of the non-innocent: here the more knowing and responsible protagonist must protect and maintain the innocence of some secondary character, some child in his bubble.

But there are other innocents abroad in the world.

The Beauty of Being Frozen by Trauma: Heavenly Cities and Spaces in Burnett's *The Secret Garden* and Other Narratives

An ecstatic space lies at the center of the classic childrens' novel *The Secret Garden* by Frances Hodgson Burnett. The story of a little girl named Mary, it begins with a powerfully traumatic Dantean moment; when Mary is ten, both of her parents are killed in a cholera outbreak at their estate in India. She is abandoned on the empty plantation and nearly starves to death.

The small, undernourished, penniless, ugly and embittered girl is then sent to her neglectful uncle's estate in England. On the estate she discovers her uncle's son Colin, who is an equally neglected and embittered child whose mother died at his birth and who is thus rejected by his father.

She then discovers a secret garden, a construction of Colin's mother. The garden is now hidden; it was walled up years ago by Colin's still-grieving father. Thanks to the generous care of a working-class family that lives on the estate, Mary slowly comes out of her shell of bitterness and hatred. Mary's finding of the key to the garden, her healing there in the garden, and her project to heal the crippled Colin make for a purgatorial drama that takes up half the novel and marks her own transformation into a loving, happy, caring child. Interestingly, though, her dramatic arc ends before her entire story does. Her story's final act is a heavenly tale of her machinations to heal others, a strategy that leads to the regeneration not only of the garden, and not only of Colin and then of his father, but the healing even cuts across British class lines between bitter lords and servants and then even includes other species. It becomes a true utopia, a microcosm of heavenly conflict-resolution on earth.

It is important to see how differently this sentimental space works from the ones considered so far. Mary does not need to emotionally 'work through' the garden, the way that for example Ripley must face her monsters and Brody must enter his bunker. Mary does not need to face her fears or guilt in this space. Instead the garden is itself what is to be found, what she must herself cultivate and what should then be shared. It is what is given first to Mary so she can heal and regain her generosity and hope, and then it is what she can give to Colin and then give to his father. The garden, embodying her own innocence and lost mother's love, is opened by her to include this new family. Through her new-found innocence and hope, Mary expands her Dantean space of healing and love to include others.

As we have seen repeatedly, a Dantean character is often facing a trauma from childhood, and the same is true of many innocents. For example, consider the peculiarly–charming and enchanting world of *Amelie*: what underlies this film's nostalgic, innocent and enchanting air, so similar in some ways to *The Secret Garden*? The parallels are obvious: both *The Secret Garden*'s 8-year-old girl protagonist and the 8-year-old Amelie in the film's first acts share a sudden traumatic loss and abandonment by parents. As a result both characters are in a sense frozen at this age unless they can work through their traumas by building a space that represents the dead mother. And both succeed, Amelie by transforming Paris into a childlike zone of love and playfulness, a Dantean space that returns her father's love to her and produces her new lover. Similarly, Mary, the bitter little heroine of *The Secret Garden*, achieves this by searching for, then finding and then sharing the garden, this Dantean space which then grants her a new substitute loving mother, father and family. In the end Mary's Colin's and his father's bitterness has been melted, replaced with a contagious social circle of openness, trust and care.

Both examples suggest to us yet again that innocence is a crucial aesthetic category. Quite different from ignorance and immaturity, and somehow avoiding any of the older tropes of purity and timidity that earlier innocent women too often embodied, our two characters embody a newer form of *generative* innocence.[4] In these two narratives it is an active attribute, a form not just of hope but of potentiality, a freedom from cares that allows a character to be active in certain ways. This crucially allows them to craft, enact and bring into being the remarkable positive social agendas and social spaces of *Amelie* and *The Secret Garden*: it is central to their ability to create an empathetic space of community. And unlike our earlier spaces of empathetic compassion, these two rather unique examples offer Dantean spaces that more than one person can occupy at a time. Like Bernini's ecstatic version of St. Teresa, they are communally empathetic, open to be shared experiences, emblems of a body of empathetic social practices that should be adopted, and like all of our examples their actions and spatial projections are intended to be enzymatic, to be spread, to grow into a larger and more inclusive world.

And so it seems that certain kinds of Dantean space can perhaps have a positive social affect, helping us overcome alienation. Could we ever somehow harness the positive side of this spatialized empathetic machinery in our ethics, politics and social efforts? Could such narrative spaces help us overcome our own worst angels?

Innocence and Communal Empathetic Space in Video-Games

By now it is clear that ecstatic spaces can take place in literature, plays, movies and television, or really in any form of narrative that features characters in places. And as of 2013, ecstatic space has at last come to the world of video-games.

This marks a break. For the most part, one-dimensional characters anchor most first-person shooter video-games: these are dispassionate characters driven by external objectives like "kill all the monsters" with little of the real internal emotional conflict that is needed to build empathetic spaces. As we have noted, this is of course a mas-culinized form of character with a long history in the West. And yet Oliver, the protagonist of the 2013 video-game *Wrath of the White Witch*, may illustrate the most effective use yet of empathetic space in a video-game.

Oliver's story will sound a bit familiar by now. In the opening narrative, his mother is killed in a car accident that is partly his fault, and this trauma leaves him grief-stricken. But when his tears magically transform his doll into Drippy, the king of the fairies, Oliver is given a magical purgatorial offer. If he saves Drippy's world from its problems of depression, lack of enthusiasm and alienation then he may be able to bring his mom back to life.

Not surprisingly, Drippy's world turns out to be a wonderfully crafted Dantean space imbued with the longings he has for his dead mother. Moreover, Oliver's route through the world is all about doing good for the creatures he finds: he has to, for example, cheer up an animal king who is depressed, to not only make friends but to bring friends together. The world is all about creating community and our own communal empathy is triggered as Oliver advances through its levels and through his own grief. This video-game has gained the highest ranking by video-game critics, but what is more interesting is the unusual emotional effect it has had on its reviewers; many speak of how it is the first video-game to actually make them cry. But the machinery seems familiar to us: once again Dantean space is grafted onto a highly empathetic innocent. Having lost a parent, and feeling responsible for her death, he seeks purgatorial actions and to recreate the loving caring space of her arms. Elements of Bruce Wayne, of Amelie, of Mary and others are all here.

Escaping Dantean Space

We conclude by considering why and how all of these examples show a protagonist bringing other characters into an enchanting social space that is in fact a new form of social commons where they can bond in new, positive and social ways. We ask if and how stories with ecstatic space might engender actual ecstatic spaces in the world. Can actual places become productively enchanted? In other words, can they be granted a specific narrative meaning like the spaces we find in these stories? Can an ethics of care be spatialized via a certain kind of narrative architecture? Does *Amelie's* Paris somehow reflect or channel the situationist energies and dreams of the Paris Spring of 1968?

These may seem like impossibly utopian questions, perhaps even incoherent ones, until we consider a few facts. Today, even sixteen years after its release, *Amelie* still drives people to haunt Montmartre in the hope of re-experiencing the film. This and other examples from cinema tourism show directly how actual places can become entangled with and be enchanted by narratives that feature powerful Dantean spaces. When we then consider the emotions of *Amelie's* ecstatic spaces we remember how Amelie's Paris is enchanting and powerful precisely because it promises to its characters (and to the viewer) new relationships, new forms of human empathy and of human potential and a new richness of social capital.

What, then, are the limits of these forms of narrative enchantment in the actual world? Can actual spaces become ecstatic spaces? Can they then produce social bonds? Can a social commons become a shared secret garden? Is the mass ecstatic movement inspired by St. Teresa's diaries worth a closer look today? Might such forms of narrative architecture actually help transform our social and political world?

Examples of Innocence in Europe and American Stories

Let us step back and try to see the outlines of our complex tradition of the innocent.

The innocent has been empowered in our culture since at least the New Testament, which features a rather prismatic Jesus who is an innocent in at least three different senses. First, we have the open-hearted innocent figure who has no boundary to his empathy: this version returns in later figures like St. Francis of Assisi who felt even the pain of small animals. However, Jesus's actions upending the money-lenders' tables embodies a second and entirely different kind of innocent figure; the revolutionary who can topple a corrupt culture. This tradition descends through the history of innocent warriors like Joan of Arc.

But Jesus also embodies a third kind of innocent, one we might call the remarkably-clear-eyed innocent; in the modern period this figure returns in the fable "The Emperor's New Clothes" fashioned by Hans Christian Anderson in 1837. When the boy in the fable cries out that the Emperor has no clothes, his cry spreads like wildfire across the entire crowd. Not understanding the power relationships that keep everyone else from pointing out that the emperor is naked, the innocent's observation indicts the tailors, the courtiers who promoted this blinkered lie, the cowardly adults who have acquiesced in it, the arrogant foolish emperor, and essentially the very idea of rulers. It is both a celebration of the innocent as a truth-teller and as the revealer of a potent anti-hegemonic, anti-monarchial truth that Anderson himself tried to walk back in later fables (Zipes 2005).

A mix of these kinds of innocents haunt the pages of nineteenth century European literature.

This innocent is usually a very active and inspiring figure, capable of selfless acts and comporting himself without judging others. He is often able thus to walk safely among very angry, vicious and torn human beings, doing small favors for them that they do not expect. And, being an unthreatening figure, he can inspire a form of sympathy and confession in twisted, lonely people. He can safely enter the dens of murderers where no-one else would survive, even as we empathetically fear the delicate glass of his innocence will be shattered by the horrors and meanness of such fallen places. Sometimes the innocent's very childlike comportment can remind a wizened, worldly character of an earlier time, a childlike moment when they weren't as tortured by anxieties and guilt as they now are, and this can give them moments of respite, reflection and sometimes even transporting them back to long-forgotten memories of an innocent time that they sorely need to recall, triggering a re-evaluation of their choices in life.

All of these facets make innocents great main characters for exploring fallen worlds, as we see with the main character of many Dickens' novels such as *David Copperfield*, *Great Expectations* and *Oliver Twist*, but they also serve Fyodor Dostoevski, that adult version of Dickens, in the stories of Alyosha in *The Brothers Karamazov* and Prince Myshkin of

The Idiot, the main characters in two of his most celebrated novels. In all of these examples, our innocent character is in some real sense pure and unspoiled by the crimes of the world, which means that all of our characters have in some sense had a highly-protected childhood before being tossed into their respective worlds.

Yet Dostoevski's open-hearted innocents are also often singularly clear-eyed, possessed of sight and insights that the non-innocent lack. Alyosha can see people's deeper wounds and fears while Prince Myshkin can see the traumas of some characters and thus love or care about them in ways that no-one else can.[5]

We lack such figures in the American tradition, where most of our famous 'innocents' are not only basically idiots in the dumb-as-a-post sense but who also lack any social ethic. Take, for example, the genial stupidity of Forrest Gump: his 'common-sense' conservative values, acts of bravery and good business sense by contrast reflect quite a shallow version of the social. Here is a character thrust by the screenwriter into highly charged historical situations like the Vietnam War, the anti-war movement, the treatment of veterans and the spread of drugs and AIDS, among which Gump deploys a bag of simple moralizations that guide him to right actions that are intended to throw everyone else into moral relief as selfish. If Gump is an innocent it is an innocence of the Reagan age, a stripped-down version of Heartland values that borders comically on the plain old dumb: even the dumb can succeed in America if they just stay clear of the embitterments of actual history, project a sunny disposition, stop complaining and show real grit. Another common illusion of innocence is found in Chauncey Gardner, the mentally diaphanous hero of *Being There* (1979), but this character is by contrast a pure cypher, a blankness onto which other project their hopes. These are ignorant, morally infantalized characters and not innocents in our sense.

This flattened sense of innocence in American storytelling goes back some way. The ignorant innocent is there in Faulkner's *As I Lay Dying* and the cynical innocent is there in Gatsby. The realistic portrait of the destruction of innocents extends to at least Henry James, from his frail Daisy (*What Daisy Knew*) to his Isabel Archer in *The Portrait of a Lady*. These characters lose their happy innocence to discover how soul-killing the world can actually be. No-one would ever strive to be one of them. Even Twain's Huck Finn shows a very fitful grasp of the innocent. Finn shows a brilliant coming-of-age arc halfway through the first half of the novel, exhibiting great moral courage and sense when he apologizes to

Jim on the raft and maturing as he witnesses the brutal feud between the Grangerfords and the Shepherdsons, but all this story with its marvelous sense of character development is then thrown away as Huck soon collapses back into an inexperienced boy amusingly played as a fool by a wiser world, then shifts inexplicably back into a racist cruel boy, torturing Jim for no reason. Huck Finn's nonsensical character-arc resembles the unchanging innocent clown of Cervantes more than a modern character: not surprisingly, both novels have an episodic plot composed of brilliant clown-driven subplots.

None of these figures resembles the European tradition of the ecstatic innocent, which features a host of world-changing figures who bring salvation by presenting a radical new vision of how to comport yourself. Arguably descended from the preternaturally wise child Jesus, from the cult of Mary, and from later instantiations such as St. Francis, these open innocents change ordinary people who feel trapped in a life, showing them there is always another way to be. The sense of confederateship, of friendship and companionability, of joy and happiness that St. Teresa, Alyosha, Prince Myshkin and Amelie bring to socially-isolated figures is only part of it: the innocent also brings a sense of potential, a sense of different futures, of escape from being hated and judged as well as a release from being hateful and judgmental. The innocent brings and provokes care, returns the bitter and the guilty to a childlike time before life brought its withering moments. This is the socially infectious nature of such characters. Found across the tradition from Manzoni to *Game of Thrones*, they are often touchstone characters that transform the arcs of those they meet.

Game of Thrones begins as an innocent-killing, empathy-eating machine. Like *House Of Cards*, its Macchiavellian world initially tossed every empathetic character who cared about social bonds or offered social trust into a meatgrinder. Here innocence is a fatal ignorance. But in later seasons an axis of innocents rises. Among its wide-eyed leaders we might count Samwell Tarly, Jon Snow and the show's Joan-of-Arc Daenarys Targaryen. All three exhibit a plastic intelligence, an ethics of care, a reservoir of trust and other attributes of the knowing innocent that make them empathetic leaders in this bitter, guilt-laced world of precarity and cynicism. However, the show never uses Dantean space, tending instead to alternate between dramatic space and pure genre spectacle: committed to a naturalism punctuated by the fantastic, it rarely enters the emotional POV of any of its many characters, and so this world can never look ecstatically-innocent in the European sense.

And this hints at the division between the American innocent and the ecstatic innocent. American innocents cannot really project a Dantean space because there is a dearth of sensibility in them. Lacking a Dantean moment in childhood, they just seem simply inexperienced. Unlike Amelie, there is no sense of being frozen in a brighter social horizon: there is only a hangover of childhood, a lack of maturity, which is a radically different problem of character from that faced by the European innocent. The American innocent is simply lagging behind the wizened, bitter characters who surround him, but as the race continues he will surely catch up. By contrast, the ecstatic innocent stops the race. She is grounded in certain specific experiences and wisdoms and thus possesses the power to bend the world back towards herself.

Why do Americans have no real tradition of ecstatic innocents even if both traditions show great allegiance to the figure and model of Jesus, the ur-innocent? We can credit the difference to many causes but there is a distinct division in the Catholic and the Protestant traditions of innocents, perhaps in part because as we've noted the Catholic tradition also cultified the Mother Mary, another ur-innocent who was however more purely associated with healing, feeding, mercy and other specifically-caring actions and relationships. But aside from shearing away this proto-care-ethic, there are other related impulses in the protestant-leaning US culture such as its related commitment to individualism and a corresponding fear of the social, combined with an aesthetic impulse towards naturalism and an associated fear of sentimentalism. American culture has been awash in wars of empathy for generations. Though we saw glimpses of this quasi-Rousseauesque character in some of our ecstatic religious communities like the Shakers and the Oneida community, it is not until the counterculture appeared that dreams of a specifically *generative* innocence would reappear. Now innocence is raised again as a value, an aspect of character to be cultivated and protected, and once again innocents are seen as socially-positive agents of a socially infectious utopia.

We might argue that the stories of ecstatic innocents are marked by another commonality that separates them from the American literary tradition: a difference over clear oppositions. The stories of Dostoevski are marked by clear oppositions between good and bad and serve a pedagogical function. In some ways he seems very opposed to the morally-muddy aesthetic of modernism, which feels more observational and 'real' precisely because its worlds do not feature clear moral dichotomies. This contrast them with the nineteenth-century novels as it distinguishes them from the simple oppositions of the children story genre, which Dickens never really escapes and where audience members are trained to identify with the inexperienced and the powerless as they gain power over their worlds. The innocent serves very different roles if he faces a world with a moral compass than if he is tossed into an amoral universe.

OUR EMPATHETIC ARGUMENT

And so our account of Dantean space ends by showing that this has not simply been a series of investigations about narrative architecture in film and television: instead, these interrogations actually lead us into many rich questions about the aesthetic construction of character and of the social. But looking back now, perhaps we might identify an overall argument with certain clear social and political imperatives. That overall argument can be summarized from start to finish as follows:

1. **The phenomenon**: In a Dantean space a character is surrounded by a physical-yet-metaphorical manifestation of the character's actions and life. Here the character is both within a space and simultaneously *within her- or himself* because the space itself is **a physicalized cage of the character's traumas, passions and conflicts.**

2. **Its construction**: This space is usually informed by a moment in the character's past which involves a deep trauma. Because the character's psyche is somewhat trapped or frozen psychologically in that moment of trauma, it inflects later dramatic experiences in life creating a double-lensed sense of narrative space. Thus in such spaces spectacle embodies the axis of the story present with the character's charged personal history, creating a storied sublime marbled with the deepest anxieties, hopes and fears of the character's psyche.

3. **History**: Though examples of Dantean space can be found across our trans-media experience, in novels, films, television, documentary, video-games and even sculptural tableaus, this aesthetic was codified by Dante in his *Inferno* through the memorable examples of Ugolino, Capaneus, Francesca and others.

4. **Its uses**: Such physical and sensupus expressions of the character's emotions serve as highly-powerful engines of the **empathetic machinery** of the plot. Now location, production design and other aspects of narrative place all communicate the character's immediate emotional perspective to the viewer. This has many uses in film and television because it provides:

(a) *Heightened empathy*: Because such spaces utilize spectacle to embody character, thus offering a powerful sublime marbled with the deepest anxieties of the character's psyche, this creates a mirrored emotional subjectivity where even the space of a scene helps bond viewers to protagonists. Because Dantean spaces entangle us sensuously with the fears and hopes of the character in a far more effective and empathetic way than other techniques—such as typical exposition or flashback—they suture us into the emotional point of view of the character in an immediate, non-verbal and uniquely-powerful way, making us cry and hope and fear and dream in unison with the protagonist. And because these films have this unique power to inscribe fear, hope and desire, they can often communicate and inscribe deep *social* hopes, fears and anxieties, which makes such sites of specific interest to researchers interested in the social implications of narrative.

(b) *Rising tension in story construction*: When they are not present throughout a narrative (as they are in *Amelie* and *Batman*) active Dantean spaces are usually **found in the ultimate or penultimate scenes** of the drama (*Aliens, Homeland*) As such cathartic scenes, they are often the conclusion of the rising action of a plot and thus the moment of the clearest expression of the story's antagonisms as well as the moment of greatest empathetic emotion in the viewers, the space of emotional catharsis.

(c) *Entanglement with actual places*: Because this account shows how location and place can become a powerful glue by which viewers are sutured to a protagonist, it also helps explain how and why viewers can become so deeply tied to a specific location or city by narratives that present them as Dantean spaces. For example, this explains the phenomena of *Amelie* and *The Third Man*, two films that for decades now have triggered continuous and strong waves of cinema tourism, driving large numbers of fans to their respective locations with the hope of repeating the intense experiences of those films.

5. **Social implications**: This account raises a number of further questions, not least of which is the implications of this model for the ideas of the personal and the social self and of the construction of the public commons:

(a) *Negative*: On the one hand, this account raises the question: Is Dantean space bad for us? As we experience narratives with Dantean space, a form of machinery with a specific historical and cultural pedigree in the Western tradition, are we also being inscribed with a particular form of self-interpretation, one with its own history of alienation and social atomization? Are such negative forces, so present in the roots of Dantean space itself, also an effect of this form of aesthetic participation? And does this model of narration carry forwards certain Western constructions of the self into other narrative traditions? Does Dantean space 'colonize' the self of the foreign Other who experiences it?

(b) *Positive*: On the other hand, are there developments within the tradition of Dantean space that offer social theorists and filmmakers a unique political and social tool? The examples of *The Secret Garden* and *Amelie* feature positive, socially–welcoming, enchanting Dantean spaces that in fact overcome social atomization and alienation. They do so by arguing for a new and gendered conception of innocence, an innocence of re-enchantment that is not about ignorance but about human potential and an ethics of care, an innocence that can be spatialized and imbue places and therefore entered into and socially shared. Can such hopeful, positive, welcoming spaces play a role in creating a new and empathetic form of the social commons, so under attack today in our globalized economy? Could ecstatic spaces be good for us?

Empathy Reconsidered

Threaded through this overall argument, we suggested that the history of our dramatic forms (and the empathies they offer) is twinned both with the construction of the Western self and with the history of our morality. This last history is perhaps easier to untwist than the more subtle question of the self, a construction that if it even exists is made of the material of the imagination, a material admittedly as delicate and hard to perceive as the wings of mayflies. Largely avoiding that active debate,[6] for now we have focussed on excavating the machinery of empathy, since this can serve as a mirror not only of the Self and what it sees in others but also a mirror of what it wants the Other to be in its quietest and most buried dreams. This is socially and politically important because all empathetic machinery is designed to get us to draw analogies between others and ourselves. In fact, our moral traditions, which claim to be metaphysical revolutions of self-evident validity, are arguably to some degree based on the creation of specific narrative innovations for triggering and channeling empathy towards some topics, histories, identities and social groups and away from others. Arguably, the dominance of guilt or bitterness or innocence, and the chain of artistic tropes that each brings in its train, is also a signifier of deeper shifts in our culture, of deep shifts in social bonding or of the severing of bonds, just as the tropes of Dantean space, of alienated space or of ecstatic space themselves contain deep, emotionally-convincing empathetic propaganda about the need for individualism or for communal bonds.

Moreover, we might see our three categories of drama—dispassionate, dramatic and Dantean—as themselves often serving political movements. On the one hand we can draw analogies between a tendency towards dispassionate forms of narrative and being drawn towards an ethos and politics that wishes to simply banish empathetic reactions from our social calculus by labeling them irrational, fragile, infantile, feminine and childlike. Such movements might label their opponents "weak-minded," "woman-hearted", or "snowflakes" for their foolish calls for social empathy. Is this a conservative trope? Is there perhaps a reason that authoritarian rulers, who tend to speak of and set one clear dispassionate goal for their societies, tend to be memorialized by highly dispassionate monuments and iconography?

When considering such questions, we realize that both racism and sexism are also essentially deep forms of highly channeled compassionate and communal empathy. In fact while promising to deliver a deep and true community, they also confine empathy: they require that we become quite dispassionate towards the subjects that they determine are not to be experienced or narrativized. Like every narrative we have discussed so far, like all cultural efforts to create in- and out-groups, they too are confines on how to hear stories and what stories to hear: they are imaginative sphincters, channels of a subject's personal analogies, only here put on a tight laser-like beam that leaves whole groups in the dark.

For these reasons we have finally focussed on the unchannelled openness of innocence, which with all its risk of sentimentality and its elevation of childlike wonder, seems today a potentially more social form of empathy than guilt or bitterness. Perhaps this is why we find the call for a re-enchantment of the world so convincing: theorists like Bennett and films like *Amelie* argue that that is needed for us to re-establish a healthy moral relationship with each other and with our world. As Bennett (2001) notes, modernity has been a project of disenchanting the world, of withering the subject's relationship to it and to each other, with dire results because in fact "the mood of enchantment may be valuable for ethical life". She observes that "in the cultural narrative of disenchantment, the prospects for loving life—or saying "yes" to the world—are not good. What's to love about an alienated existence on a dead planet?" In such a light these films and stories of re-enchantment, which carry in their train a longing to re-create affective bonds, now seem like a struggle to re-establish not only an escape from the modern but to also re-invent an ethics to resist the atomization of modernity. In ecstatic space the two efforts are joined through communally empathetic narratives.

But whether we embrace guilt, bitterness or innocence as gyroscopes for our character, we need to decide how empathetic we want our neighbors and our culture to be. And for that reason we need to focus on Dantean space. Its aesthetic implications must be explicated because just as this aging, rootless, embittered moralist intended some eight hundred years ago, Dantean space now extends into ours and enfolds us all. At the time he began writing *The Divine Comedy*, Dante was essentially a failure, a bitter man cut from his social roots and without a city, lost like the narrator is in his very first canto. It seems clear from his writing that Dante hated his time and wanted desperately to change it and that he felt that the 100 cantos of his *Comedy* could do exactly that.

And for once at least a poet has achieved his worldly wish: Dante's poetry has in fact changed the world. His inventions have had a remarkably outsized emotional and social impact because when we consume and imagine these emotionally powerful Dantean spaces, we also construct, self-inscribe and reinforce Dante's pre-Renaissance ideas about the self, responsibility and community. Dante's characters are the narrators of their lives in more than one sense: each story and its resulting punishment or reward illustrates Dante's idea of free will and of the self as a mechanism for achieving narrative cohesion over the course of a life. This is deepened by the empowering force of purgatorial self-understanding—in Purgatory your fate is constructed and narrated by your own willful acts, but you can change your arc by your own efforts. It is possible to sense the seeds of both the Protestant work-ethic and of liberal capitalism here, and that is why one chapter of this book was titled "How *not* to think like Dante Alighieri".

Dantean moments are clearly real, a given aspect of being human. Dantean space, on the other hand, is not. It is instead a complex aesthetic invention that we use to make sense of our memories, our laws, our sense of responsibilities, and even the vagaries of life under late capitalism. Of course, by doing so, we existentially make Dantean space real. The modern self is to some degree a construct, a cultural collusion, a kind of software we use to make sense of our mental hardware, our culture's expectations, our neighbors, our loves and our laws. We can construct a Dantean space for ourselves and others, and this space will allow us to have many kinds of adventures and experiences: it is a life-logic that can give us a whole new realm of self-directed projects. In that sense Dantean space is real: it is certainly real to the extent that, as Blake succinctly said, the Altering Eye alters all. As a form of self-understanding it is an altering of our vision of ourselves, which then alters the world, it is a wire-frame that we use to sculpt our lives, and it is a very successful, infectious construction that now undergirds much of our social cohesion.

But once we examine the complex story architecture that Dante helped craft and that we now inhabit, once we know how he has altered our eyes and our world, we are left with some crucial questions. Whatever ontological status we grant it, we still ask ourselves: is Dantean story space actually the best way to make sense of ourselves? Or is it too wedded to alienating ideas of guilt, individualism and the self? Are these altered eyes revealing life in new, beautiful, and tragic detail, or is this an embittering, guilt-spreading form of moral, social and aesthetic blindness?

And so Part III of this book has necessarily been deconstructive. We have argued that Dante invented fundamental parts of the Neo-Aristotelian framework in which today's writers, filmmakers and video-game designers think and work. But perhaps this is exactly why Dante must be deconstructed: perhaps we should fear him for the very same reasons Bertolt Brecht says we should fear Aristotle, for their inventions of the protagonists and the building-codes and zoning laws of today's story space. What if Brecht is right? What if NeoAristotelian vehicles are themselves disempowering and alienating? What if they are destructive of our frayed social fabric? What if our protagonists are very bad for us? In short, should we enthusiastically celebrate Dante or should we instead purge ourselves of his dark machinery?

These questions are pressing because, thanks to its viral spread in our novels and films and video-games, for good or bad and whether we acknowledge it or not, Dantean machinery now clicks and clatters and rumbles along inside us all.[7] And yet so does the machinery of empathy. By using empathy in story to show how a better Space is possible, some artists and writers offer us a doorway for escaping Dantean space.

NOTES

1. In *The Interpretation of Cultures* (1973), the anthropologist Clifford Geertz described culture as "a system of inherited conceptions expressed in symbolic forms by means of which men communicate, perpetuate, and develop their knowledge about and attitudes toward life."
2. This scene shows the protagonist glimpsing another community, one endowed with a feminized ethics of care. The barn being raised is in a sense her secret garden that she asks him to enter: because he will have to renounce violence to enter, it will change his character and heal him in certain ways if he accepts. In the end he realizes that it is a place where he with his violent ways does not belong.
3. Gaston Bachelard pioneered the phenomenological approach to architecture and materials, most notably in his lyrical classic text *The Poetics of Space.*
4. See Giaccardi and Magatti (2014), for an excellent discussion of their concept of generativity.
5. To judge from their work and writing, the painters Vincent van Gogh and Marc Chagall seem to be also striving for a kind of innocent-yet-social sensibility, even willing to risk sentimentality as they pursued an ethics of care and communal empathy. In this way they did not simply share that modernist drive of striving to see the world as a child does, the way for example a Paul Klee does. Klee has no obvious social commitments while they both were deeply committed to a sense of fighting prejudice, economic disparity and social hate. By striving not only to see the world with the fresh eyes of a child but to also behave with a childlike openness and vulnerability, they fit into this overall trend in European thought that Amelie also expresses.
6. See for example Goldman (2002, 2006) versus Gordon (1995a, b) and (2000), Heal (2003) and Stueber (2006, 2012). For the debate on intersubjectivity and mirror neurons, see Allen (2010), Borg (2007), Csibra (2009), Debes (2010), Goldman (2009), Hickok (2008), Iacoboni (2011), Jacob (2008) and Stueber (2012a). Some of this debate can be characterized as a philosophical one revolving around the question: is

empathy a resonance between the subject and the Other or is it a direct perception of that Other's emotional states?

7. Dedicated to Anna Francesca, our creature of the future.

BIBLIOGRAPHY

Alighieri, Dante. 2006. *The Divine Comedy*, trans. and ed. Robin Kirkpatrick. London: Penguin.

Aristotle. 1986. *Poetics*, trans. A. Sullivan. Chapel Hill, NC: University of North Carolina Press.

Augé, Marc. 2002. *In the Metro*. Minneapolis: University of Minnesota Press.

———. 2004. *Oblivion*. Minneapolis: University of Minnesota Press.

———. 2016. *Everyone Dies Young: Time Without Age*. New York: Columbia University Press.

Bachelard, Gaston. 1994. *The Poetics of Space*. Boston, MA : Beacon Press.

Beeton, Sue. 2005. *Film Induced Tourism*. Clevedon: Channel View Publications.

Bennett, Jane. 2001. *The Enchantment of Modern Life*. New Jersey: Princeton University Press.

Burnett, Francis Hodgson. 1961. *The Secret Garden*. William Heinemann.

Cinque, Toija, Christopher Moore, and Sean Redmond. 2015. *Enchanting David Bowie*. New York: Bloomsbury Academic Press.

D'Adamo, Amedeo. 2013. Dantean Space in the Cities of Cinema. In *Media and the City: Urbanism, Technology and Communication*, ed. Simone Tosoni, Matteo Tarantino, and Chiara Giaccardi. Newcastle upon Tyne, UK: Cambridge Scholars Press.

D'Adamo, Amedeo. 2015a. The People Beyond Mars: Using Robinson's Mars Trilogy to Understand Post-Scarcity. *Thesis Eleven* 131 (1): 81–98.

D'Adamo, Amedeo. 2015b. Ain't There One Damn Flag That Can Make Me Break Down and Cry?: On Bowie's 'Young Americans. In *Enchanting David Bowie*, ed. Toija Cinque, Christopher Moore, and Sean Redmond. New York: Bloomsbury Academic Press.

D'Adamo, Amedeo. 2017. That Junky Funky Vibe: Quincy Jones' Title Theme for the Sitcom *Sanford and Son*. In *Music in Comedy Television*, ed. Liz Giuffre, and Philip Hayword. New York and London: Routledge.

Dickens, Charles. 2002. *Great Expectations*. London: Penguin Classics.

Dostoevski, Fyodor. 2003. *The Brothers Karamazov*. London: Penguin Classics.

Dostoevski, Fyodor. 2004. *The Idiot*. London: Penguin Classics.

Geertz, Clifford. 1973. *The Interpretation of Cultures*. USA: Basic Books.

Giaccardi, Chiara, and Mauro Magatti. 2014. *Generativiti di Tutto Il Mondo. Unitevi!* Rome: Feltrinelli.

Gilligan, Carol. 1982. *In A Different Voice: Psychological Theory and Women's Development.* Cambridge, MA: Harvard University Press.

Hollan, D.W., and C.J. Throop. 2011. *The Anthropology of Empathy: Experiencing the Lives of Others in Pacific Societies.* New York: Berghahn Books.

Noddings, Nel. 2002. *Educating Moral People: A Caring Alternative to Character Education.* Vermont: Teachers College Press.

Ostrom, Elinor. 1990. *Governing the Commons: The Evolution of Institutions for Collective Action.* Cambridge, UK: Cambridge University Press.

Tronto, Joan C. 2005. An Ethic of Care. In *Feminist Theory: A Philosophical Anthology,* ed. Ann E. Cudd, and Robin O. Andreasen. Oxford and Malden, MA: Blackwell Publishing.

Zipes, J. 2005. *Hans Christian Andersen: The Misunderstood Storyteller.* London: Routledge.

Glossary

Alienated space: a narrative space that through its design, look and feel expresses some external or internal disjunction between characters and their world.

Bleached dialogue: dialogue that intentionally contains little or no dramatic meaning.

Character: character, in both life and literature, is composed of the tendencies in the motives, actions and reactions of a person. To discern such heuristic "tendencies" in a person is to discern the predictive patterns in the desires, hopes, dreams, approaches, impulses, tactics and techniques of that person.

Character arc: the clear changes in a character's tendencies (or the failure of a person to change her or his tendencies) in the face of the conflicts in the story.

Character use of music: a use of music that conveys something of the tendencies of a character in a way that informs us of her past or predicts how she will behave. It is opposed to the emotional use of music which more simply informs us of what a character is feeling or may even more simply inform us of what *we* ought to be feeling in a dramatic beat or moment.

Characterological manifold: any element in a story can have at least one and as many as six dimensions of meaning as described in the manifold.

Chronotope: a concept invented by Bakhtin and used often by narrative theorists, the chronotope is grounded in the Kantian concept

© The Editor(s) (if applicable) and The Author(s) 2018
A. D'Adamo, *Empathetic Space on Screen*,
https://doi.org/10.1007/978-3-319-66772-0

of the space—time manifold. In this concept there is a specific form of space and time that is warped by the nature of place in ways that carry across narrative representations of such places. For example there is the chronotope of the bar, allowing us to compare bars across different narratives to discover cultural concepts embedded in such constructs. In this book we differentiate the concept of the characterological manifold from the Kantian roots of the chronotope to clarify that ours is a very different, character-based form of space.

Dantean space: a space in a narrative that empathetically expresses and embodies the internal conflicts of a character.

Dantean moment: a central emotional moment in a person's life whose power of joy and/or pain is so strong that the person's sensibility is affected and shaped by the experience. As the example of Miss Havisham shows, such moments can even freeze a person's sensibility in a specific situation and space.

Dispassionate, dramatic and Dantean: a dispassionate character is a character with an external conflict with no or a very weak and non-determinative inner conflict. A dramatic character is a character with both an external and an internal conflict. A Dantean character is a character with an internal conflict that is projected outwards and embodied in the narrative space where we find them.

Dispassionate space: a space hosting characters that have external objectives but no clear internal conflicts. Such spaces tend to use and embody spectacle, often becoming the expression of their characters' dispassionate nature.

Dramatic space: a space in a narrative where the characters have an internal conflict they are struggling with but where the backdrop does not express that conflict.

Ecstatic space: a space crafted or curated by a character that embodies an ethics of care and which heals the internal conflicts of characters. One example is the garden in the novel and film *The Secret Garden*.

Emotional use of music: a use of music that expresses and heightens the moment-to-moment emotions of a character. It can be contrasted with the Character use of music, which expresses and informs us about a character's tendencies and not simply her emotions.

Empathetic space: an empathetic space exists in a moment of a story which (1) arouses some intense level of empathy in us and in which (2) the space itself is somehow expressing that empathy by embodying the hopes and/or fears of the character. In general, the space becomes more intensely empathetic the more it movingly expresses the emotional conflicts of a character. While empathetic space needn't express memory, both Dantean space and ecstatic space are forms of empathetic space that express a strong memory from the past.

Empathy, communal vs. compassionate: Compassionate Empathy can be triggered by feeling some compassion for a character's situation and can involve no relationships among characters. Communal Empathy on the other hand is triggered by witnessing the character build relationships, and most powerfully by seeing her do something good for someone else at some cost to herself.

Machinery of empathy: a list of identifiable story tactics, attributes and situations that are found across stories and that cause us to feel intense moments of empathy towards characters.

Rings of intimacy: a series of concentric rings of trust, rings of revealing character tendencies. One version of the rings would start with the widest ring representing people in general, then a smaller ring of neighbors and colleagues, then a smaller one of friends, then of close friends, then of family, of lovers, and perhaps finally of the beloved. Different people and societies will construe these rings in slightly different ways. Many dramas involve a large disturbance in the rings of trust.

Self-abasing space: a clearly unpleasant space that a protagonist has engineered or sought out and now treats as a kind of nest that he does not want to leave. The space is a kind of mirror of what the character feels he deserves or has become, a willingly-chosen space of self-judgement. Examples can be found in the film *Barfly* and Camus' novel *The Fall*.

Shade: a shade is a person who is absent from a story or from the main part of a story and who is so badly missed by a character that he or she cannot get over the loss. An empathetic figure of hauntology, a shade takes us inside the sensibility of a character trapped in a sense of loss. We may go inside the space of the shade as we do in many Dantean spaces: in this case many elements of the story then signify the lost future, the hopes and dreams that were torn away when the shade figure left the character's world. Unlike a ghost who can operate in the story like a character, shades do not operate directly on the actions of a story but rather through engendering a mood and presence of loss. We see only glimpses of a shade and usually never see the shaded figure's face.

Shaded space: an empathetic spatial frame of hauntology that takes us inside the sensibility of a character trapped in a sense of loss, usually because of the death of a beloved.

Showcase space: a space in a narrative where everything is new and unmarked by human touch or inhabitance, creating the eerie and alienated feeling that the characters live or work in a showcase. The tv show *Mad Men* uses showcase space to indicate deep internal disjunctions in its main characters.

Third space theory: A spatial theory by Oldenberg that divides human space into Work Space, Home space and the Third Space. The Third space is the realm of social discourse, common areas and other spaces not included in work or home. Oldenberg argues that the quantity and quality of such Third Spaces indicates the social health and power structures of a culture.

Tryst space: the location in a romantic relationship where the couple has their first scene of revealing vulnerabilities and asking for commitments from each other.

A BACKWARDS FOREWORD:

Rationale: The Question of the Bed-sheet

Perhaps it's appropriate for a book that focuses on how the past lives on in the present to end with a foreword that is delayed to the end. But I wanted to look back over this path and then forwards to where any work on film theory and practice should: towards stories not yet fashioned, films not yet made, shows not yet staged and cultures not yet born.

First the look backwards. This book began in a class I think of as an exciting failure. I once was fortunate enough to build and run a large crafts conservatory in Los Angeles. Determined to build a new kind of school, I began hiring high-level professional filmmakers, many with Oscars and Oscar nominations but most of whom hadn't taught before. This required long conferences about how to create useful courses out of their experiences making films like *Easy Rider, Chinatown, Spiderman, What Dreams May Come, Mulholland Drive,* and many others.

Looking back, I'm honestly unsure how much I helped these luminaries in their teaching, but for me the experience became breathless on a daily basis. One experience stands out in particular. I'd started teaching while still a film student at Columbia and in my very first classes I had often described the film *Blade Runner* as a moment when seven department heads were all doing the best, most-innovative work in the field, and astonishingly all were on this film. Now as the school opened I found myself co-teaching a filmmaking course with Larry Paull, the master production designer who created the textured places and spaces of *Dirty Dancing, Back to the Future* and many other movies. Including *Blade Runner.*

Larry was wonderful to work with. He often talked about how many so-so designers "gave Great Meeting" in that they knew how to talk at great and exciting length about how a script might be realized but lacked the ability to actually make their ideas real. But he was, I realized, terrific at both, and our conversations about how the class might work were exciting.

And yet from the outset it was clear that there was a problem in our workshop class, the senior film review where we visited sets and reviewed rough cuts. Larry quickly became famous for refusing to accept arbitrarily-chosen 'props' for the dishes, bed sheets, curtains and rooms of a film but yet, true master that he is, as a first-time teacher he wasn't always following up with clear explanations of how students could improve on their poor choices. In some cases where he could, he simply stepped in, bringing in a prop or a painting reference, but he tried hard to stand back from this role so the students could learn by doing. Sometimes Larry brilliantly discussed architecture, art history or the history of fonts. But there were many cases where he simply couldn't clearly enunciate what he expected or why. This of course happens in every honest critique, and so he and the students would then turn to me for comments.

And in these moments I felt less helpful than I'd ever felt in any role as a teacher, because now I found that teaching production design was a completely different challenge from teaching writing, directing, cinematography and producing. I found that in trying to support Larry's meticulous discussion about their films' textures and myriad choices, I tended to ask about their characters' backstories and economic situation, a discussion that usually remained trapped in the box of realism. When pushed by budding designers, I would talk about the space of the film's production design, sometimes invoking LeFebvre, Kristeva and even Bachelard. Larry was in fact fascinated by this alien landscape and its clunky vocabulary of chronotopes, acoustic mirrors, poetic materials, actants and the grotesque, but at the end of the first term we both knew the truth: we had not yet answered what I began to call the Bed-sheet Question.

The Bed-sheet Question can be put as follows: why does the bed-sheet in *Amelie*'s bedroom have a richer phantasmagorical presence than a bed-sheet in a neorealist film like, say, Ken Loach's film *I, Daniel Blake (2016),* and yet Loach's spectacle is completely right for his film? Why must an alleyway in the city of *Batman* feel more operatic, more imbued with Wagnerian malevolence and gothic grimness, than an alleyway in *Spiderman*? What determines the unity of any successful spatial spectacle with its particular characters and story? We can all see that the backgrounds in comedies are usually intentionally flatter and less interesting than those in most dramas, horror films and thrillers, but why is this? And why are the settings in dramas so different from those in most summer blockbusters?

I talked at great length in those years about the Bed-sheet Question with Larry and also with our fellow faculty Anna Thomas and Richard Sylbert, with Ellen Mirojnick and Donn Cambern, Maysie Hoy and Bill Fraker, Vicky Jensen and Rolf Boda, Thom Mount and Bob Shapiro and other studio heads, with Henry Bumstead and Harold Michelson and the other countless visiting directors, cinematographers, costume designers and sound designers who had woven my favorite films but for the most part had never taught (or been trained) in a classroom. I remember great chats—Sylbert once talked about how hairstyles are the hardest thing he'd had to master when trying to create period, while Larry Paull laughed that off and pointed out the crucial role of fonts in creating a convincing sense of period. It seemed we always found ourselves far from the logic of film schools and theory programs and instead thrust deep into the actual methodologies and sensibilities of the masters of filmmaking, always working from examples without any need for some overall theories of meaning and practice. They'd often invoke intuition, which made their choices hard to justify to some executives. I remember Bob Shapiro, who had run Warners and overseen the production of *Pee Wee's Big Adventure* (a kind of landmark in using production design in the 1980s) talking about his bewilderment when reviewing dailies and having confusing chats with the film's brilliant production design team, then finally understanding certain choices only during the final screening.

After that puzzling, invaluable experience I then went on to make three very low-budget feature films, using each as an experimental classroom for a student crew. Then I returned to the classroom to teach a mixture of theory and practice courses in film and television, but all the while I was haunted by the bed-sheet question. I continued to ransack the ever-growing literature of film theory and film craft, but to me it seemed glaringly clear that most of the richest contemporary theoretical writing about narrative space never bridges the famous gap between media makers and media theorists in which I felt I was stuck.

The problem is I think that most theory accounts are generally not grounded in the specific methodologies and techniques that narrative artists use to create such spaces and therefore have little explanatory power or pragmatic robustness, while craft accounts are little more than 'how-to' guides on the treatment of surfaces and the proper organization of prop departments, usually connected to anecdotes and admonishments to "put the story first". Neither approach answers the Bed-sheet Question: though it is now decades since LeFebvre opened the rich conversation about space, we still seem to lack a conceptual frame that can explain why certain forms of design, cinematography and overall spectacle arise around certain stories and not others. One result of this is that filmmakers cannot dialogue with narrative theorists. Another is that in both worlds we still struggle to understand the concrete specifics of how the actual core concepts of our story-forms might themselves be gendered, racist and alienating. Outside of the prosaic methods for indicating genre and for constructing 'realism,' can we elaborate any useful general rules to help explain why certain design choices possess spectacular power and others do not? Can we define story space in ways that are useful, explanatory and productive? And if we cannot, then how can we ever begin to explain the spectacular and phantasmagorical machinery of cinema?

And so this book. This is an attempted answer to the question that Larry and I faced about Amelie's bed-sheet and Loach's teacup and Hitchcock's room and *Batman*'s alleyway and the homes of *Homeland*. The intent is to link the terms and methodology of the makers of all these narrative forms to the terminology and concerns of cultural theory. I hope to help bridge these two camps for many reasons. On the one hand I strongly believe that most theoretical readings can be deepened when grounded in the methodologies and building-codes of the working architects of narration. At the same time though, I also argue that to make new and convincing works, story-crafters must themselves understand the history and the social implications behind their range of dramatic techniques. Whether you're a novelist, filmmaker, game-designer, media theorist, reader or viewer, you pay attention to the coffee-cup and the window and the wallpaper because their connection to the main character, the genre, the plot, the backstory, and the form of spectacle this all generates is not only helping to suture us all into this story but is also shaping our conception of ourselves and others.

But finally, there is also a redemptive intention here. It's true that whenever we can deconstruct the foundations of narrative space and spectacle, we also help reveal how these spaces encode our deep convictions about the self and social relations—and are thus also deeply implicated in our social and gender alienations. And this can be a productive, generative understanding: if we can grasp the techniques then not only can we then better critique and construct such spaces but, as the conclusion of this book suggests, perhaps we can also then culture the seeds of a rich spectacular space, an under-explored ecstatic space which offers new social and aesthetic possibilities to both theorists and storytellers.

And that is the utopian conviction of this book. I believe that today's theorists do not simply want to grasp our contemporary culture nor do today's story creators simply want to build it. In my experience they also yearn to create a new, more social and less gendered culture that they can love.

INDEX

Printed by Printforce, the Netherlands